LITERATURE, RELIGION, AND
POSTSECULAR STUDIES

Lori Branch, Series Editor

Walker Percy, Fyodor Dostoevsky, and the Search for Influence

Jessica Hooten Wilson

THE OHIO STATE UNIVERSITY PRESS
COLUMBUS

Copyright © 2017 by The Ohio State University.
All rights reserved.

Library of Congress Cataloging-in-Publication Data
Names: Wilson, Jessica Hooten, author.
Title: Walker Percy, Fyodor Dostoevsky, and the search for influence / Jessica Hooten Wilson.
Other titles: Literature, religion, and postsecular studies.
Description: Columbus : The Ohio State University Press, [2017] | Series: Literature, religion, and postsecular studies | Includes bibliographical references and index.
Identifiers: LCCN 2017030187 | ISBN 9780814213490 (cloth ; alk. paper) | ISBN 0814213499 (cloth ; alk. paper)
Subjects: LCSH: Percy, Walker, 1916–1990—Criticism and interpretation. | Fiction—Religious aspects—Christianity. | Dostoyevsky, Fyodor, 1821–1881—Influence.
Classification: LCC PS3566.E6912 Z976 2017 | DDC 813/.54—dc23
LC record available at https://lccn.loc.gov/2017030187

Cover design by Larry Nozik
Text design by Juliet Williams
Type set in Adobe Minion Pro

∞ The paper used in this publication meets the minimum requirements of the American National Standard for Information Sciences—Permanence of Paper for Printed Library Materials. ANSI Z39.48-1992.

9 8 7 6 5 4 3 2 1

For my husband

CONTENTS

Acknowledgments ix

INTRODUCTION 1

CHAPTER 1   Failed Imitation in *The Charterhouse* and *The Gramercy Winner*   21

CHAPTER 2   Faithful Re-membering in *The Moviegoer*   41

CHAPTER 3   Modeling a Holy Fool in *The Last Gentleman*   59

CHAPTER 4   Borrowed Critiques in *Love in the Ruins*   86

CHAPTER 5   "Outdostoevskying Dostoevsky" in *Lancelot*   112

CHAPTER 6   Echoed Prophecies in *The Second Coming* and *The Thanatos Syndrome*   134

CONCLUSION   Imitation Versus Anxiety: A Christian's Response to Harold Bloom's *The Anxiety of Influence*   160

Bibliography 163

Index 170

ACKNOWLEDGMENTS

PROVIDENCE INTRODUCED me to Walker Percy in 2003 at the Witherspoon Fellowship in Washington, DC, where we read and discussed *The Thanatos Syndrome*. The book's depiction of apocalypse caused by good intentions haunted me for years, but I never sought to study Percy further. He was a good storyteller, I thought, not a literary figure. Then, Professor Ralph Wood at Baylor University assigned *The Moviegoer* in a course on Catholic renascence. Ralph pressed me to include Percy in my first book on Dostoevsky and O'Connor, advice I initially refused. After completing that first book, however, I spent the next summer investigating Ralph's hunch that Dostoevsky had a profound significance to Percy. That research journey not only unveiled more than I expected but also converted my view of Percy; here was an author offering as much instruction as delight.

The book owes debt to more people than I will be able to name, for as I argue, writing is so much a composite of the many other writers whom we have read. In addition to Ralph Wood, I'd like to thank Sarah Jane Murray, who encouraged tying the idea of this second book to Dostoevsky's influence rather than to my previous writing on O'Connor. To John Wilson, the editor of *Books and Culture,* thank you for showing me how to make my project matter by encouraging me to define influence itself. Thank you to Lori Branch, the series editor, who gave pages of feedback to my initial proposal and who saw potential in the project, despite the enthusiastic but incoherent first draft. Similarly, Margy Thomas Horton, the editor at Scholar Shape, brought forward the argument regarding a Christian theory of influence, and to her I owe the greatest debt for making the book the lucid version that it currently is. The research was originally funded by the University of Mary Hardin-Baylor, most notably by Steve Oldham, the provost at the time, who saw this book's potential. My student assistants Annaleta Nichols and Maribelle Perrigo also contributed to preparing the manuscript for publication. They are editors-in-training with whom I have had the honor to work while they are undergraduates. Thank you, as well, to John Brown University, not only for supplying these great assistants but also for the summer scholar's grant to help me complete my work on this book.

I am grateful to Mary Pratt Lobdell and Ann Percy Moores for the permission to print unpublished notes from their father's papers and letters, housed primarily at the Southern Historical Collection at the Wilson Library at the University of North Carolina-Chapel Hill. All of the unpublished archival material that I use from the Percy papers is copyrighted by Mary Pratt Lobdell and Ann Percy Moores. In addition to Chapel Hill's library, I received permission from Vanderbilt University's Special Collections and the Princeton Fireside Library's Rare Book and Special Collections where some of Percy's correspondence, as well as letters about or to Percy from Caroline Gordon and Allen Tate, are held. Thank you is also owed to Louisiana State University Press for their permission to reprint a new version of my chapter on Dostoevsky and Percy's *The Moviegoer*, which first appeared in the collection *The Moviegoer at 50* (LSU Press 2016).

Lastly, I wish to thank my family, especially my husband, Jonathon Wilson. We were dating when I began researching this book, were engaged when I started writing; I finished the first draft a month before our daughter was born, and I submitted it for review merely a week before our son was born. He has been with me through the entire process of this book's making, and although he will never read it, he deserves credit and thanks for any good that it accomplishes.

INTRODUCTION

~

ON A PORCH in Athens, Georgia, teenage Walker Percy sat reading *The Brothers Karamazov*. It was Christmas time, the porch was his grandmother's, and the book was a gift from his close friend Shelby Foote. Later Percy would describe the volume as "the big fat Random House edition, fat as a Bible, its pages pulpy, crumbling at the corners and smelling like bread."[1] This object, a decayed pile of pages recording the spiritually intense story of three Russian brothers, and this place, a homey veranda in the mild midwinter of a Depression-era American South, were fusing in the young man's imagination, coalescing into an unforgettable memory that would become a touchstone throughout Walker Percy's long career as a novelist.

For Percy, even then, reading Dostoevsky was an experience of such visceral power that it took on a religious dimension. Certainly it was no accident that Percy likened the size and weight of his copy of *The Brothers Karamazov* to the Bible. And sure enough, at other key moments in Percy's life, he continued to take up Dostoevsky for periods of deep and meditative reading. As a medical student nearly dying of tuberculosis in the 1940s, as a Catholic

---

1. Decades after that Christmas discovery, Percy would recall how, from his very first reading of *The Brothers Karamazov*, the characters felt as real as next-door neighbors: "And how can I disconnect Ivan and Mitya from reading about them sitting in a swing on my grandmother's porch in Athens, Georgia, in the 1930s?" Percy, Introduction to *Walker Percy: Novelist and Philosopher*, xviii.

convert taking up fiction writing in the 1950s, and later as an increasingly celebrated novelist through the 1960s, 1970s, and 1980s, Percy continued to sit with his well-worn copies of *The Brothers Karamazov*, *Notes from Underground*, and other works, thinking about Dostoevsky's transcendent themes and studying how Dostoevsky concretized those themes in fiction that held a seemingly miraculous appeal for the masses. Walker Percy himself asserted in 1989, "I suppose my model is nearly always Dostoyevsky."[2]

This study takes as its theme the influence of Dostoevsky upon Percy. But that influence is considered in an unorthodox way, not as a static "X influences Y" relationship but as a dynamic, subtly shifting, lifelong engagement between the two authors who lived a century and a continent apart. As Dostoevsky himself said, "Man is only a creature in development, . . . someone not finished but transitional."[3] Over the six decades of his adult life, Percy would turn over and over again to the works of Dostoevsky, each time with slightly different preoccupations, attitudes, and perspectives. In his own work, he would try on Dostoevsky's influence in a variety of distinct ways. To investigate the relationship between Percy and Dostoevsky in its full complexity is to understand both authors more fully, and ultimately, on a much broader scale, to reimagine what it means for one literary writer to influence another.

Walker Percy remains one of the greatest American novelists of the twentieth century. His first novel won the National Book Award in 1962; his second was nominated; his next four topped the bestseller lists and continue to be read for leisure and taught in classrooms. Sympathetic critics and admiring readers do recognize that Percy manages not only to capture the imagination of his own time but also to create works that transcend his time and place; these readers applaud his work for its sophisticated interrogation of existentialist philosophy, its Southern character, and its treatment of Catholicism. Yet scholars have done little to understand how Percy—a former medical student with no creative writing training—became such a great novelist. Some dismiss him as having written the same novel over and over. Others appreciate his philosophical depth while contending that he was hit or miss as a literary artist.[4] However, Percy did receive acclaim for his fiction, and one of the keys to Percy's success as a thinker and writer was Dostoevsky. Scholars are generally aware that Dostoevsky held some interest for Percy—for the latter did

---

2. Percy, *More Conversations*, 224.
3. Frank, *Writer*, 409.
4. In a review of 2014 books, editor of *Books and Culture* John Wilson remarks offhandedly, "Walker Percy, whom I revere, was very much hit-and-miss as a novelist." Such sentiment may be provoked by assessments such as Ralph Wood's negative review of *The Thanatos Syndrome* or Jay Tolson's indictment that "Percy was no longer at the top of his powers" at the end of his career (*Pilgrim in the Ruins*, 452).

publicly express admiration for Dostoevsky in letters and interviews, claiming numerous times that Dostoevsky was his model or crediting the Russian for the ideas in his novels.[5] However, as I will show, previously unknown archival documents show a far deeper relationship than has been recognized.[6]

In Percy's papers at the University of North Carolina, Chapel Hill, one finds frequent references to Dostoevsky scrawled across the manuscript pages of Percy's novels, pages upon pages of handwritten notes in Percy's copies of Dostoevsky's novels, and annotations in nearly all of Percy's personal editions of the famed Russian's works. *The Idiot* alone contains almost thirty pages of comments, handwritten by Percy. In the summer of 2011, deep in those Percy archives, I opened one of Percy's folders labeled "Misc—Save for Book," and there behind an unpublished short story, I discovered a sheaf of notes on Dostoevsky's *The Possessed, The Eternal Husband,* and *Notes from Underground.* The wealth of notes and annotated volumes in the Percy archives makes abundantly clear that Dostoevsky meant a great deal to Percy. The question that remains to be pursued is, what is the scope and shape of that influence? And beyond that, why does literary influence matter at all, in this case or any other?

Walker Percy read Dostoevsky because the great Russian writer had succeeded in doing precisely what he himself wished to do: Dostoevsky wrote novels that spoke to his time and place, or as Percy put it in a 1989 interview, Dostoevsky "illustrated and incarnated the most powerful themes and issues and trends of his day."[7] And in Percy's own writing, he strove to do the same. Percy's updating of Dostoevsky's protagonists include a retired civil servant from St. Petersburg (*Notes from Underground*) who becomes a retired lawyer from the NAACP living on Belle Isle (*Lancelot*), and a Russian Prince living

---

5. Before 2012 the only article dedicated to the connection between Percy and Dostoevsky was a brief eight pages by Lewis Lawson that examined Percy's *The Moviegoer*. Percy's biographers mention the Dostoevsky connection several times over, though again without much explanation. Yet the amount of time and energy that Percy spent with Dostoevsky's texts appeared more significant than even his reading of Kierkegaard, which was undoubtedly influential on his fiction, especially his early novels—and has been mined extensively. Maria Bloshteyn concludes her essay on Dostoevsky's influence on Southern writers with an allusion to Percy: "The key to the dilemma of why southern readers tend to choose Dostoevsky over Turgenev and Tolstoy . . . appears obvious: only in Dostoevsky's novels are the 'Ultimate Questions' given such priority" ("Dostoevsky and the Literature," 20). More recently two scholars have explored the connection more fully: John Desmond in "Fyodor Dostoevsky, Walker Percy and the Demonic Self" and Farrell O'Gorman in "Confessing the Horrors of Radical Individualism in *Lancelot*: Percy, Dostoevsky, Poe."

6. On the Percy library stacks, the works of Dostoevsky occupy thirteen spots. Three of them are anthologies of his short novels, so that there are seventeen total works lining his shelves, not counting the oft-quoted copy of *The Brothers Karamazov* that has disappeared from his library.

7. Percy, *More Conversations*, 224.

abroad (*The Idiot*) who becomes a Southern heir traipsing around New York (*The Last Gentleman*). John Desmond affirms this connection: "Writing about the present crisis, Percy constantly looked back to Dostoevsky as a model for both themes and narrative strategies."[8]

As the proceeding chapters will show, even though Percy's works were profoundly influenced by Dostoevsky's, they differ in two fundamental ways. First, whereas Dostoevsky created panoramas, Percy's works focus on individuals. Percy himself would explain, "The common thread that runs through all of my novels is of a man, or a woman, who finds himself/herself outside of society [and this character] use[s] his very outsideness as a way of seeing things in a different way."[9] The second and more significant adaptation, for the purposes of this study, is that Percy shifted the mode from tragic to comic, from bleak to hopeful.[10] Joseph Schwartz calls Percy's endings affirming and credits Dostoevsky, in part: "[They] are always special in the affirmation (and sometimes celebration) they give to the reader. I think he is indebted principally to Dostoevsky and Tolstoy for this."[11] While one could argue for hope in the epilogue to *Crime and Punishment* (though not before that coda) and in the "Hurrah!" of the boys in *The Brothers Karamazov*, Dostoevsky's endings are overall more haunting—the sadistic and isolated narrator in *Notes*, the murder of Nastasya in *The Idiot*, Stavrogin's suicide on the final page of *The Possessed*—and even within the aforementioned seemingly positive examples, we have protagonists in prison, sick, and insane. Perhaps due to the superficial differences among the texts, very few readers of Percy have ever taken much notice of the close relationships among Dostoevsky's tragic Russian grand narratives and Percy's comedic Southern American portraits.

The neglect of this subject is surely attributable to the fact that, for most scholars today, talking about creative influence is like trying on clothing that is long out of fashion. In 2008 the *Modern Language Quarterly* devoted a special edition of their journal to influence. The editor Andrew Elfenbein introduced the topic by noting the "paucity of places to look for interesting recent work on others."[12] For Elfenbein and the contributors to this issue, there was a "seri-

---

8. Desmond, "Fyodor Dostoevsky, Walker Percy, and the Demonic Self," 89.
9. Percy, *More Conversations*, 275, 281. Percy retraces all of his previous novels and classifies each hero as an outsider in a different way—"Binx Bolling, the king of laid-back, cool, outsider; or Will Barrett, who's a much more disturbed outsider; Lancelot, who's downright violent" (*More Convsations* 281)—and he connects them with his latest novel, *The Second Coming*, in which there are two outsiders, Barrett and Allie.
10. The exception, *Lancelot*, in which he "outdostoevsky[s] Dostoevsky," is discussed in chapter 5.
11. Schwartz, "Will Barrett Redux?," 45.
12. Elfenbein, "Defining Influence," 433.

ous gap in the contemporary construction of literature scholarship" around this issue of influence. Elfenbein concludes, "Although it [influence] remains a building block of critical investigation . . . and of critical practice, . . . it rarely rises to the level of explicit discussion."[13] Still, there once was a time when artists embraced creative influence as inevitable and even desirable. Later in this chapter, I will discuss how and why influence studies fell out of fashion, and I will argue that a new approach to influence studies is urgently needed in our own time.

DOSTOEVSKY IN PERCY'S WORLD

Among the British literary elite of the early twentieth century, there sprang up a "cult of Dostoevsky": Virginia Woolf, D. H. Lawrence, Joseph Conrad, and other modernist novelists read Dostoevsky with intense energy and interest. Even among the masses, Dostoevsky's novels were plucked off the shelves like new releases as quickly as Constance Garnett could translate them. By the 1920s, the Americans were as addicted as their British counterparts to Dostoevsky's fiction. Between 1928 and 1938, the Modern Library edition of Dostoevsky's *The Brothers Karamazov* outsold every other title on the list.[14] Producers from Hollywood to Broadway transferred Dostoevsky's work to screen and stage. Within Percy's lifetime, *The Brothers Karamazov* (1964), *The Idiot* (1966), *The Possessed* (1969), and *Crime and Punishment* (1979) were produced as TV mini-series, and *The Brothers Karamazov* (1958) was released as a film starring Yul Brynner. Russian literary critic A. N. Nikoliukin contends, "After the First World War, Dostoevsky suddenly proved alone the most influential writer in America."[15]

Given the qualities that make Dostoevsky's novels distinct, it seems paradoxical that Dostoevsky could find such mass readership. He raised and prioritized transcendent questions: Does God exist? Do demons exist, and if so, what power do they have over us? He was unapologetically Christian. Yet one American audience was perfectly amenable to his peculiar fiction: readers in the South.[16] Southerners had an affinity for Dostoevsky's grotesque style, his

---

13. Ibid.

14. On January 31, 1938, *Time* magazine cited the publisher Bennett Cerf's assertion that "Dostoevsky's *The Brothers Karamazov* is the most popular of the Modern Library's 257 titles, [and] has sold 120,000 copies in ten years."

15. Nikoliukin, *Vzaimosviazi literature Rossii,* 239.

16. McCullers: Only ten years before Percy began writing, Southern novelist Carson McCullers claimed modern Southern writers seem "rather to be most indebted" to Russian

sense of place, and his spiritual magnetism. It would be this latter quality that most captivated Walker Percy.

The striking parallels between Dostoevsky's Russia and the post–Civil War American South were not lost on Southern readers. In Carson McCullers's 1941 essay, "The Russian Realists and Southern Literature," the Georgian novelist explains, "The circumstances under which Southern literature has been produced are strikingly like those under which Russians functioned."[17] Both societies were plagued by nearby progressive cultures whose members sought to impose outsider values; both had recently suffered major military defeats that reminded them of their limitations; both cultures were rather late in abolishing slavery and did so within two years of one another; and both were haunted by a religious past that no longer seemed relevant.[18] That famous Southern woman writer, Flannery O'Connor, wrote of the South as "Christ-Haunted"; Percy would revise her modifier to "Christ-forgetting."[19] These Southern readers recognized the "spiritual urgency"—to use a phrase from the dust jacket of Percy's *The Moviegoer*—of Dostoevsky's fiction.

The cultures of both the Russians and the Southerners were saturated by the Judeo-Christian tradition, regardless of whether individual members ascribed to the Christian doctrines. In Steiner's depiction of nineteenth-century Russia, it was an apocalyptic bedlam in which "the kingdom of God had moved terribly close to the declining kingdom of man."[20] Political pamphleteers adopted religiously charged language, and Russian novelists assumed tones of corresponding spiritual intensity. Similarly, in the post–Civil War American South, people grew up on stories of the Old Testament and the Civil War, and those ghosts haunted the writers. As a result, the writers were distinguished from their Northern counterparts by what Flannery O'Connor calls the "vision of Moses' face as he pulverized our idols" (*Mystery and Manners*

---

realists, in which she includes Gogol and Tolstoy but centers on Dostoevsky ("Russian Realists and Southern Literature," 15).

17. Ibid.

18. In 1861 Russia abolished serfdom, and two years later America followed suit with Lincoln's "Emancipation Proclamation" in which slaves were set free, the most affected region being the American South. These violently abrupt changes in class system concurred with parallel military disasters: Russia in the Crimean episode and the South in the American Civil War.

19. "Christ-Haunted" is a modifier O'Connor used in a 1960 interview, and Percy borrowed and amended with "Christ-forgetting" in his 1978 *Love in the Ruins*. A comment that echoes O'Connor's description of the South as "Christ-Haunted," found on the Vintage International 1998 edition of *The Moviegoer* dust jacket, reads: "Percy managed to combine Bourbon Street elegance with spiritual urgency of a Russian novel."

20. Steiner, *Tolstoy or Dostoevsky: An Essay in the Old Criticism*, 43. George Steiner writes in his famous critical discussion *Tolstoy or Dostoevsky*, "The Russian mind was, literally, God-haunted" (43).

59).[21] O'Connor encourages her fellow Catholic novelists that, in the future, they "will know that what has given the South her identity are those beliefs and qualities which she has absorbed from the Scriptures" (*Mystery and Manners* 209). Although Percy would hesitate to adopt the title "Southern writer" as much as Flannery O'Connor did, he did recognize the essential value of the place-ness of the South for his writing. In the essay "Why I Live Where I Live," he once confessed, "I miss the South if I am gone too long" (*Signposts* 4).[22]

PERCY'S ENCOUNTERS WITH DOSTOEVSKY

As this study shows, the life's work of Walker Percy is partially defined by his relationship with, and his changing engagement in, the work of Dostoevsky. The nature of the influence cannot be understood in static terms; rather, the ties between the two authors must be tracked through time, through a close comparison of their texts and a careful mining of Percy's archives. What such work reveals is that both authors were concerned with the existence of God and of evil, the question of what it means to be human (particularly autonomy versus authority), and the tension between faith and science.

In the 1940s, Percy was a young medical student who had been raised without concern for church, faith, or Christianity in general. Then, through contact with cadavers during his residency, he contracted a life-threatening strain of tuberculosis. Quarantined at Trudeau Sanitorium, he began reading as though his life depended on it. Drawn to the existentialists, he picked up Dostoevsky not for the spiritual themes but because the Russian was, at the time, grouped with such existential writers as Sartre and Kierkegaard. Notwithstanding his teenaged discovery of Dostoevsky, Percy's upbringing had not prepared him for spiritual inquiry; his guardian, the highly regarded literary figure William Alexander Percy, was a Stoic humanist. In any case, the illness ultimately catalyzed not only a revolution in spiritual beliefs but also a change in profession. Like Dostoevsky before him, who had spent seven years imprisoned in Siberia, Percy's confinement at Trudeau made him a new man. Both Dostoevsky and Percy underwent suffering and exile before converting to Christianity: the former to Russian Orthodoxy and the latter to the Roman Catholic Church.

For Percy, it was precisely the feeling of death's nearness while at Trudeau that inspired him to read works about how to live. Percy would later recall, "I

---

21. In-text citations are used for primary sources that I cite throughout the book. *Mystery and Manners* by Flannery O'Connor will have in-text citations.
22. *Signposts in a Strange Land* by Walker Percy will be cited in text throughout the book.

found myself reading what I should have been reading in college and didn't. I started with Dostoevsky."[23] According to Percy's biographer Jay Tolson, Percy "read like a person who was trying to define his subject, searching among his favorite writers for clues."[24] Percy clarifies why he entertained such a rigorous syllabus of authors: "I read *The Brothers Karamazov* in Greenville high school and was tremendously affected, but I abandoned it then for science (like Ivan in the book)."[25] Percy refers to Ivan Karamazov, who is said to have been first regarded as a "student of natural science" and later recognized in "literary circles" (*Brothers Karamazov* 11).[26] In his notes from this period, Percy often speaks of Dostoevsky and his characters in familiar terms, showing how much he internalized the texts themselves and applied the works to his own life. Percy was also reading voraciously in philosophy and literature in an attempt to answer what he later calls "ultimate questions" (*Signposts* 202).[27]

One book that he reread at this time was Dostoevsky's *Notes from Underground* (*Pilgrim in the Ruins* 183). Suffering tuberculosis in confinement, Percy must have been fascinated by Dostoevsky's novella about a "sick man" living isolated underground. The story follows the unexplainable, purposeful self-destruction of a man who calls himself "a sick man . . . a wicked man" who doesn't "know a fig about [his] sickness" and is not sure what it is that ails him (*Notes* 3).[28] The Underground Man, as he refers to himself, defies the wisdom of doctors who treat him as though his illness were of an unseen cause. In 1943, when Percy updates a friend on his health, he writes, "My lesion, as they call it, appears to be healed. . . . [My] only handicap being a colossal disgust with myself."[29] The word "disgust" was also used in Percy's translation of the Underground Man, who uses the word to describe himself and others half a dozen times in the novel. Percy invokes the Underground Man by connect-

---

23. Percy, *More Conversations*, 136.
24. Tolson, *Pilgrim in the Ruins*, 183. Tolson assumes the annotations in Percy's edition of *Notes* are from when Percy read the novella in Trudeau. However, the questions Percy makes in the margins as well as the corresponding page numbers marked between the incongruent editions suggest those are later annotations from when he taught *Notes* as part of a course on alienation at Louisiana State University. For instance when Percy writes about "Kafka's hero" in the margin, he does so because he is drawing connections between another assigned reading on his syllabus. Moreover, he writes the question in the margin that Tolson cites, "If D were alive, who would he attack?" directly in his teaching notes from 1972.
25. Percy, *More Conversations*, 136.
26. *The Brothers Karamazov* by Dostoevsky will be cited in text throughout the book.
27. In his 1983 essay on Herman Melville, Percy writes, "Dostoevsky impresses Southerners [because he was not] afraid to deal with ultimate questions" (*Signposts in a Strange Land,* 202).
28. *Notes from Underground* will be cited in text throughout the book.
29. Percy, qtd. in Tolson's *Pilgrim in the Ruins*, 177; cites the letter to Ned Boone, Oct. 2, 1943, Southern Historical Collection (SHC).

ing his physical with his spiritual ailment. Dostoevsky's novel explores the internal workings of the human being: The Underground Man willfully defies reason and thus calls into question the nature of freedom and the propensity for evil in human beings. Although not the singular influence, this book did shape Percy's understanding of his own need for redemption.[30] Along with the philosophical explorations of the existentialists, the "dramatic form" of Dostoevsky's novel made Percy cognizant of the unexplainable in human nature.

Thus it was that Dostoevsky played a key role in Percy's conversion to religion and to fiction writing. Through Dostoevsky, Percy recognized that his reading was changing his life and that literature answered the questions that science could not. In the same year that he became a Catholic, 1947, he also declared himself a writer. Tolson credits *Notes* for Percy's concurrent life changes: "The story [*Notes*] set wheels in Percy's mind turning: Could one really write a story this way?"[31] Percy has no fewer than five copies of *Notes from Underground* in his library; over the course of his life, he taught the novel at least twice and used it as a model for two of his own novels, *The Moviegoer* and *Lancelot*. This novella, Tolson writes, was "the beginning of Percy's career as a moralist" and the fuel that fired Percy's interest in writing novels.[32]

As a recent convert in the 1950s, Percy's primary concern in reading Dostoevsky was to learn how to write fiction full of conviction. He regarded literature as the medium that had brought him from death to life, and he wanted to author life-restoring works himself. In his 1951 notes for *The Charterhouse*, Percy jots down the question, "Is there or is not there a God and Christ incarnate. If so, then what reason can be given for not making him the center of our lives?"[33] Like an echo from Dostoevsky, this question arises again and again in Percy's novels. In *The Moviegoer* the possibility of God must overcome not only the despair and malaise of the protagonist but also the sentimentality and hypocrisy of many American Christians. In Percy's second novel, two characters replay the dialogue from *The Idiot* as Sutter asks Bill Barrett whether he believes in God; these characters live in a world that has a powerless Christ like Myshkin, one that emphasizes the divide between the body and soul. Percy then accepts the Dostoevskian prediction that without God, the demonic reigns; demons inhabit both *Love in the Ruins* and *Lancelot*.

---

30. In the Underground Man, Percy sees the reflection of his own spiritual dearth. Tolson underscores the influence of *Notes*: "One cannot overestimate Percy's debt to Dostoyevsky's *Notes from Underground* for setting forth, in compelling dramatic form, the connection between human perversity and human freedom" (*Pilgrim in the Ruins*, 208).
31. Ibid., 183.
32. Ibid., 208.
33. SHC 164.21.

However, at the conclusion of all of his novels, Percy imitates the hope found in *The Brothers Karamazov,* and Percy's last two works are even more hopeful than his previous endings hinted. In *The Second Coming,* love, which in the Christian faith comes from God—whether or not the source is acknowledged—triumphs. And, in *The Thanatos Syndrome,* the Father Zosima character preaches the final words louder than any Ivan-Karamazovian protest.

A major theme that Percy drew from Dostoevsky was an awareness of the power of art to transform in an age when most people placed their trust in science. In his 1985 "Diagnosing the Modern Malaise," Percy explains how he applied his medical training to his search for answers to transcendent questions through reading and writing. In so doing, the aspiring novelist fashioned himself as a diagnostician for what was wrong in the world and with the people living in it, starting with himself. Percy recalls, "What did at last dawn on me as a medical student and intern, a practitioner, I thought, of the scientific method, was that there was a huge gap in the scientific worldview.... What it is like to be an individual living in the United States in the twentieth century" (*Signposts* 213). Percy had discovered this gap in the 1940s when he became engrossed in the existentialists. Later in the same essay, he explains that Dostoevsky convinced him that "*only* the writer, the existentialist philosopher, or the novelist can explore this gap with all the passion and seriousness and expectation of discovery" (ibid.). While science can tell about things, art offers insight into the nature of the human being, although occasionally the two fields may lead one to oppositional conclusions. It was from Dostoevsky that Percy gleaned this theme that would become so central to his work. From Dostoevsky's fiction, Percy learned how to embody his faith in fiction; that is, he developed an incarnational aesthetic. In his own fictional worlds, Percy would reveal how the theological prophecies of Dostoevsky played out in the twentieth century. As I will show, the aesthetic method by which Percy learned to incarnate these ideas is as significant as the ideas themselves.

APPROACHES TO INFLUENCE STUDIES

In the summer of 2011, I had dinner at the Italian restaurant Volare in Chicago with a few friends. Beneath the reverberating hum of the "L" train, while eating enough garlic and drinking enough red wine to begin emitting Italy from our pores, we discussed literature, politics, religion, and anything else worthy of debate. The subject of my book on Dostoevsky and Percy came up. I related to these friends, two professors and an editor and his wife, my exhilarating discovery of Percy's obsession with Dostoevsky, which I had recently uncovered in his manuscripts and papers. I couldn't contain my excitement and was rambling with blushing cheeks and hurriedly gesturing hands when one of my friends, the editor, interrupted me. "But why does it matter?" he asked. My ecstasy was instantaneously muted, and he took another bite of pasta. Yet, seeing my perplexed and disappointed expression, he continued, "It seems like you should make a bigger argument about what *influence* even means." He stressed the word *influence*. His suggestion continued to gnaw at me as I began writing this book. What I realized in the process of writing was that this book mattered most because of what it revealed about influence.

My study of Dostoevsky and Percy responds to a secular assumption about human nature that plays out in a couple of ways in literary studies: the sovereignty of the individual as it affects the motivation of the author as well as, for the reader, the necessary death of the author. Influence studies are unpopular because, to the modern mind, they disenfranchise writers of originality. In an investigation into the discrimination of influences, Andrew Elfenbein writes, "A lingering mythology of genius resists the usefulness of such a description [of influence] by insisting that the minds of great authors are unique; to describe them in terms of general processes elides the specialness that makes them worth studying in the first place."[34] However, in Jay Clayton and Eric Rothstein's *Influence and Intertextuality in Literary History,* they question such "normative judgments about originality."[35] They cite two eighteenth-century works that posit "originality" as the "key to a work of literature and the only true sign of an author's genius."[36] These works seem to foreshadow the obsession with originality among nineteenth-century authors, who prided themselves on individual and unique means of expression, so that any admission of having learned from or emulated one's predecessors was to discredit one's own unique voice.

In *The Anxiety of Influence* (1973), Harold Bloom's seminal study on the nature of literary influence, he argues that strong poets wrestle with their predecessors in order to create works by which they may establish their immortality. The conflict with former authors stems from a need to establish the self as apart from any "parent" poet, a self-made poet, in other words, the victory being artistic autonomy. Bloom relies on romantic poets, with a few contemporary examples, such as Wallace Stevens, for his evidence. His explanations are fraught with defensive phraseology—"necessary rebellion," "poetic

---

34. Elfenbein, "On the Discrimination of Influences," 483.
35. Clayton and Rothstein, *Influence and Intertextuality in Literary History,* 12.
36. Edward Young's *Conjectures on Original Composition* (1759) and William Duff's *An Essay on Original Genius* (1767). Clayton and Rothstein, *Influence and Intertextuality in Literary History,* 5.

misprision," and "agonistic struggle"—because he believes influence to be both unwanted and unavoidable. Bloom summarizes his thesis thus: "*Poetic influence—when it involves two strong, authentic poets,—always proceeds by a misreading of the prior poet, an act of creative correction that is actually and necessarily a misinterpretation.*"[37] By opposing, completing, discarding, or reworking the original, a poet "misreads" and "misinterprets" his antecedent. According to Bloom's theory, a writer will not imitate another volitionally, and thus, a study of influence must uncover the ways in which a writer has tried to overcome his predecessor.

On the other side of the pages, from the reader's perspective, editors Jay Clayton and Eric Rothstein look back at the change in literary theory from one of influence studies (pre-1950) to intertextuality studies. In the former, the author was of great significance, including beliefs, historical context, and intention, but the latter tries to reclaim the role of the reader by focusing on the object, the text itself. It should be noted that the advent of intertextual criticism—namely the publication of "Word, Dialogue, and Novel" (1966) by Julia Kristeva—was shortly followed by Roland Barthes's publication of "Death of the Author" (1967). The congruence of the two ideas makes sense, for no two sovereigns may occupy the same space. If readers are to take precedence, they must first dethrone the author. I am grateful to part of Bloom's project, namely, his insistence on the import of the author, in contrast to his intertextual and deconstructionist colleagues. "Poems are written by men," Bloom insists, "and not by anonymous Splendors."[38] However, I have undertaken my reading of Dostoevsky and Percy with quite different presuppositions about human beings. In contrast to these goals of authoritative autonomy and the good of individualism, this book suggests that authors create the best work when they humbly recognize those models whom they consciously or subconsciously emulate, and, consequentially for readers, a recognition of this imitation produces greater understanding—with all the humility that word entails (literally, to stand under rather than over such texts).

Before the aforementioned nineteenth century and modern writers became so fixated on originality, a host of Christian authors—Dante, Chaucer, and Shakespeare, to mention a few canonical names—wrote by intentionally drawing upon their literary forerunners. Taking Chaucer's *Troilus and Criseyde* as an example, we can see influence forward and backward: for the Elizabethan theater, Shakespeare adapts Chaucer's poem, which Chaucer borrowed from Boccaccio, who probably based his *Il Filostrato* on Benoît de

---

37. Bloom, *Anxiety*, 30. Emphasis in original.
38. Ibid., 43.

Sainte-Maure's *Le Roman de Troie,* which claims in its prologue to be drawn from the memoirs of an eyewitness in Troy.[39] None of these writers felt the pressing necessity of originality. Rather, these writers considered the value of the work to be its benefit for readers. When they themselves read, they discovered truth; and thus, in their own writing, they felt compelled to recapitulate the stories for new audiences, so that each new generation could experience the stories afresh.

These poets did not desire originality any more than they desired recognition. For instance, the twelfth-century Anglo-Norman poet, known to us only as Marie de France, purports in her prologue that she draws from ancient stories because "beneficial things" should be retold. Marie explains that the ancients "express themselves very obscurely so that those in later generations, who had to learn them, could provide a *gloss* for the text and put the finishing touches to their meaning."[40] To "gloss" the text does not mean to "complete" the poem, as Bloom describes the method of *tessera,* in which a poet "antithetically" rewrites the antecedent poet with "another sense, as though the precursor had failed to go far enough."[41] Instead, both the writer and the reader acknowledge that truth, being beyond the complete comprehension of one person, may only be illuminated in part by each successive writer and reader.

Pre-Enlightenment poets, primarily Christian artists such as Dante or Milton, defined "influence" according to its Latin root "inflow" meaning "an emanation or force coming in upon mankind from the stars," in Bloom's words.[42] In *The Divine Comedy,* Dante moves from a consideration of "one's own star" as the guide, the artistic muse drawn from the self, exalted by Brunetto Latini, Dante's teacher in *Inferno,* to acknowledge the stars as emblematic of divine inspiration to which Dante will submit: "Already were all my will and my desires turned . . . by the Love that moves the sun and the other stars."[43] He enacts what Bloom refers to disdainfully as "Christian teachings of sublimation."[44] Chaucer and Milton behave similarly. At the conclusion of *Troilus and Criseyde,* Chaucer begs God, his "maker," to make his "little tragedy" into a "comedy," the word alluding to Dante's poem.[45] And Milton, initially imitating earlier epics with his call to the "Muse," modifies the term

---

39. Sarah-Jane Murray discusses this in the opening chapter of *From Plato to Lancelot*: Benoît gives credit to a discovered manuscript by Trojan Dares, "a supposed firsthand witness to the fall of Troy" (38).
40. Marie de France, *Lais of Marie de France,* 41. Emphasis mine.
41. Bloom, *Anxiety,* 14.
42. Ibid., 26.
43. Dante, *Inferno,* 1.xv.55–56 and 3.33.143–45.
44. Bloom, *Anxiety,* 10.
45. Chaucer, *Troilus and Criseyde,* 5.256.

with the word "heavenly" and conflates it with the Holy Spirit as he seeks its instruction for his poem.[46] These pre-Enlightenment poets appear to operate by an understanding of influence far different from the modern definition.

The problem for twentieth-century writers or critics such as Bloom stems from a misreading of the phrase "X influenced Y," which prioritizes the former over the latter. As art historian Michael Baxandall[47] points out, the grammar mistakenly attributes authority to the wrong party: "If one says that X influenced Y it does seem that one is saying that X did something to Y rather than that Y did something to X. But . . . the second is always the more lively reality."[48] For example, although it is true that Virgil influenced Dante, rather than focusing primarily on the Roman forerunner, the more interesting study would assess how Dante pays tribute to Virgil. Although grammatically passive, the *influencee* is the active agent and is properly the subject of the study, as in the case of Dostoevsky and Percy.

One way to understand the shifting influence of Dostoevsky upon Percy is that the former is manifested in the work of the latter, in accordance with how Percy remembers Dostoevsky, consciously or subconsciously, during any given moment of writing. This model of influence is something like what George Steiner describes in *Real Presences*: "The presence, visible solicited or exorcized, of Homer, Virgil and Dante in Milton's *Paradise Lost*, in the epic satire of Pope and in the pilgrimage upstream of Ezra Pound's *Cantos*, is a 'real presence,' a critique in action."[49] By drawing on his predecessors, according to Steiner, a poet can "make the past text a present presence."[50] The new text is a "critique in action" of the old, not in the sense of finding fault, but in the sense of bringing that text into the present moment. Indeed, when it comes to literary influence, one author's working upon another nourishes the predecessor as much as it feeds the work of the progenitor.

Steiner uses the metaphor of digestion to describe one poet's consumption of an earlier one. The later poet makes the earlier poet's work her own, and then she produces work that bears resemblance to the original: "It is through this internalized 're-production' of and amendment to previous representations that an artist will articulate what might appear to have been even

---

46. Milton, *Paradise Lost*, 1.6.
47. Baxandall, *Patterns of Intention*, 58–59.
48. Bloom contends that the later poet may win the contest match with his antecedent or may even produce a work that rewrites the original better. However, his theory insists on seeing two writers as against one another, rather than as a gift from the forerunner or willing selflessness on the part of the later poet. For Bloom, this kind of mentor relationship only produces weak poets: "Where generosity is involved, the poets influenced are minor or weaker" (*Anxiety*, 30).
49. Steiner, *Real Presences*, 12–13.
50. Ibid., 13.

the most spontaneous, the most realistic of his sightings."[51] One example of George Steiner's "internalized reproduction" occurs in Percy's last novel, when he unknowingly represents a work of O'Connor's that he read almost thirty years prior. In *The Thanatos Syndrome,* Father Smith asks the protagonist Tom More whether he knows "where tenderness always leads," answering his own question with the haunting revelation, "To the gas chamber."[52] In a 1989 interview with Percy, Scott Walter catches the author by surprise when he assumes that Percy intentionally alluded to O'Connor's introduction to *A Memoir of Mary Ann,* where she writes that "tenderness . . . ends in the fumes of the gas chamber."[53] After hearing the shared quote, Percy responds, "I'm amazed. I would happily admit that I did that consciously because I'd love to give her the credit."[54] Although Percy owned and lightly annotated his copy of O'Connor's essay, he did not recall purposefully quoting her. Despite being taken aback by the similarities in the two passages, Percy declares he would "happily" grant O'Connor influence had he realized it. Percy has no professed anxiety concerning influences on his work, especially those that he chooses.[55]

For his part, Percy often spoke of his influences in a tongue-in-cheek tone. Upon the success of his first published novel, *The Moviegoer,* he says offhandedly, "All this happened to the novelist and his character without the slightest consciousness of a debt to St. Augustine or Dante" (*Signposts* 193). Percy implies that he was in fact indebted to his Christian predecessors, but that in his naïveté, he was initially unaware of it. In the same year that Percy penned this essay, he affirms his desire to emulate the European existentialists: "They created living characters who illustrated the themes of philosophy. So I said, why not do that in the South?"[56] Percy determined to follow the form of the writers he admired—without trying to fit into a formula—while drawing his content from his own time and place. Tolson writes, "Percy realized, he could not simply rewrite *Pilgrim's Progress* or Dostoevsky."[57] So rather than set out on his own as though he were the human race's first storyteller, Percy turned

---

51. Ibid., 17.
52. Percy, *Thanatos Syndrome,* 128.
53. O'Connor, *Collected Works,* 830–31.
54. Percy, *More Conversations,* 229.
55. In his 2012 *Anatomy of Influence,* Bloom clarifies that it is not the poet who will feel anxiety but the work itself will experience it: "Influence anxiety exists between poems and not between persons" (4). However, this later addendum seems contrary to his insistence in *Anxiety of Influence* that "a poet's stance, his Word, his imaginative identity, his whole being, *must* be unique to him and remain unique, or he will perish, as a poet" (71). The stress in the former book is on the poet, the one, Bloom argues, who fears death and thus undertakes a competition with his literary forbearers.
56. Percy, *Conversations,* 217.
57. Tolson, *Pilgrim in the Ruins,* 212.

to the masters to help him discover his voice. Throughout his career in fiction, Percy repeatedly looked to Dostoevsky in particular as the artist who could model for him how to create stories drawn from his faith that would speak to his own secular age. Percy actively *absorbs* Dostoevsky's work, a term that Foote uses in Percy's eulogy: "Walker *absorbed* his preceptors."[58] Whatever Percy admired in other authors became part of who he was, the way that he saw the world, and thus the way he depicted his own worlds. In an interview near the end of his life, Percy asserted, "Whatever you believe, whatever you think, is the way you are, and what you are informs your novel."[59] For Percy there is no contradiction between imitation and originality; he appears to have no interest in that dichotomy that so captivated the romantic poets.

While much work has been done in the academy since the romantics in terms of influence, such as the development of intertextuality studies, deconstructionism, new historicism, postcolonialism, and so forth—all of which challenge the autonomy of the author—these trends do so to the detriment of the author's agency. To use an apt cliché, they throw the baby out with the bathwater. The author becomes subject to a variety of forces, and thus the text is a byproduct of outside "influences." Instead I want to examine the way Percy *chooses* to submit his work to the example of a previous master. Percy desired to imitate one whom he deemed better than himself. By doing so he suffers no anxiety, for his act is a willful meditation upon the success of his predecessor. Moreover, Percy never claims to rival Dostoevsky because the goal is not focused on his personal success as an author.[60] Rather Percy begins writing as a means to extend truth to other seekers. Because Percy found such truth outside of himself, he never claimed authority over it. Writing, for Percy, is continuing a conversation that others have started about the nature of reality and predicament of human existence. He chooses Dostoevsky as the ultimate conversation partner—not to mention Kierkegaard, Sartre, Nietzsche, and others—and he offers his contribution to the discussion. There is a relationship between Dostoevsky and his novels, and Percy, his novels, and his readers. Rather than Percy standing in opposition to his master, he is in communication with him and places him in communication with us.

As readers, we too, must realize the fault in trying to deny the role of the author in our reading. Our paradigmatic assumptions about our indepen-

---

58. *Correspondence*, 304. Emphasis mine.
59. Percy, *More Conversations*, 224.
60. However, in Percy's satirical interview with himself, "Questions They Never Asked Me So I Asked Myself" (1977), he feigns protest against the subject of Dostoevsky's influence: "*Do you have any favorite dead writers?*" Percy queries himself and answers, "None that I care to talk about. Please don't ask me about Dostoevsky and Kierkegaard" (*Signposts*, 399). Through irony, Percy admits to these two writers as his "favorites" and thus his most significant influences.

dence will blind us to a full appreciation of the text. In his analysis of René Girard's theory on secular culture, Scott Cowdell writes,

> The independent buffered self is in reality a fragile metaphysical poseur and the modern romantic individual is an illusion. . . . Our myth is one of cool individualism, and of a pride in our metaphysical autonomy that Girard traces from the Renaissance to become the underlying principle of every new Western doctrine since the Enlightenment.[61]

Cowdell pulls the term "independent buffered self" from Charles Taylor's definition of "secular" in *A Secular Age*. Somewhat in line with Girard, Taylor proposes that "secular" includes a belief in a sovereign self. Yet, as Cowdell indicates, this pride is illusory. Just as the authors cannot help but be influenced by those who came before, nor can readers ignore the reality of interdependency.

Both Dostoevsky and Percy desired to write novels that would compel change in their readers. Neither would want their reader to see only as they saw or parrot their intentions in the text. To be the best reader of either author, however, is to imitate the way they read. Standing humbly beneath these works of literature allows them to rain down truths into our consciousness that then become integrated into our way of seeing the world. Hopefully by showing how Percy read Dostoevsky, I've proposed a theory of influence that stands in stark contrast to most postsecular assumptions about literary relationships. More significantly, a look at how Percy imitated Dostoevsky should be a model of humility for all of us. For only in renouncing our claims to be sovereign selves may we see fully as we ought.

OVERVIEW

This book will examine Percy's six published novels as well as his two unpublished works in order to understand the evolving nature of his relationship to Dostoevsky. In each of Percy's novels, he distills the themes that Dostoevsky had portrayed on a panoramic scale, narrowing the focus to individual men struggling with alienation and the question of God's existence. Along with this change in scale, Percy also shifted the mode from tragic to comic, and it is the nature and consequences of this change that are articulated in the chapters to follow. After decades of denying the usefulness of studying writerly influence, literary scholars can benefit from recovering this approach in order to under-

---

61. Cowdell, *René Girard and Secular Modernity*, 45.

stand the origins and meanings of literary texts. To study an author's influences is to discover, paradoxically, what in the writer is most original.

In the first chapter, I hunt for traces of Dostoevsky in Percy's unpublished novels, hints that foreshadow Dostoevsky's later significance to his work. Notes on Percy's first novel, *The Charterhouse*, indicate that Percy was reading Dostoevsky primarily for his ideas and not his art. Among other influences, Percy was trying out the ideas and styles of Mann and Wolfe. In *The Gramercy Winner*, Percy drew heavily on Colin Wilson's *The Outsider*, which was itself influenced by Dostoevsky's fiction, as he began to develop the alienated protagonist who would become one of his fiction's distinctive features. Because Percy had no formal training as a novelist, he sought the influence of other writers; however, at that point, he failed to find the model that he needed, and the two novels he produced are bloodless and flat. I conclude the chapter with a brief outline of "incarnational realism," an aesthetic Percy learned from Dostoevsky and implemented in his later fiction.

In chapter two, I look at Percy's faithful (re)membering of Dostoevsky in *The Moviegoer*. Specifically, Percy both remembers (models) and re-members (reassembles) Dostoevsky's *Notes from Underground* in order to develop his own mid-twentieth-century novel. During Percy's very act of writing, he came to realize that Dostoevsky would be, and had to be, the central influence on his work. *The Moviegoer* evinces both the polyphonic form and, more importantly, the incarnational aesthetic of *Notes*. Essentially Percy brings his predecessor into the present moment, midcentury America, creating a novel that is no less original for having found inspiration in Dostoevsky.

Chapter three presents a close analysis of *The Last Gentleman*, Percy's most direct and intentional copy of a Dostoevsky novel, *The Idiot*. In the novel, Percy crafts a protagonist in the "holy fool" tradition, modeling Barrett on Myshkin, who in turn is modeled on Don Quixote. Through close examination of the parallels between Percy's novel and Dostoevsky's *The Idiot*—including the two protagonists' "strangeness"; their journeys from orphanhood to adoption; and their abstracted, "angelic" love of idealized women—I demonstrate that Percy learned from Dostoevsky how to create novels that made Christianity palatable to a modern audience. *Don Quixote* served as their shared inspiration in constructing their romantic protagonists. Disappointed with readers' misunderstanding of *The Moviegoer*, Percy was determined that in this, his second novel for publication, readers would be elevated with affirmations of Christianity—specifically the doctrine that Christ is the only source of goodness—even if they were tinged with satire, and this is why Percy turned Dostoevsky's tragic ending into a hopeful one.

Unlike Percy's first two published novels, which explored the inner life of a single alienated individual, Percy's third, *Love in the Ruins,* attempts a vast Dostoevskian scope, taking on the spiritual sickness of an entire nation. Percy models his apocalyptic setting and suicidal protagonist on Dostoevsky's *Demons.* As chapter four shows, even though Percy's attempted "big one" turned into yet another story of an individual protagonist,[62] Percy still manages to revive Dostoevsky's themes and questions and apply Dostoevsky's critiques of his own society to twentieth-century America. The mode of literary influence that is exemplified in *Love in the Ruins*—borrowing one writer's critiques and applying them to one's own time—is possible because the ills that plague one society are, all too often, the result of universal spiritual sickness rather than isolated contingencies.

In chapter five, we examine Percy's darkest novel, *Lancelot,* in which he pushes the Russian novelist's signature themes—violence, sexuality, tortured conscience—further than Dostoevsky himself ever did. In *Lancelot,* Percy draws on the characters, plot, and themes of *Notes from Underground, Crime and Punishment,* and *The Brothers Karamazov,* darkening them to a point that he "outdostoevsk[ies] Dostoevsky."[63] In doing so Percy critiques the problems of his own era and conjures a glimmer of hope. This chapter demonstrates how profound influence can occur unintentionally. We see in *Lancelot* how Percy, having read and digested Dostoevsky's work, came to construct, without intending to, a novel that is more Dostoevskian than the Russian's own work.

The final chapter considers Percy's fifth and sixth novels, *The Second Coming* and *The Thanatos Syndrome,* which are sequels to his earlier fiction. In these works, Dostoevsky still resonates, though more elusively. *The Second Coming* shares Dostoevsky's concern that language was being misused for heretical ideologies, and *The Thanatos Syndrome* demonstrates how violence arises from this degradation of language. For this final novel, Percy gave credit to Dostoevsky for the idea. Because Percy saw how certain issues had evolved since Dostoevsky's time, he realized that in these last books, he must do more than chronicle Dostoevskian prophecies. He must make his own.

If this book succeeds, it will erase the tarnish on the idea of influence and highlight aspects of Percy's work that often are underrated. For too long

---

62. In at least half a dozen of his letters to Shelby Foote, Percy refers to "the big one," the novel to outdo all novels, using *The Brothers Karamazov* as his ideal. He uses this phrase to refer to *Love in the Ruins* as he is brainstorming and planning the novel (*Correspondence,* 129).

63. In a letter dated Sept. 25, 1976, Foote tells Percy that he hopes to accomplish this feat in his next novel (*Correspondence,* 219). Percy had already completed *Lancelot.*

has the romantic preoccupation with originality prevailed, a poetic philosophy that is frankly an illusion. Since influence is unavoidable, it should not be downplayed but celebrated. Unpacking the layers of influence in a body of writing should enhance the meaning in the work. It is with this assumption that I have sought to evoke every whisper of Dostoevsky's name from Percy's fiction. Although Percy named many other influences—Kierkegaard, Faulkner, and Walter Miller, to list a few—the goal of this study is to focus on one particular influence. And the choice of Dostoevsky is not random. It was this author from whom Percy learned how to captivate his non-Christian readership with fiction saturated by a Christian vision of reality. Not only was his method of imitation in line with this Christian faith but also the aesthetic mode and very content of his narratives centered on his knowledge of Christ. The influence of Dostoevsky on Percy, then, becomes significant as a modern case study for showing the illusion of artistic autonomy—and absolute autonomy in general—and the strength of choosing a good model. Each chapter looks at how Percy set about becoming a novelist with emphasis on his modeling of Dostoevsky. My hope is to revitalize influence studies, especially as they relate to our religious assumptions about aesthetics, and by doing so with Percy as my exemplar, to uplift novels that have something to add to theological discussions. I hope readers will become excited by this way of thinking about literary influence, and after reading this study, dust off their copies of *The Brothers Karamazov* or *The Thanatos Syndrome* to read them again, with fresh eyes, ready to glean more truth about the world we live in.

CHAPTER 1

~

Failed Imitation in *The Charterhouse* and *The Gramercy Winner*

WALKER PERCY'S first two unpublished works bear the faintest traces of Dostoevsky's influence. Although turned toward both the Catholic Church and the life of a novelist by Dostoevsky's powerful fiction, Percy did not initially imitate his spiritual and literary forerunner. One may expect that, as a new convert, Percy spent hours poring over Aquinas's *Summa*. Instead, he dedicated more attention to atheist writers such as Sartre, Proust, and Thomas Mann. The latter two figures were probably recommended to him by his close friend Shelby Foote, who had established himself as a writer between 1949 and 1952 with a handful of novels. However great these writers are, their fiction failed to provide the model that Percy needed, one that allied his new beliefs with his new vocation.

In his first two novels, Percy tries to write an imitation of Wolfe or Mann with Christianity capped on top, and the combination crumbles. Neither Mann nor Wolfe could provide models for Percy's fiction because neither shared Percy's Christian philosophy. Their novels could not teach him how to create conversion narratives, show salvation, or illustrate any of the sacraments of the Church because neither author adhered to Percy's faith. In both the notes from the first attempt and the manuscript pages of the second novel, Percy searches for a model of the kind of fiction he wants to write. Percy sought to unite his philosophy with a narrative, ideas with images, the universal with the particular, and to bring higher truths to the forefront. Whereas other literary models that he mentions in interviews, such as Mark Twain and Ernest Hemingway, could write exemplary realistic fiction, and his philosophic mentors, such as Sartre and Kierkegaard, could create noteworthy existential allegories, neither the novelists nor the philosophers combined the two in the way that Percy desired.[1] It is easy to imagine that the memory of that charmed Christmastime reading of *The Brothers Karamazov* as a teenager pulled Percy back again and again to the worn copies of Dostoevsky's novels for inspiration.

At this point in Percy's development, he was no longer reading Dostoevsky merely for plot, as when he was a teenager; and yet, neither was he reading Dostoevsky for art. Instead Percy was in a middle stage of maturation, focused solely on Dostoevsky's ideas.[2] Percy read the Russian as a thinker, specifically a Christian existentialist, mining the motifs, themes, and ideas from the novelist to use in his own work. Despite Percy's deep engagement with Dostoevsky's ideas, however, he had not yet attained the necessary craft to embody the theology. Having recently converted to Catholicism, Percy had determined to write novels as a means of exploring the truths about the world that had been revealed to him via his new faith and his reading of great literature such as Dostoevsky's. His first two novels, never published, manifested the themes and archetypal characters that would interest him throughout his career.[3]

---

1. Percy, *Conversations*, 275.

2. It is likely that Percy's philosophical transition from Tolstoy, the pseudospiritual author, to Dostoevsky, the Christian novelist, coincided with his conversion to Catholicism in 1947. In his essay, "From Tolstoy to Dostoyevsky in *The Moviegoer*," Lewis Lawson asserts that it was Tolstoy, not Dostoevsky, who was Percy's "model when he began to write fiction" (411). Of the two references to Tolstoy in Percy's notes, the first calls the opening chapter of *War and Peace* "genius" and suggests it as a "model for scene of social gathering" (SHC 164.27). Notes such as this one reflect Percy's search for a model for writing fiction, but the half a dozen mentions of Dostoevsky suggest Percy considered him a more worthwhile possibility than Tolstoy. Later he would advise Foote to consider the beginning of *The Brothers Karamazov* because it "work[s] eminently" better than *War and Peace*: "Frankly I never thought the opening of *War and Peace* worked—a monstrous bore in fact, cocktail party conversation!" (Sept. 10, 1980, *Correspondence*, 268). In this letter, he overturns his earlier esteem of Tolstoy in favor of Dostoevsky.

3. Percy's general approach is from *The Brothers Karamazov*. In his notes for this first novel, Percy tries to unravel the "difficulties of introducing the 'Catholic thing' into novel" (SHC 164.19), turning to Dostoevsky's example for aid. He observes: "Brothers Karamazov. D's device. A religious approach, but no secrets, no subtleties. Concede all to begin with; evils of church etc. Even a mocking tone, to disarm hostile reader" (SHC 164.26). Perhaps the note refers to Ivan's or his father Fyodor's mockery of the church: Ivan insinuates that the Roman Catholic

As this chapter will show, Percy's first two attempted novels went no further than imitating Dostoevsky in an amateurish way: the characters are unreal, the action stilted, and the ideas flat on the page. *The Charterhouse* and *The Gramercy Winner* did not embody Percy's philosophical revelations so much as disembody them. As Caroline Gordon put it, the characters seemed like abstract, floating heads in a grayish unreality.[4] In Percy's late essay "Physician as Novelist" (1989), he describes his initial efforts at novel writing as two poor *imitations* (*Signposts* 193). He recalls wondering, after his two failed imitations, "Why not forget about other writers, however distinguished, and go your own way? . . . Wasn't this what Newton and Darwin and Freud had done in science?"[5] Percy was asking the questions rhetorically, for as a scientist, Percy would have been accustomed to learning from those who preceded him.[6] The seventy-three-year-old Percy would declare that his thirty-something self had attempted to take the lone-artist approach and had ironically "landed squarely in the oldest tradition of Western letters: the pilgrim's search outside himself (*Signposts* 193). Indeed, in Percy's first two unpublished novels, the influence of Dostoevsky is already perceptible; Percy's original impressions of Dostoevsky were intermingled with two other works that were themselves influenced by the Russian novelist. Karl Stern's autobiography *Pillar of Fire* (1951) would inform the transcendent themes of *The Charterhouse*, while Colin Wilson's *The Outsider* (1956) would provide the prototype of what was to become Percy's signature protagonist in *The Gramercy Winner* and later novels.

Church is spiritually bankrupt, and Fyodor publicly lambasts the Russian Orthodox clerics. Either way, Percy recognizes how Dostoevsky employs the polyphonic technique—a method Percy later adopts—to raise religious issues without alarming his secular audience.

4. Although Gordon and Allen Tate appreciated the religious themes in Percy's first attempted novel, *The Charterhouse*, both of them agreed the novel lacked tangibility. In a letter dated Dec. 11, 1951, Gordon advises him "to realize that <u>nothing</u> happens in a vacuum" (SHC 387.3). She preaches, "A novelist has no business with thought at all—unless he can translate it into action. Your concern is primarily with your hero's sensations and emotions. . . . But his thought cannot substitute for action" (ibid. 15). Tate concurs with Gordon's assessment in his own letter to Percy (Jan. 1, 1952), repeatedly instructing him how to give "characters a little more life" and make certain ones "three-dimensional" (ibid. 426.2). In addition to sending encouragement and advice, the two writers interceded on behalf of Percy's novel with publishers, but editors rejected it for similar concerns.

5. Ibid., 193.

6. Granted Newton was not the first to use the metaphor "standing on the shoulders of giants," and as a reader of Catholic theology, Percy may have also been familiar with the phrase from Bernard of Chartres, who originally penned it.

DISEMBODIED CHARACTERS IN *THE CHARTERHOUSE*

All that remains of Percy's first effort at writing a novel is approximately twenty typed pages of sporadic notes, written from 1951 to 1952, in which he plans a manuscript he entitles *The Charterhouse*. Percy probably began writing the manuscript shortly after joining the Catholic Church; Tolson describes the book as making a "decidedly Catholic argument."[7] Percy worked on the novel for almost five years before destroying the manuscript. Although the plot of *The Charterhouse* remains a mystery, fragmented episodes have been pieced together to indicate that the trajectory of the narrative seems to be the protagonist's potential conversion.

Scholars have pieced together a sense of *The Charterhouse*'s plot by studying Percy's notes and the comments of people who read the manuscript.[8] The story, which centers on the potential conversion of the protagonist, Ben Cleburne, begins with Ben's return home from a sanatorium and his befriending of a Jewish convert to Catholicism, Ignatz Kramer. The two men carry on several nondescript interactions, and then Ben undertakes a pilgrimage to South America. There, Ben decides to operate a filling station—a fantasy that Percy's later protagonist, *The Moviegoer*'s Binx Bolling, would also entertain—and he marries a girl named Abbie. Percy's notes on the novel mention a funeral, probably that of Ben's father; a jail; a golf course; and a game of cards. But the driving tension of the novel, as the novel's few readers have recognized, is Ben's suffering from the feeling that he is spiritually dead. The fragmented notes on the novel suggest that in the end, even though Ben seeks the help of Ignatz and of a psychiatrist, his spiritual development is ultimately thwarted.

The novel is blatantly Christian from the outset. On the first page of *The Charterhouse* manuscript, Percy's first note reads, "The tremendous compelling figure of Christ on His Cross, overshadowing everything in these times."[9] While writing the novel, Percy knew his contemporaries would resist the unapologetic spirituality of his work; and yet he was determined to compose

---

7. Tolson, *Pilgrim in the Ruins*, 197.

8. Because no manuscript for *The Charterhouse* survives, our knowledge of the text derives from Percy's notes; from the comments by those who read the novel—Gordon, Foote, Percy's family, and a handful of potential editors; and from Percy's marginalia from the books that he read during these years. According to biographer Patrick Samway, who interviewed Percy about the early novel, "Though we do not know the book's outcome, it is clear that it centers on a young man who wants to develop the spiritual part of his nature" (*Walker Percy: A Life*, 145).

9. Percy, SHC 164.1.

a story that deliberated upon religious issues. For this first attempt at a novel, he chose the Christian genre of the conversion narrative. Indeed he turns not only to Dostoevsky but to an early twentieth-century German neurologist and psychologist, Karl Stern, who after surviving life in Nazi Germany recounted his conversion to Catholicism in the autobiography *Pillar of Fire* (1951).[10] In Stern's autobiography, he draws heavily on Dostoevsky's novels to interpret his personal suffering, justify his conversion, and explain the evil that he witnessed at war. Although Stern's primary allusions to Dostoevsky are to *The Brothers Karamazov* and *The Idiot,* many other passages also recall *Crime and Punishment,* including his description of a foolish conversion, of the murderous impulses within all humans, and of his use of psychology. According to Percy's notes,[11] in which he mentions *Pillar of Fire* four times, he consciously based the Ignatz figure on Stern's book: "The lesson of Pillar of Fire. Jew in face of anti-Semitism can become Catholic."[12]

In Percy's heavily annotated volume of Stern, he drew double lines in the margins to mark the passage depicting Stern's conversion. That conversion, in Stern's account, took place during a visit to a psychiatrist: "When I first lay down on the couch I was a convinced dialectic materialist; when I arose from the couch for the last time I was absolutely convinced of the primacy of the Spirit."[13] The sudden and unexplainable conversion that Stern describes is similar to that of Dostoevsky's protagonist, Raskolnikov, in *Crime and Punishment.* However, Percy must have taken note of Stern's caution in the introduction to *Pillar of Fire*: "To write the story of a conversion is a foolish undertaking, for the convert, the 'turned-around,' is a fool."[14] Stern explains that the convert, because he believes in unseen realities, miracles, or revelations that transcend reason, will appear to be like Don Quixote. The ultimate question causing the division between fools and others is "whether Jesus of Nazareth is Christ incarnate."[15] Stern uses the authority of Dostoevsky to bolster the importance of the question, writing, "Dostoevsky once said that it is the one question on which everything in the world depends."[16] In reaction to

---

10. Foote recommends the novel to Percy in a letter dated Oct. 17, 1950, and Percy has annotated his copy in his library. In Percy's *Charterhouse* notes, he mentions Stern second only to Dostoevsky (2.278).

11. Percy, SHC 164.20.

12. Percy underlines twice Stern's conclusion, which follows a quote by Father Zosima: "Psychoanalysis has reaffirmed that which the Church has taught all the time; namely that potentially there is inside every man a den of murderers and thieves" (*Pillar of Fire,* 297).

13. Ibid., 154.

14. Ibid., 3.

15. Ibid.

16. Ibid.

Stern's opening paragraph, Percy writes in his notes, "Is there or is not there a God and Christ incarnate. If so, then what reason can be given for not making him the center of our lives?"[17] Whether Percy asks this question of himself or intended this question to be placed into the mouth of a character is unclear, but either way, his raising of the question is itself significant. Percy would return to this question in his unpublished novel *The Last Gentleman*, in which the protagonist appears like Don Quixote and yet fails to live with any concept of incarnation or the embodied soul.

As for how Percy was reading Dostoevsky at this time, the fledgling novelist's notes suggest that his understanding of the Russian writer was simplistic. The second page of notes begins,[18] "Dostoievski's [sic] way of creating characters from his own complexity. The Brothers. He is all three. Priest, atheist, worldling."[19] This note suggests that Percy is discovering how Dostoevsky draws a multiplicity of fictional characters from his own person, using autobiography to compose not one protagonist but competing characters. However, Percy reduces the complex characters of Alyosha, Ivan, and Dmitri (assuming those are the three characters to whom he is referring with the phrase "priest, atheist, worldling") to one-word descriptions. These notes suggest that, at the time, Percy read Dostoevsky to extract the existentialist ideas from the story but missed the incarnational aesthetic—the very element that would later captivate him. Instead of round, dynamic characters driving the novel, Percy's notes reveal a fascination with disembodied ideas.

One ambiguous line in *The Charterhouse* notes is illuminated by Dostoevsky's *Crime and Punishment*. The line is a context-less piece of scribbled dialogue: "Ben: (jokingly): And how will I know when Grace acts within me? Ignatz: you will not want to kill a man."[20] The line recalls a moment in *Crime and Punishment* when Raskolnikov decides to kill a woman without reason or motive, merely to enact his philosophical nihilism. By the conclusion of the book, Raskolnikov converts suddenly and confesses. The confession is inspired by Raskolnikov's hearing of the story of Lazarus,[21] then wandering down the St. Petersburg streets; when "a certain sensation seize[s] him all at once [and takes] hold of him entirely—body and mind" *Crime and Punish-*

---

17. Percy, SHC 164.21.
18. Unfortunately pages 2–18 are missing of the 1–36 numbered pages, so what appears as the second page of notes is numbered 19.
19. Percy, SHC 164.19.
20. Ibid.
21. Inside the back binding of his copy of Colin Wilson's *The Outsider*, Percy writes: "166—he too [Raskolnikov] like Lazarus needed to be raised from the dead." On page 166, he has squiggled a line by the reference to *Crime and Punishment*.

ment 525).[22] Raskolnikov, transformed by this seizure of faith, bows to the earth, kisses it, and confesses his murder. The suddenness of the transformation inspired Percy, but his own attempt to depict such a conversion in *The Charterhouse* failed, in turn, to enthuse any of his early readers—his family and friends.

Percy had begun writing *The Charterhouse* in the very year that he joined the Catholic Church; the quick turn to fiction writing did not allow him time to acquire the skills necessary to submit his art to his faith. As an example of Percy's immature art, one plot note in Percy's papers reveals a trite solution to a complex problem: "The only way Ben can avoid killing his father and killing himself with guilt is to become a Christian. Then he may still disagree with his father, leave him, but still honor him."[23] Percy imagines Ben combating his extreme hatred of his father and desire to commit patricide with the seemingly banal action of conversion. Percy seems in these notes to be reducing the story of Dostoevsky's greatest novel, *The Brothers Karamazov*—which Percy himself calls "maybe the greatest novel of all time"[24]—to a thesis that Christianity overcomes parricide. Percy would later come to believe that a novel should not have a thesis; in 1974, for example, he tells Barbara King, "Nothing would be worse than a so-called philosophical or religious novel which simply used a story and plot and characters to get over a certain idea."[25] And yet, as a young novelist writing in the 1950s, Percy committed this very misuse of the novel genre. This is the reason that Percy's first attempt at novel writing fell short.

Percy's friends and supporters were concerned about this particular failing. Foote worried that Percy's newfound answers in his faith interrupted his creative search, declaring, "No good practicing Catholic can ever be a great artist."[26] Gordon, in her twenty-page letter of advice to Percy, offers one option to improve his writing (Dec. 11, 1951): "About all we can do is observe the practice of the masters."[27] Among the examples of masters, she specifies Dostoevsky: "I imagine Dostoevski's [sic] devoutness accounts in part for the amazing variety and spontaneity of his creations. Very little of his energy was misspent in figuring out the things that our contemporaries feel it their duty to figure out."[28] As Gordon saw it, because Dostoevsky adhered to a shared

---

22. *Crime and Punishment* by Dostoevsky will be cited in text throughout the book.
23. Percy, SHC 164.29.
24. Percy, *More Conversations*, 224.
25. Idem, *Conversations*, 89.
26. *Correspondence*, 20.
27. Percy, SHC 387.1.
28. Ibid. 387.20.

faith, even if not denominationally, the Russian Orthodox "master" was suitable for Percy to follow. Later in the same letter, Gordon emphasizes the likeness between Percy and Dostoevsky: "You are Catholic and therefore have some notion of what it's all about."[29] Both Dostoevsky and Percy "had some notion" about the creation of the world, the purpose of human beings, and the nature of God—and this notion would be the key to Percy's development as a novelist. As Percy worked to improve, he could choose no better "master" to emulate than one as devout as himself. From the start, they already had this one essential characteristic in common.

THE OUTSIDER-PROTAGONIST IN *THE GRAMERCY WINNER*

In Percy's second novel, *The Gramercy Winner*, he appears to be attempting to relate the discoveries he had made while on bed rest with tuberculosis at Trudeau in the early forties. Percy ceased working on *The Gramercy Winner* in 1954.[30] Although the novel was never completed or published, several of the characters, incidents, and themes in *The Gramercy Winner* foreshadow later novels.[31] The most important revelation in this novel, though, is the character of the protagonist. The extant project notes reveal that Percy was beginning to develop the protagonist who would become, in one variation or another, a character in each of his proceeding novels: an outsider who is able to see what other characters cannot. In constructing this character, Percy was strongly inspired by Colin Wilson's *The Outsider*, which was itself informed by Dostoevsky.

This second novel is set in a sanatorium outside of New York. Paralleling Percy's own biography, the protagonist, William Grey, lies bedridden, recovering from tuberculosis while others his age fight abroad in World War II. Most of the "action" of the novel is understated and hardly dramatic, centering on conversations between Grey and a lieutenant named Sutter, his wife Allison,

---

29. Ibid. 387.13.

30. Percy also identified other influences on these two novels. He referred to his two unpublished novels as "much more traditional sort of apprentice novels. One of them was heavily influenced by Thomas Wolfe, and the other was influenced by Thomas Mann" (*More Conversations*, 40). In this early fiction, Percy tries and fails to imitate a variety of literary mentors, including Tolstoy and Thomas Mann, and follow the advice of friends, namely Caroline Gordon and Shelby Foote.

31. Superficially he uses the names Sutter and Allison again in *The Last Gentleman* and *The Second Coming*. Percy reworks the conclusion of the novel in which a sick character is baptized on his deathbed in *The Last Gentleman*.

and later, at another recovery center, two doctors named Van Norden and Scanlon. At the start of the novel, Grey relishes the knowledge "of the heart of things, namely molecules and atoms" that science provides.[32] Only after his encounters with the experts themselves, the infallible scientists, does Grey begin to doubt the absolutism of their knowledge. *The Gramercy Winner* suffers from the same weakness as *The Charterhouse*. Percy focuses more on ideas than on stories, creating incorporeal characters that inhabit blank spaces, not taking action, making choices, or engaging with one another. Yet even though this novel fails to model Dostoevsky in any meaningful way, the outsider protagonist whom Percy is developing would recur throughout the rest of Percy's published novels.

Although rather dull as heroes go, Will Grey would become the trace outline for the "outsider" type found in most of Percy's subsequent novels. Will's quarantine away from society grants him an outsider-looking-in perspective. Percy himself would assert in a 1983 interview, "The common thread that runs through all of my novels is of a man, or a woman who finds himself/herself *outside* of society. . . . The reader is supposed to recognize the *outsider* in himself, and to identify with the alienated values of these characters."[33] In multiple interviews and essays, Percy describes the "outsider" as the alienated individual whose location on the margins of society allows him or her a different perspective on the world.

Percy identifies several sources of "the outsider," among them "Kierkegaard in philosophy" and "Dostoevsky in fiction." Both exhibit "a particular man who finds himself in some fashion isolated from the world and society around him, a society which in both the philosophy and the fiction is viewed as more or less absurd" (*Signposts* 218). A third source, Colin Wilson's nonfiction work *The Outsider,* is of particular interest in this discussion because it draws heavily from Dostoevsky. Wilson's work popularized existentialism by exploring the characters and artists who exemplified this philosophy. In an article on Kierkegaard and Dostoevsky, George Pattison calls *The Outsider* "the most influential work of literary criticism in Britain [and in America] in the 1950s" (239).[34] Despite the mockery it later received for its extremism and colloquial style, *The Outsider* initially made bestseller lists and was lauded by reviewers. Percy has scribbled all over his 1956 edition.

---

32. Percy, SHC 162.6.
33. Percy, *Conversations*, 281. Emphasis mine.
34. According to a *Time* magazine review on *The Outsider* (Jul. 2, 1956), four printings in Britain sold out in three weeks. Wilson writes in his 1965 postscript that it reached bestseller lists in both countries and was translated into fourteen languages within eighteen months.

Wilson, originally a student of atomic physics, first undertook an investigation of the mystery of human existence using the scientific method, but then, after reading Dostoevsky's *The Possessed,* he began plumbing novels to collect his data.[35] In his treatise on the archetype of the outsider, Wilson declares that this theme "is present in everything that Dostoevsky wrote."[36] Wilson establishes the Underground Man of Dostoevsky's *Notes from Underground* as the epitome of the outsider. On page twenty of *The Outsider,* which Percy has dog-eared, he underlines Wilson's thesis: "The Outsider's claim [is] that he is the one man able to see . . . that he is the one man who knows he is sick in a civilization that doesn't know it is sick."[37] Wilson maintains that the society surrounding the outsider is ignorant of its own sickness, and thus the clear-sighted outsider is the preeminent diagnostician. It seems likely that Wilson's description of the outsider reminded Percy of two sick men: himself, debilitated with tuberculosis at Trudeau, and the ill narrator of Dostoevsky's *Notes from Underground.* Percy's own experience together with his reading of *Notes* and *The Outsider* must have fueled his imagination as he invented the character of Grey in *The Gramercy Winner.*

Even though Grey suffers from tuberculosis, Percy suggests that those around him may be the "sick" ones: "If there had been anyone to see, he would have thought William, his eyes closed, his face rosy with sleep, the healthy one, and Scanlon the one sick unto death."[38] He offers the conditional clause "if there had been anyone to see" to underscore the blindness of those around Will. In this instance, Scanlon represents the unaware society who suffers sickness greater than Will's tuberculosis. Moreover, in his sickness, Grey seems to have discovered something that gives him the illusion of health. In his introduction to Dostoevsky's short novels,[39] Thomas Mann, whom Percy imitates in *The Gramercy Winner,* writes, "Certain attainments of the soul and the intellect are impossible without disease."[40] Percy applies Mann's premise about Dostoevsky to himself. He recognizes that his sickness may have offered himself and his character insight into the transcendent purpose of life. Here tuberculosis represents a spiritual malady, and as Grey dies from the former, he recovers from the latter. His sickness sets him apart from those around him, but not as one who is more worthy.

---

35. Wilson reveals these autobiographical details in a pretentious postscript to a 1965 reprint of his book.
36. Wilson, *Outsider,* 157.
37. Ibid., 20.
38. Percy, SHC 163.331.
39. Percy has underlined much in Mann's introduction.
40. Mann, Introduction to *The Short Novels of Dostoevsky.*

Before Grey dies, he converts in a scene that parallels the conversion of another outsider, Raskolnikov in *Crime and Punishment*. In the epilogue of Dostoevsky's novel, Raskolnikov appears in a similar situation to Will Grey; he lies ill in the prison hospital. Under the influence of his fever, Raskolnikov dreams that the "whole world was doomed to fall victim to some terrible, as yet unknown and unseen pestilence" (*Crime and Punishment* 547), from which all will perish—this is the sickness unto death that Kierkegaard and Jesus refer to. These dreams torment him all during his illness, which, not coincidentally, occurs from Lent to Holy Week, a time that culminates in the resurrection of Jesus Christ on Easter Sunday. In the Catholic Church, on this Sunday, proselytes are baptized. In the final scene of *The Gramercy Winner*, Scanlon baptizes Will with a glass of water before the latter passes into a coma. For Catholics, baptism is when the self dies and the spirit is reborn. When Raskolnikov leaves the hospital, he opens the gospels "from which [Sonia] had read to him about the raising of Lazarus" (*Crime and Punishment* 550). Dostoevsky aligns Raskolnikov with Lazarus, calling him also "risen." In the final paragraph, Dostoevsky concludes with a reference to beginning: "But here begins a new account, the account of a man's gradual renewal . . . his acquaintance with a new, hitherto completely unknown reality. It might make the subject of a new story" (551). Percy seems to have subconsciously undertaken Dostoevsky's subject for his new story.

In comparison to Raskolnikov's conversion, Grey's baptism feels contrived. Roughly ten pages before, Grey professes nihilism: "The one thing I have been absolutely sure of all my life is that one day I was going to know something. . . . I found out. . . . The secret is that there is nothing."[41] In contrast with Raskolnikov, who practices nihilism at the beginning of Dostoevsky's novel but undergoes transformation near the end, Grey reverts to it. On his deathbed, he expresses "absolute" conviction that "there is nothing." Not only is Grey's conversion unprepared for in the novel, its resolution seems too tidy. Percy himself, reflecting on his penultimate novel, *The Second Coming*, asserts, "A writer cannot get away with theological revelations. It doesn't work in a novel and maybe it never did."[42] He does not mean that writers should leave theological truth unrevealed, but that a writer should never spell out the message in a thesis statement. When writing *The Gramercy Winner*, however, Percy had not yet learned this lesson.

Even if he did not quite succeed at it yet, Percy was learning a subtle technique. In an interview with Peggy Castex, Percy describes his method for

---

41. Percy, SHC 163.328.
42. Percy, *More Conversations*, 49.

revealing theological truth as follows: "So what you do is suggest something and then you back off from it and you have an interplay between an inkling that such and such may happen and that such and such is the way you discover who you are."[43] Percy sounds as though he discovered this method by studying the success of *Crime and Punishment*. First, Raskolnikov's transition occurs gradually: Sonia reads the story of Lazarus to Raskolnikov three-quarters of the way through the novel, which initiates stirrings in him. However, not until the final pages of the epilogue does Raskolnikov then return to the gospel story. Second, the protagonist never affirms the Nicene Creed or becomes a missionary in Africa, rather Raskolnikov *questions* whether or not he may feel the same convictions as Sonia or share her aspirations. Even though ellipses follow his unanswered, open-ended questions, Dostoevsky fills the epilogue with inklings for discovery.

INCARNATIONAL AESTHETIC

Percy was troubled after the completion of *The Gramercy Winner*. He was nearing forty, had finally determined what he wanted to do, and yet found himself unable to succeed at it. He could have taken heart that Dostoevsky was forty-five when he penned *Crime and Punishment*, after which he would go on still to write *The Idiot, The Possessed*, and *The Brothers Karamazov*. Instead he took a break from writing fiction to draft a few philosophical essays. Although seeing his name in print was quite a coup d'état for the would-be writer, Percy knew that such material would never reach his intended audience. If his ideas were to have any transformative power, they needed to be embodied—or incarnated—in fiction, as Dostoevsky had done.

Intellectually and content-wise, the incarnation was central to Percy's ambition as a novelist, but in order to accomplish himself as an artist, it must become the guiding principle of his aesthetics. Percy was transformed by his reading of Dostoevsky, and he desired to transform others. In an essay on Dostoevsky's "incarnational realism," Paul Contino has argued that Dostoevsky "*sought* to inspire spiritual transformation in his readers."[44] After his delivery of his speech for the Pushkin memorial (1880), hordes of fans accosted Dostoevsky to thank him. "We've become better people since we read *The Karamazovs*," they cried. From this account, Contino theorizes that *The Brothers Karamazov* has the potential to better its readers "ethically, spiritually, and aesthetically to the extent that we are able to discern and reflect

---

43. Ibid.
44. Contino, "'Descend,'" 132.

'the image of Christ' that the novel presents."[45] Similarly, Percy never hid his moralist agenda from readers, and he indicates that Dostoevsky motivated such an agenda.[46]

Dostoevsky's novels were transformative because they, as Percy notes, "*incarnated* the most powerful themes and issues and trends of his day."[47] Percy's use of the word "incarnated" is more than a vivid verb choice; it signals the theological source of Dostoevsky's aesthetic. Although some scholars have accused Dostoevsky of writing mere parables or unrealistic allegories, the majority of readers are persuaded by the tangibility of his fiction and recognize in it, the radiance of the incarnation.[48] Critic George Steiner claims, "In Dostoevskian worlds, the image of Christ is the centre of gravity."[49] And Romano Guardini, a theologian whom Percy read and admired, compares Dostoevsky's works to Rembrandt's paintings where "the central point [is] 'nowhere' because it [is] everywhere, as diffuse as light."[50] In his study of Dostoevsky's form, Robert L. Jackson writes, "At the center of Dostoevsky's Christian aesthetic—as it becomes more explicit in his notebooks and *belles letters* in the last decade of his life—is the image of Christ."[51] Jackson references Dostoevsky's notebooks where he emphasizes not the moral teachings of Christ but the very fact that "the Word became flesh."[52] Dostoevsky himself referred to his style as "higher realism;" he writes in his notebooks: "I am only a realist in the higher sense; that is, I portray all the depths of the human soul."[53] Motivated by the enfleshment of Christ, Dostoevsky's higher realism may well be called "incarnational realism," as Contino describes it or an incarnational aesthetic.[54]

Whereas philosophers such as Kierkegaard may have gifted Percy with the worldview through which he wanted to write—the ideas about modernity,

---

45. Ibid.

46. In a letter to Caroline Gordon after the publication of *The Moviegoer*, Percy asks, "How does a Catholic fiction writer handle the Catholic Faith in his novel? (Actually the only reason I can raise the question now is that I see the glimmerings of an answer.) Dostoevsky knew the answer" (quoted in Samway, *Walker Percy: A Life*, 224).

47. Percy, *More Conversations*, 224.

48. One case in point of the Russian perspective that reduces Dostoevsky's novels to allegory is an article by Vladiv Slobodanka entitled "Dostoevsky's Major Novels as Semiotic Models," which was presented at the Proceedings of the Russian Colloquium, University of Melbourne (August 1976).

49. Steiner, *Tolstoy or Dostoevsky*, 291.

50. Guardini, "Legend," 58.

51. Cited by Contino, "Incarnational Realism," 131.

52. Jackson, *Dialogues with Dostoevsky*, 287.

53. Simmons, *Introduction to Russian Realism*, 104.

54. Contino "Incarnational Realism," 132.

God, and the self that he wanted to disperse—Dostoevsky showed him how to embody these ideas in fiction. Percy's first two novel attempts were too abstract and allegorical, full of propaganda rather than art. One could imagine *The Charterhouse* with its overt Catholic agenda probably read like a Romanized Aesop's fable. If Percy continued down this track, he would produce little more than parables with direct messages. What he needed was embodiment, indirection, and a full aesthetic experience for the reader. From Dostoevsky, Percy learned the incarnational aesthetic, which I will outline here but will more fully explore in the rest of the book. The incarnational aesthetic that Percy gleaned from Dostoevsky thoroughly informs his characterization, is partially structural, and most significantly, alters his way of creating his worlds or, rather, imitating this one as Dostoevsky depicts it. Moreover, while Percy desired that his moralizing be effective, he chose these subtle, indirect means by which to accomplish his task.

At this stage in his vocation, Percy was attending a master class in writing through his correspondence with Caroline Gordon and Shelby Foote, not to mention his reading of Allen Tate and Jacques Maritain. When Gordon received Percy's first novel attempt in 1951, she was impressed; here was the kind of novel that she had been looking for. A new convert herself, she was anxious for great Catholic fiction to arrive to combat the secular drivel, as she saw it, lining the bookstore shelves. However, she chastises Percy for one great error, which has been previously mentioned: falling for the "sin of the age, angelism."[55] Here she alludes to Maritain who blamed René Descartes for introducing a division into the human consciousness between the coexisting angelic and animal natures. Percy not only would go on to read and annotate Maritain's *The Dream of Descartes* but also to gloss the text in numerous ways throughout his work, most notably in *Lost in the Cosmos* in which he elaborates on the problem of the Cartesian split.

Gordon's accusation may have incited Percy's search toward a better way of writing, a way of not separating the angel from the beast but of understanding the pull between the two natures that comprise us. After all, one of the reasons that Percy became a Catholic was that he bought Thomas Aquinas's claim that the body and soul cannot be understood as separate entities.[56] We are not pigs or gods or ghosts in machines, to use Percy's language (*Love in the Ruins* 104).[57] Rather, we are some mysterious combination of both the angel

---

55. Percy, SHC 387.1.
56. Under the influence of Art Fortugno, a Roman Catholic resident at Trudeau, Percy read Aquinas and found Christianity—for the first time—intellectually plausible. He was impressed with Aquinas's logic (Tolson, *Pilgrim in the Ruins*, 171).
57. Dr. Tom More insists that we are "not pigs nor angels."

and animal, of transcendent and immanent. And thus if Percy was to write convincing fiction—especially works that revealed the truth he attributed to his Christian faith—then his aesthetic needed to correlate with his ideas. The content must match the form; the soul must be embodied.

In an earlier letter from Gordon, she advises Percy to "imitate the Almighty" by "mak[ing] one's word flesh and dwell among men." If he can't do that, then she tells him, "you'd better not try to write fiction."[58] Gordon's ultimatum set a high standard for fiction writers: to imitate the Incarnation itself, word becoming flesh. What she meant was what Maritain had explained in *Art and Scholasticism*, another text that influenced Percy's aesthetic understanding. Maritain writes, "The brilliance of the form, no matter how purely intelligible it may be in itself, is seized *in the sensible and through the sensible*, and not separately from it."[59] Like Gordon's dictum to imitate the Incarnation, Maritain emphasizes the fleshliness of writing, of making ideas concrete realities as perceived through this world of our senses. In contrast to Percy's first two novels, in which the action was more or less interior or abstractly occurring between talking heads, his later fiction would follow this advice, making those same philosophical drives to be tangible, smell-able, taste-able, and so on.

Shelby Foote directs Percy's attention to Dostoevsky as the master example for how to accomplish such embodied writing. He flings out Dostoevsky like a life raft to his flailing artist friend: "Look at *The Brothers Karamazov*: tremendous narrative drive and strong enough to support any mass of theory he cared to pile on it."[60] There are no floating heads in Dostoevsky's novel. Because of its particularity, *The Brothers Karamazov* possesses the philosophical power that Percy desired for his own writing. Following this book recommendation, Foote specifies that Percy should write about New Orleans, set the novel during Mardi Gras, end it on a holy day, and include characters from his own personal life—all of which Percy eventually does to write *The Moviegoer*. If the latter advice was so persuasive, it may be concluded that the former admonition—check out *The Brothers Karamazov*—was equally convincing.

Years later, reflecting on his success as a novelist, Percy would outline the features of his incarnational aesthetic, which moved him from the weak dramas of abstract allegory to the potent and concrete realism of his pub-

---

58. SHC 387.3.

59. Maritain, *Art and Scholasticism*, 25.

60. Tolson titles this section of correspondence between Foote and Percy, "Master to Apprentice." It is within these letters that Shelby instructs Walker in how to write. The master he looks toward most often is Dostoevsky (*Correspondence*, 47).

lished works. Percy is explicit about the primacy of the Incarnation for the way he writes:

> The fact that novels are narratives about events which happen to people in the course of time is given a unique weight in an ethos that is informed by the belief that awards an absolute importance to an Event which happened to a person in historic time. In a very real way, one can say that the Incarnation not only brought salvation to mankind but gave birth to the novel. Judeo-Christianity is about pilgrims who have something wrong with them and are embarked on a search to find a way out. . . . The incarnational and sacramental dimensions of the Catholic Christianity are the greatest natural assets to a novelist. (*Signposts* 362)

From this description (as well as what can be found in his fiction), Percy outlines the anthropology that stems from his incarnational aesthetic: the particularity of the person, time, and place, and things in the world; the "predicament" as Percy calls it, which is, for him, a feature of original sin; and finally, characters as wayfarers, pilgrims, or searchers. Percy credits this "recipe for the best novel-writing" (*Signposts* 369) to Dante and Dostoevsky.[61] The former is the archetype of a Catholic writer, one who embodied Aquinas's worldview in *The Divine Comedy* and who was often cited by Tate, Gordon, and Maritain as the quintessential incarnational realist. However, since Percy only read *Inferno*—he admits to struggling to get further than that in his letters—we can conjecture that the latter, Dostoevsky, would be the writer who taught him the most about this type of writing.

First, Percy acknowledges the Incarnation as the source for novel writing because it invests the particularity of individual humans here and now with great worth. He claims, "The intervention of God in history through the Incarnation bestows a weight and value to the individual human narrative which is like money in the bank to the novelist" (*Signposts* 178). Because the Divine chose to lower himself into human form as a carpenter's son in the Middle East during the Roman rule of Herod the Great, so too Percy could find purpose in telling the story of a young man wandering through Santa Fe in the 1960s. Writing incarnationally did not consist of recording the prayers and good deeds of nuns and priests inside a church building. Rather, because of the Incarnation, for Percy, the South suddenly became as worthy of a setting as ancient Jerusalem had been.

---

61. In this particular quote, Percy is speaking about the anthropology that Dante and Dostoevsky assume about their characters, that of wayfarers.

Second, Percy discovered that the Christian story placed every character in a predicament. He argues that any novel that begins by admitting this predicament—this sense that something is wrong or something is missing—is illustrating original sin. The Christian anthropology sees "man as a creature in trouble" (*Signposts* 369), or to use biblical language, human beings as fallen. Percy quips, "I don't recall reading a good novel which was informed by a Marxist belief in an inexorable dialectic of history . . . or a good novel informed by a preoccupation with the mechanisms of one's own psyche" (*Signposts* 369). As opposed to the Marxist, Freudian, or Hindu worldviews, only the Christian worldview allows for a narrative in which a particular person faces the problems of reality and must choose how to act: Peter Augustine Lawler and Brian A. Smith claim in *A Political Companion to Walker Percy* that "Percy explains that the novel itself is a Christian medium."[62] Whether or not these novelists admit to a Judeo-Christian worldview, for Percy, these stories are closet Christian narratives.

Third, characters must be wayfarers or pilgrims, unsettled in this home that is not their home. Percy's famous images of this are drawn from Robinson Crusoe or Rip Van Winkle: characters are out of sync with their worlds, castaways, exiles, and outsiders. Although Percy workshopped this character in *The Gramercy Winner*, it comes to fruition in *The Moviegoer* (mostly with the aid of *Notes from Underground*). Percy describes *The Moviegoer* as "a modest restatement of the Judeo-Christian notion that man is more than an organism in an environment, more than an integrated personality, more even than a mature and creative individual. . . . He is a wayfarer and a pilgrim" (*Signposts* 246). Percy's protagonists are all searchers on a journey—Binx Bolling, Will Barrett, Lancelot, and Tom More. They have a mysterious telos encoded into them because of the *imago dei*, and thus they seek the end for which they were made. Percy credits this "view of man as wayfarer" from Dostoevsky (*Signposts* 369).

In addition to these anthropological motivations, Percy's incarnational aesthetic can be found in how he organizes his narratives. For instance, *The Moviegoer* exemplifies a structural pattern popular throughout the great works of Christian literature, including in Dostoevsky's *The Brothers Karamazov*. Dostoevsky emulates this element of the incarnation in his organization of *The Brothers Karamazov*.[63] The epigraph is from John 12:24: "Except a grain of wheat fall to the ground and die." Jesus' words here to his disciples, though mysterious, foreshadow his descent to ascent journey, which they will

---

62. Lawler and Smith, *Political Companion*, 1.
63. Contino, "Incarnational Realism," 179.

soon witness. For Dostoevsky, the structure becomes emblematic for all of the brothers' journeys in the text. Those who are initially high must fall low in order to be raised up higher. Other Christian writers have followed this same pattern: Augustine in his *Confessions* falls to hedonism before ascending to his role as Bishop of Hippo; Dante the pilgrim descends into the inferno before he is able to ascend Mt. Purgatory and ultimately up to Paradise. Although counterintuitive and paradoxical, such a movement becomes commonplace in Christian literature in imitation of the incarnation. Binx will follow this trajectory in *The Moviegoer*.

Finally, and probably most significantly in Percy's work, the incarnational aesthetic showcases a world of contradiction in which horror often accompanies beauty. The blood of the cross precedes the rolled-away stone. In Dostoevsky, the death of a child leads readers to a small gravestone where young mourners begin to believe in the resurrection. For Percy, slit wrists herald the joy of living, and an abscessed tooth moves a man toward marriage. Critic Franklin Arthur Wilson notes, "Walker Percy uses the unlikely images of a dung beetle, bowel movements, the death of children, and even genocide to express the sacramental presence of God in the often traumatic mess of human existence."[64] Such grotesque combinations were not out of the ordinary in Southern fiction (nor Russian literature, for that matter), but for Percy as for Dostoevsky, these combinations resonate with the Incarnation; they stem from a God who defiled himself to be born, and even lower than that, to be birthed in an animal stall and executed as a criminal.

Dostoevsky's and Percy's style embody the juxtaposition of ingrate and saint: both proscribed to an incarnational view of the world, which influenced the type of art they created. Incarnational artists perceive the transcendent or sublime in the natural world around them and portray this paradoxical reality. Eric Auerbach in *Mimesis* describes this "mingling of styles" as "harshly dramatized through God's incarnation in a human being of the humblest stations, through his existence on earth amid humble everyday people and conditions, through his passion which, judged by earthly standards, was ignominious."[65] According to the New Testament authors, God became one of the lowliest of human beings, born in a manger amid filth and animals and killed among criminals. Not only does the everyday world then become exalted and capable of portraying divine truth but also the "worst of sinners" becomes a potential conduit for grace. Dostoevsky calls his incarnational art "higher realism." In his notebooks, he describes

---

64. Wilson, "Bible Notes," 197.
65. Auerbach, *Mimesis*, 41.

his art as seeking through "utter realism to find the man in man. . . . They call me a psychologist; this is not true. I am merely a realist in the higher sense, that is, I portray all the depths of the human soul."[66] According to Bakhtin, Dostoevsky wanted to showcase the entire human person—flesh and spirit, ugly and beautiful, sinful and charitable—whereas nineteenth-century psychologists would divide one into objective pieces, disregarding a soul altogether. Like Dostoevsky's, "Percy's imagination uses paradox not to provide a meretricious journalistic surface for his narrative but to explore the richness and contradictory forces at work in a single human life."[67] For Dostoevsky and Percy, the incarnation gave potential to the lowly and ugly to be raised up and become beautiful. Their fiction overcomes the paradox of either "insect or hero," in the Underground Man's terms, or "beast or angel," in Percy's, by showing how their characters may transition by grace from insect to hero or beast to angel.

This aesthetic method achieved the moralizing that was Percy's goal, though it did so indirectly. Percy credits Dostoevsky with mastering the skills of "guile, indirection and circumspection" in fiction.[68] Through Dostoevsky, Percy learned how to incarnate the truths of his faith in a way that would subtly affect his readers and would make them step out of their apathy and question the status quo. The transformation that Dostoevsky caused among those readers in St. Petersburg over a century ago could be emulated in the late twentieth-century South—albeit with a bit of tweaking.

CONCLUSION

After Percy finished writing *The Gramercy Winner*, he felt discouraged and depleted. His old friend Foote writes him an encouraging letter infused with Dostoevsky. Quoting the epigraph to *The Brothers Karamazov*, Foote expounds on the necessary sacrifice of artists: "We could all be great writers, perhaps, except that we know the cost; and few are willing to pay it. . . . 'Except a grain of wheat fall to the ground. . . . If it die not . . .'"[69] Foote's point in quoting this biblical allusion is that art could proffer salvation. Percy was not convinced by this argument, but still Foote's sermon rings true for Percy in another sense: Percy needed to do what he wanted his characters to do. In order to write the novels he hoped to write, he must first die to self and be resurrected as a bet-

---

66. Cited in Bakhtin, *Problems*, 60.
67. Webb, "Binx Bolling's New Orleans," 22.
68. *Correspondence*, 258.
69. Ibid., 96.

ter creature. Indeed, Percy later describes his renewal as a writer as being like that of a man who has overcome the "sickness unto death": "The slate is wiped clean. It is almost as though discouragement were necessary, that one has to encounter despair before one is entitled to hope" (*Signposts* 189–90). Descent, in the Christian model, is a necessary precursor to ascent. It is in this spirit of renewal that Percy would begin writing his third (though first to be published) novel, *The Moviegoer*. Taking up his pen once again, Percy sounds like a man who has been baptized from the sins of his earlier work and is now rising like Lazarus to begin a new story.

CHAPTER 2

Faithful Re-membering in *The Moviegoer*

A TWENTY-SOMETHING young man, living underground but peering keenly out at the world labors, composes a confessional narrative for an unseen audience. In his writing, the young man rages against the secularism of the contemporary world; particularly disgusting to him is the way in which modern science has encouraged the reification of human beings into mere objects to be studied empirically. As the man composes his narrative, he tries on an alternative perspective, one that is more romantic than that of his contemporaries. He searches for the unexplainable or even, the transcendent. This description of an isolated, confessing, romantically inclined young man could apply equally well to two different characters: he is the Underground Man in Fyodor Dostoevsky's *Notes from Underground* (1864), and he is Binx Bolling in Walker Percy's *The Moviegoer* (1961). The latter character is essentially a reimagined version of the former. When Walker Percy published his first novel a century after Dostoevsky, he was remembering the great Russian's work and re-membering (reassembling) it in the midcentury American present.

The mode of influence in *The Moviegoer* is more conscious, more attentive than in *The Charterhouse* and *The Gramercy Winner*. For his part, Percy described the ending of *The Moviegoer* as a "gloss" on *The Brothers Karamazov*, yet that is not the most significant Dostoevsky source for Percy's *The*

Moviegoer.[1] That designation, as I will show, goes to *Notes from Underground*. In this novel, Percy is not merely recalling Dostoevsky and playing with his ideas; he actually picks apart and reassembles the pieces of Dostoevsky's works into a story that, through creative amalgamation, is brought to life anew in the present.

When Percy sat down to write *The Moviegoer* in 1958 "on that back porch of that little shotgun cottage in New Orleans," remembering was not what he consciously set out to do. He has said that he did not intend to invoke Dostoevsky (nor those other philosophical writers whom he was reading deeply at the time, Sartre and Kierkegaard). Rather, in Percy's own description, what he set out to do was to "translate" philosophical ideas into fiction. In an interview with Malcolm Jones (1987), Percy recalls the process of starting *The Moviegoer*: "So it just occurred to me, why not take these ideas I'd been trying to write about, in psychiatry and philosophy, and translate them into a fictional setting in New Orleans."[2] Yet the method by which he would accomplish this translation remained a mystery to him even after he finished writing the novel.

Percy wrote *The Moviegoer* after years of working on philosophical essays. He only began writing *The Moviegoer* when it seemed to him that he had forgotten all previous sources. Emerging from his submersion in philosophy, Percy drafted *The Moviegoer* in about a year. In hindsight, he described his new writing process as an exercise in primal discovery: "One begins to write, not as one thinks he is supposed to write, and not even to write like the great models one admires, but rather to write as if he were the first man on earth ever to set pencil to paper" (*Signposts* 190). To support his decision to discard all conventional notions of fiction, Percy quotes John Barth's declaration that it is "no longer permissible to write nineteenth-century novels" (190)—including, perhaps, the novels of Dostoevsky. Forty years after the success of *The Moviegoer*, Percy claimed, "It was the first thing I wrote that I felt was my own voice."[3] Despite Percy's claims of originality in *The Moviegoer*, though, the book is unmistakably marked by the style and thought of Dostoevsky.

At this moment in Percy's career, as he became a full-fledged novelist, his key discovery was learning how to write a story rooted in time and place. By adopting the (re)membering mode of influence, Percy was able to write concretely. Percy explains in a 1985 essay, "Diagnosing the Modern Malaise,"

---

1. Percy, *Conversations*, 66.
2. Percy, *More Conversations*, 175. Percy makes no mention here of Shelby Foote who gave him the idea to set his novel in New Orleans. Foote writes to Percy (May 1951): "New Orleans is right in your back yard and it has everything. . . . Fling us into that melee—something is bound to happen" (*Correspondence*, 47).
3. Percy, *Conversations*, 40.

that the job of the novelist is to depict a protagonist, and that this protagonist ought not to be viewed "as specimen Homo sapiens alienatus pinned like a dogfish to a dissecting board, but rather as an individual set down in a time and place and a predicament" (*Signposts* 218). That is to say, the protagonist must be (or must seem to the reader) a real, living, breathing human being.[4] Percy's prior novels, *The Charterhouse* and *The Gramercy Winner*, did not succeed for precisely this reason: the characters were—literally and figuratively—on dissecting boards.[5]

This reading of *The Moviegoer* takes up two suggestive remarks made by reviewers of the novel. First, there is Lewis Lawson's notion, expressed in 2003, that *The Moviegoer* represents Percy's "conversion" from Tolstoy to Dostoevsky. According to Lawson, the conversion happens in the narrative itself, following a trajectory that parallels Binx's conversion. The second insight with which this chapter is concerned comes from Brainard Cheney, who in his 1961 review for *The Sewanee Review* described the novel as a restorative work that reassembles the discarded *imago dei* in the human person. Cheney briefly noted that the novel invoked ideas from Dostoevsky's fiction, especially *Notes from Underground*. Both Lawson's and Cheney's remarks indicate that a few readers, at least, recognized that *The Moviegoer* bore the influence of Dostoevsky. Until now, no other scholar has taken up this crucial theme for closer examination.

In *The Moviegoer*, Percy remembers and re-members Dostoevsky, both imitating him and revising him. Two examples of Percy's adoption of Dostoevsky's art are his aesthetic of incarnational realism and his polyphonic technique. Percy not only remembers, or faithfully imitates; he re-members, or reassembles something new. Percy's protagonist, like Dostoevsky's, reaches an

---

4. In a 1983 interview, he asserts that Dostoevsky's method most influenced him: "Dostoyevsky in his idea of people obsessed with ... some idea or something, or find themselves in a certain situation, a terrible predicament, and behave accordingly" (*Conversations*, 275). A few years later, he describes his own method in parallel terms: "What happens to a young man in a certain situation with no beliefs in particular [when I] put him down in a kind of middle class suburb in New Orleans" (*More Conversations*, 217).

5. Before Percy began writing *The Gramercy Winner*, Foote advised him to forego the abstractions of *The Charterhouse* and his onetime model, Mann's *Magic Mountain*: "Look at *The Brothers Karamazov*: tremendous narrative drive and strong enough to support any mass of theory he [Dostoevsky] cared to pile on it." Foote also advises Percy to focus on his concrete surroundings: "New Orleans is right in your backyard.... Use yourself.... Something is bound to happen" (*Correspondence*, 47). In another letter, Foote held forth on the role of philosophy in fiction: "The philosophy must be submerged, used naturally as it proceeds from character; having been assimilated it has therefore been 'forgotten,' and having been 'forgotten' it has become truly a part of the man" (96, emphasis mine). Yet when Percy begins *The Moviegoer*, he describes the experience as setting out on his own: "All past efforts are thrown into a wastebasket; all advice forgotten" (*Signposts*, 189).

existential crossroads but takes a different path: Binx Bolling chooses to ascend rather than to follow the infamous descent chosen by Dostoevsky's antihero. In this reimagined ending, Percy goes beyond remembering (recounting) Dostoevsky to achieve re-membering (reassembling) him. In the very act of writing *The Moviegoer,* Percy discovered who would be arguably his most significant model. It could not be Sartre or Mann; rather it must be a fellow Christian. In Dostoevsky, he found his ideal model, and in *The Moviegoer,* he would discover how to write from the inspiration of another while retaining (or discovering for the first time) his voice.

REMEMBERING DOSTOEVSKY

How exactly does Percy's text remember Dostoevsky's? To start, Percy constructed a novel that shares profound parallels with Dostoevsky's. Some of these parallels were alluded to at the outset of this chapter, but they are worth discussing in greater detail. First, of course, the protagonist/narrators are similar in both superficial and profound ways. They confess to the reader but never definitively commit to a single view of the world. At the time of the major narratives, both protagonists are in their twenties, young men observing the world. The authors of both novels are men in their forties—Dostoevsky, forty-three, and Percy, forty-five—who understand their narrators from the inside as well as from the distance of age and thus are able to write their naive protagonists with a sort of double consciousness. The two protagonists also live underground, Dostoevsky's literally and Percy's figuratively. Moreover, both novels are written in the confessional mode to an unseen reader. Binx offhandedly uses the language of confession in the very first paragraph: "I confess I do not find the prospect [of visiting my aunt] altogether unpleasant" (*The Moviegoer* 3, emphasis mine).[6] The Underground Man parodies the features of a confession throughout his narrative because he does not desire to repent or be transformed through the act of telling his story. For both authors, the confessions are based on their own life events; Dostoevsky describes the project to his brother as "a confession—a novel that I wished to write after everything, so to say, I have had to live through myself."[7] Meanwhile the original title of Percy's novel was "Confessions of a Moviegoer," which Lawson offers as evidence that Percy "intended to pay homage to Dostoyevsky."[8]

---

6. *The Moviegoer* by Walker Percy will be cited in text throughout the book.
7. Frank, *Writer,* 405.
8. Lawson, "From Tolstoy to Dostoevsky," 414.

Given the centrality of memory to the mode of influence that I have termed remembering/re-membering, it is worth noting that memory itself is a crucial theme in both *The Moviegoer* and *Notes from Underground*. The protagonists of both novels regard memory as a faculty that offers a means of transcending one's flawed and finite human experience.

The Moviegoer begins with three different instances of Binx remembering. First, Binx introduces his Aunt Emily to the reader by sharing his memory of the conversation they had after the death of his brother Scott. He remembers the setting vividly: "On one side [of the street] were the power plant and blowers and incinerator of the hospital, all humming and blowing out a hot meaty smell" (*Moviegoer* 4). By depicting the scene in such a sensory way, Percy achieves the concreteness that his first two unpublished novels lacked. Binx remembers details about the world around him and his own insides: "My heart gave a big pump and the back of my neck prickled like a dog's" (ibid.). Binx's internal response is as real as the smell from the hospital or the feel of Aunt Emily's hand squeezing his. In this example, remembering brings the past into the present reality. Yet this particular memory is ironic, for in the conversation that Binx remembers so vividly, his aunt counsels him to forget the tragedy of his brother's death.

The second instance of remembering is triggered by the first. Binx's memory of himself at age eight reminds him of a movie he had seen a month before about a man who lost his memory. Binx remembers that the man's memory loss resulted in the loss of everything else, "his family, his friends, his money. He found himself a stranger in a strange city" (*Moviegoer* 4). While Binx recognizes that the movie was meant to be a tragedy, he himself envies the amnesiac character's "fresh start."

Suddenly, without explanation, Binx's attention shifts to a third memory, the memory of his date, Linda. From this rapid sequence of memories, it becomes clear to the reader that Binx is avoiding some sort of knowledge about the power of memories. For example, his failure to reflect upon why he appreciates the amnesiac suggests that, for Binx, memory operates mysteriously within him, and to understand it would demand more of him than he is ready to give. Ultimately, memory provides Binx with the clues that guide his search, offers the means of restoring his fragmented self, and promises the possibility of a transcendent reality.

Memory is an equally important theme in *Notes from Underground*. Dostoevsky emphasizes the role of memory in the very structure of the novella: it is divided into two books, one that occurs in the present and one that recounts a memory from twenty years before. The Underground Man draws attention to the substance of this confessional narrative being his own memories: "Even now, after so many years, all this comes out somehow none too well in my recollections" (*Notes* 129). The Underground Man's "recollections" make the past vivid before him, so that he reexperiences the initial shame of his earlier actions. Yet for all the shame he feels, the Underground Man proposes that he "perhaps come[s] out even more 'living' than" his readers because he has attempted to carry to an extreme his free will, which readers do not "carry even halfway" (130). In short, the Underground Man believes that his memories of the past, however painful, may offer him some sort of redemption. This is not unlike Binx Bolling's belief that memory offers a means of building a coherent self and transcending temporal reality.

Another similarity between the Underground Man and Binx Bolling is that they face essentially the same dilemma. Surrounded by enthusiasm for modern science, they do not share the faith of those around them. They are troubled by modern scientists' reification of the human being, and they feel drawn toward alternate worlds of romance. For the Underground Man, it is books that fuel and structure his romantic retreat from the world. For Binx Bolling, as the novel's title implies, it is movies. Both protagonists, even as they feel pulled toward fantasy, wonder whether a third option exists. For Dostoevsky that "something better" is Christ—although that section of the novel was excised by censors before publication. For Percy, as mediated through the character of Binx, the answer is the Incarnation.

Both the Underground Man and Binx recognize the limits of modern science and sometimes show an outright disgust for it. Dostoevsky's antihero spends the first half of the novella lambasting scientists' restriction of the definition of man to what may be discovered in "test tubes" or according to "tables and directories" (*Notes* 25). Such a definition cannot account for free will, which may not always follow reason. Binx too is concerned with the limits of science: When he tries to conduct scientific research, he discovers what Percy calls "the gap" overlooked by science (*Signposts* 213). Binx recounts how a "peculiar thing happened" (*Moviegoer* 51): he becomes more interested in the way sunlight stretches across the laboratory or the way the building creaks in the heat. His lab partner, Binx sardonically declares, has the blindness necessary for those who will succeed in research; however, Binx "do[es] not envy him. . . . For he is no more aware of the mystery which surrounds him than a fish is aware of the water it swims in" (52). Binx's realization echoes Percy's biography in which he too recognized the limits of science.

As they reject modern science, both the Underground Man and Binx are pulled toward romantic escape. The Underground Man's definition of a romantic is one to which Binx consents:

The properties of our romantic are to understand everything, to see everything, and to see often incomparably more clearly than our very most positive minds do; not to be reconciled with anyone or anything; but at the same time not to spurn anything; to get around everything, to yield to everything, to be politic with everyone. (*Notes* 46)

The list continues, but this abbreviated version highlights their shared notion of a romantic, what Binx also terms a "moviegoer."

In *Notes from Underground,* books stimulate the narrator's romantic tendencies, making him feel paradoxically "stirred, delighted, and tormented" as well as "bored" (*Notes* 48). When he interacts with his colleague, Zverkov, for instance, he imagines himself a hero in a romantic novel, dueling with a rival for a perceived indiscretion (*Notes* 85). The novel is rife with evidence that Percy equated the act of moviegoing with romanticism. In the first version of the novel, Percy subtitled his *Confessions of a Movie-Goer* with "from the Diary of the Last Romantic." In the published text, he makes the term "moviegoer" synonymous with "romantic," as when Binx meets the "romantic" on the bus and observes: "He is a moviegoer, though of course he does not go to movies" (*Moviegoer* 218). For both protagonists, then, the retreat from modern science means an attempt to escape into fictional narratives.

For the twentieth-century Binx, the texts' mediating effect—distancing him from the world by romanticizing it—is the same. The movies allow him an escape from real life, from the unseeing frenetic activity of ants on an anthill, to use the Underground Man's terms (*Notes* 33). Binx refers to those around him, including himself, using the names of film stars, such as "Mickey Rooney" or "Marlon Brando." In the original manuscript, the protagonist writes, "I must confess that when I come out of a movie, for some time afterwards . . . I am Gregory Peck" (*Moviegoer* 10). At one point in the published novel, Binx sits on a bus and imagines it as "if it were a movie": "The bus would get lost or the city would be bombed and she and I would tend to the wounded" (13). Yet in the same moment that he imagines the film version of life in his head, he knows how "it is": movies are not reality. This rationalization does not, however, save him from living as a moviegoer, from participating in life as fantasy as much as the Underground Man did.

For both the Underground Man and Binx, the desire to escape into romance—the problem with the modern world—is that scientific humanists have limited what it means to be human to what can be observed empirically. In his review, Cheney likened Percy's novel to Dostoevsky's novella: "In *Notes from Underground* scientific humanism is first exposed. . . . In the world of

The Moviegoer, however, it has already been abandoned and our hero stumbles amid its shards and glimmering confusion."[9] On the other hand, romantics' deification of humans is as problematic as scientists' reduction of them. In *The Moviegoer*, Binx blames these two connected worldviews for murdering his father: "That's what killed my father, English romanticism, that and 1930s science" (88). For Dostoevsky, the problem with both the scientific humanists and the romantics is that they neglect the free choice of the human person. Denying that human beings are objectively comprehensible or necessarily and teleologically good, the Underground Man embodies a refutation by acting irrationally, opposing psychological categories, and denying a desire for improvement.

Dostoevsky's resolution to the science-versus-faith dilemma was removed by censors before publication. The passage in question occurred midway through the novella. The Underground Man apologizes to his reader that, in his search for "something better" than the dilemma between scientific humanism and romanticism, he has found nothing. Dostoevsky would, in a letter to his brother (Mar. 26, 1864), decry the censors for removing much of this section (chapter 10), in which he "deduced the need of faith and Christ."[10] He had intended to showcase the Christian faith as the "something better" that the Underground Man is, in Frank's words, "desperately searching for": "Such an alternative ideal would thus be required to recognize the autonomy of the will and freedom of the personality, and would appeal to the moral nature of man rather than to his reason and self-interest."[11] Because the "something better" alternative that Dostoevsky proposed in chapter 10 was censored, the novel as it was published merely rejects scientific humanism and romanticism as viable worldviews, without offering an alternative. That alternative would be more fully fleshed out in Percy's *The Moviegoer* a century later.

In addition to the close parallels between *The Moviegoer* and *Notes from Underground*—evidence of Percy's remembering Dostoevsky into the present, so to speak—there is also a specific aspect of Dostoevsky's art that Percy adopts in *The Moviegoer*, the polyphonic technique. In *Problems of Dostoevsky's Poetics*, Mikhail Bakhtin credits Dostoevsky with inventing the polyphonic novel. Recognizing the applicability of Bakhtin's criticism to Percy, Michael Kobre in *Walker Percy's Voices* analyzes how Percy's novels may be categorized as polyphonic—though he does not delineate the particular connections to Dostoevsky. In his introduction, Kobre asserts, "Percy could write no other kind of fiction" than the polyphonic novel, in part, because of "his

---

9. Cheney, "To Restore," 691.
10. Dostoevsky, cited in Pevear's foreword to *Notes*, xviii.
11. Frank, *Writer*, 426.

enduring devotion to Dostoevsky."[12] He reminds readers of the strong influence of *Notes from Underground*—"a narrative that Bakhtin regards as profoundly dialogic"—on Percy's "transformation from an uninspired medical student to a novelist," then rhetorically asks, "How could he [Percy] not, then, have been affected by what Bakhtin calls 'the chief characteristic of Dostoevsky's novels,' their dialogic form and content?"[13]

Both *The Moviegoer* and *Notes* appear at first to be written entirely from the point of view of their respective protagonists, but in fact, the reader realizes gradually that the protagonist's voice is not all-controlling. In *Notes*, the protagonist calls readers into the narrative by explicitly addressing them. In *The Moviegoer*, Binx collects various perspectives on the world, like specimens in an experiment, without appropriating any one character's vision of reality. Instead he records them in a notebook. Percy admits to using the notebook form in his second published novel, *The Last Gentleman*, as a way to avoid the heavy dialogues of *The Brothers Karamazov*, and Kobre defines this as Bakhtinian "microdialogue."[14] Binx is a Dostoevskian narrator because, unlike his Aunt Emily, he does not possess a definitive view of the world. In contrast to almost every other character in the novel, all of whom seem able to make authoritative statements about the world, Binx is still searching.

The search directs the plot of *The Moviegoer*, and the moment of its initiation alludes both to Tolstoy and Dostoevsky. A pile of unfamiliar and yet familiar items from his pockets instigates a new vision for Binx. He recalls his first notion of the search, which occurred when a "dung beetle" appeared next to him as he lay under a chindolea bush in the Orient in 1951. In Tolstoy's *War and Peace*, Prince Andrei suffers a serious wound in the Battle of Austerlitz and awakes to see the enormity of the sky as though for the first time. According to Lawson, Binx substitutes the dung beetle for the sky because, by the end of the novel, he sees the world as "the great shithouse of scientific humanism where needs are satisfied, everyone becomes an anyone, a warm and creative person, and prospers like a dung beetle."[15] The insect reference, however, also recalls Dostoevsky's Underground Man who confesses how he "wanted many times to become an insect" but could not because of his consciousness: "The more conscious I was of the good and of all this 'beautiful and lofty,' the deeper I kept sinking into my mire, and the more capable I was

---

12. Kobre, *Voices*, 5.
13. Ibid., 5–6.
14. Ibid., 100.
15. Lawson, "From Tolstoy to Dostoevsky," 228.

of getting completely stuck in it" (*Notes* 7).[16] Because of his romantic awareness of the world, the Underground Man, like Binx, cannot prosper like a dung beetle. He sinks into the "mire," a word that echoes in Binx's assertion that this is "the very century of *merde*" (*Moviegoer* 228).

A second literary technique that Percy borrows from Dostoevsky is incarnational realism, which I outlined in the introduction. In *Notes from Underground*, the incarnational move from descent to ascent falters because the Underground Man *only* descends; ascent never occurs. Only in Dostoevsky's *The Brothers Karamazov*—an otherwise minor influence on *The Moviegoer*—does such an ascent take place. Later in this chapter, we will discuss the significance of Percy's departure from *Notes from Underground* on this point.

Percy's pursuit of incarnational realism began before his writing of *The Moviegoer*, but it became a prominent aspect of his first published novel. At the heart of *The Moviegoer*, is the question over God's existence, a question "in which no one has the slightest interest," and yet it is implicitly the telos of Binx's search (*Moviegoer* 14). Neither Binx's mother's side nor his father's side of the family understands his search. On the one side are those who believe in God while on the other side are those who do not: "My mother's family think I have lost my faith and they pray for me to recover it. . . . My father's family think that the world makes sense without God and that anyone but an idiot knows what the good life is and anyone but a scoundrel can lead it" (*Moviegoer* 145–46). The two sides of the question represent the ultimate either-or for Percy's fiction. Percy takes the question of God's existence as his guiding theme.

Moreover, words and images become, in Percy's novel, invested with secondary meaning, what patristic and medieval commentators would call the spiritual meaning. It is this significance that heightens the incarnational aesthetic in Percy's work. An example of Percy's exercise of incarnational realism is found at the beginning of the novel, when Binx describes a "schematic sort of bird" hovering above a school door as "the Holy Ghost, I suppose" (*Moviegoer* 10). He transfers an unexplainable feeling upon the building: "It gives me a pleasant sense of the goodness of creation to think of the brick and glass and the aluminum being extracted from common dirt" (ibid.). The allusions to the Holy Spirit, "goodness of creation," and "common dirt" recall the account in the first book of Genesis when God creates human beings from dust and deems them "good." To avoid such a conclusion, Binx thinks, "No doubt it

---

16. Although it is far-fetched to imagine that Percy would have had access to Dostoevsky's letters (he did own Dostoevsky's *The Diary of a Writer*), the image of the "dung-beetle" appears there as well. Dostoevsky calls his former mentor Belinsky a "dung-beetle" and the rest of the Petrashevsky circle "turd-eaters" (Cited by Leatherbarrow, 146). This coincidence illustrates a similarity between Dostoevsky's and Percy's perspectives.

is less a religious sentiment than a financial one since I own a few shares of Alcoa" (ibid.). Binx acknowledges the "religious" source of his thought when he tries to divest his description of any religious character. Moreover, the phrase "no doubt" suggests the opposite—that Binx himself doubts his reasons for feeling the way he does about the building. As in Dostoevsky's fiction, mundane objects, such as the school building in *The Moviegoer,* possess divine import.

RE-MEMBERING DOSTOEVSKY

Thus far I have said much about Percy's *remembering* of Dostoevsky—his faithful modeling, his writing anew the works of the novelist he so deeply admired. But remembering is only one aspect of the mode of influence with which I am concerned in this chapter. The other is re-membering by which Percy disassembles existing elements and reassembles them into something new. Both Binx and the Underground Man reach an existential crossroads during the course of their narratives, but each takes a different path: Dostoevsky's antihero follows an infamous descent, thus failing to realize fully the aesthetic of incarnational realism, while Binx Bolling chooses to ascend—so that the ending of *The Moviegoer* has more in common with *The Brothers Karamazov* than with *Notes from Underground.* It is in this reimagined ending that Percy goes beyond merely copying, or remembering, Dostoevsky and achieves a reimagination, or re-membering, of him.

In *Notes from Underground* and *The Moviegoer,* the climax occurs in similar forms, what both novelists refer to as the "catastrophe." At the climactic moment, each protagonist is offered a sort of opportunity to love. The Underground Man's chance at love comes when he invites a prostitute to visit him at home. He realizes that the abject, particular circumstances of his home do not correlate with the knight façade he had boasted of the day before. In a strange confession of his real identity as "a blackguard, a scoundrel, a self lover" (*Notes* 122), he dissembles from the character of fiction, and seeing through his mask, she discovers what he himself had not yet realized, for "a woman, if she loves sincerely, always understands": he is "unhappy" (*Notes* 123). The Underground Man chooses not to accept her love and show himself vulnerable in his misery but rather to take revenge on her. In so doing, he rejects the opportunity to ascend from the underground.

Binx's "catastrophe" (*Moviegoer* 201) is a night of impotent lovemaking with Kate. Before they begin, Binx says that he loves her, although he does not know any more than the Underground Man does about what the word "love" means. Kate only wants the "fling" without the love. Like the Underground Man, Binx wants to "do what a hero in a novel would do" (*Moviegoer* 199), but he fails. Three times he repeats the phrase "flesh poor flesh" to emphasize the literal and figurative problem with their lovemaking. This catastrophe occurs because Binx approaches Kate as selfishly as the Underground Man used the prostitute. Kate actually asks Binx to play this role toward her. She rejects "love" and seeks his tyranny over her choices. Kate sees Binx's underground nature: "You don't need God or anyone else—no credit to you, unless it is a credit to be the most self-centered person alive" (*Moviegoer* 197). However, Kate does not offer to Binx what the Underground Man views as the antidote to selfishness—love. The Underground Man understands that "for a woman it is in love that all resurrection, all salvation from ruin of whatever sort, and all regeneration consists, nor can it reveal itself in anything else but this" (*Notes* 126). The Underground Man uses religious language to discuss love; he acknowledges the redemptive character of love, which Kate, as well as Binx, denies in their sexual encounter.

If Percy had concluded his story here, he would have accomplished merely another tale of an Underground Man, albeit a twentieth-century, American version. And yet Binx, in stark contrast to the Underground Man, accepts the opportunity to love, thereby initializing his ascent. The catastrophe of Binx and Kate's night on the train provides the possibility of an awakening for Binx. Throughout the novel, Binx has tried living according to a worldview that reduces both the world and human beings to empirically provable facts, but it does not satisfy him. Desmond writes, "Paradoxically hope for [Percy's] protagonists lay in 'catastrophe,' the collapse of the fraudulent 'world' erected by scientism."[17] The world according to scientism allows Binx and Kate to disassociate their physical encounter from its spiritual reality, leaving them unsatisfied. Although Binx describes the sexual act as not "hallowed by sacrament" (*Moviegoer* 200), he ignores the "sacramental" reality. While he may not be able to ascertain what else he desires, the desire itself for, in the Underground Man's words, "something better," inclines Binx toward awareness of transcendent reality.

In the epilogue of *The Moviegoer*, Binx resembles—as Percy intended—Alyosha Karamazov more than the Underground Man. At the ending of *The Brothers Karamazov*, a small child named Ilyusha has died, and Percy parallels this moment with the approaching death of Binx's brother Lonnie. A decade after writing his echo of the Dostoevsky scene, Percy could not recall whether Lonnie was dying or had died: "Binx says, 'Well, he's dying' or 'He's dead,' I've

---

17. Desmond, *Community*, 36.

forgotten."[18] In *The Brothers Karamazov*, Ilyusha has already died, and Percy seems to conflate the two scenes in his memory. The point is not the death of the child, but the resurrection. Percy summarizes the parallels he intentionally drew between the two scenes: both have other children asking whether the dead child will rise on the last day, the protagonist in both scenes affirms the truth of resurrection, and the children in both stories then call "Hurrah!" (*Karamazov* 776) or "Hurray!" (*Moviegoer* 240). Percy may or may not have realized that in both texts the children also exclaim their love for the hero: "Karamazov, we love you!" (776) and "Binx, we love you" (240). Additionally, an echo occurs that Percy may not have intended when Kate repeats the sentimental outbursts of Kolya about how awful the child's death is. Finally, both scenes conclude with the children crying out.

But how does Binx transform from the Underground Man–like antihero to an Alyosha-type hero? On its own, the ending of *The Moviegoer* leaves unanswered questions, and yet if the epilogue is read as a gloss on *The Brothers Karamazov*, then Binx may be interpreted as a heroic Alyosha Karamazov who has overcome his doubts and chosen belief. Many reviewers regard the ending of *The Moviegoer* as "imposed upon the narrative rather than allowed to arise naturally from it," as Kieran Quinlan argues in reference to Percy's use of Dostoevsky.[19] However, this assessment misconstrues the nature of doubt, the "great perhaps" presented in the "possibility" before Percy's epilogue.

In *The Brothers Karamazov*, Alyosha exhibits a reciprocal relationship between faith and doubt. Midway through the narrative, Alyosha confesses his doubt: "And perhaps I don't even believe in God" (*Brothers Karamazov* 202). In Cardinal Ratzinger's *An Introduction to Christianity*, he explains the correlation between faith and doubt. Ratzinger records a story from Martin Buber, in which a rabbi is accosted by a young atheist scholar. The learned man rambles off the various proofs and evidence against the existence of God, daring the rabbi to contend with his indefatigable reasoning, to which the rabbi responds, "Perhaps it is true." Ratzinger explains, "In other words, both the believer and the unbeliever share, each in his own way, doubt and belief. . . . For the one, faith is present against doubt; for the other through doubt and in the form of doubt."[20] The doubt that Binx expresses before the epilogue is "part and parcel" of his faith.

Dostoevsky's epic concludes with an emphasis on the importance of "memory," and Percy follows his great model's directive by remembering his work in his own ending. In *The Moviegoer*, Binx will see an object and then

---

18. Percy, *Conversations*, 66.
19. Quinlan, *Last Catholic*, 97.
20. Ratzinger, *Introduction*, 46–47.

recall a memory, and the same phenomenon happens to Alyosha when he looks on the stone by Ilyusha's grave. He remembers an episode that occurred earlier in the narrative when Ilyusha wept for the insult his father had received at the hand of Alyosha's brother Dmitri. This memory "rose at once before his imagination" compelling him to ask the other children to never forget Ilyusha: "If one has only one good memory left in one's heart, even that may sometime be the means of saving us" (*Brothers Karamazov* 734). Although the memory that sparks Alyosha's speech about memory and salvation is a negative one, like Binx's memory in which he rejected his father, it produces good results. In the same way that Alyosha uses the memory to instruct the children, Binx's memory provides a catalyst to change his future interactions with Kate.

The ending of *The Moviegoer* also recalls *The Brothers Karamazov* in ways that must have been subconscious for Percy. In contrast to the memory of Dmitri's insult, Alyosha's saving memory is of his mother. The narrator of *The Brothers Karamazov* explains that such memories may stand out "through a whole lifetime like spots of light out of darkness" (13), a simile that connects to the content of the memory itself. Alyosha remembers his mother holding him before the icon of the Mother of God and seeking her protection: "most vividly of all" he remembers "the slanting rays of the setting sun" (*Brothers Karamazov* 13). Not until the death of his elder, Father Zosima, however, does Alyosha recognize the source of the light. While listening to the story of Cana in the memorial service for Zosima, Alyosha has a vision in which his elder shows him Christ: "Do you see our Sun, do you see Him?" (339). Recognizing Christ as the light, Alyosha escapes the "darkness of worldly wickedness" (13), as he earlier refers to it, and follows his elder's advice to "sojourn in the world" (341).

Percy attempts to diffuse such light in *The Moviegoer*. What makes Binx aware of time and place in the research laboratory is "sunlight" that comes "streaming in" and "lay in yellow bars across the room" (*Moviegoer* 51). In *The Brothers Karamazov* the slants of sunlight recall Alyosha's memory of his mother; however, there is no icon to connect Binx's recognition of light with anything transcendent. Then at the end of the novel, in the midst of Binx's "dark pilgrimage on this earth" (228) or "dark journey" (233)—a repetition that also connects with Alyosha's epiphanic moment—he sees "watery sunlight [that] breaks through the smoke of the Chef and turns the sky yellow" (231). Through this light comes Kate in her Plymouth and initiates his change.

The Brothers Karamazov also aids in elucidating how this moment causes Binx to transition from his former underground state. When Father Zosima explains to a "lady of little faith" how to overcome her doubt, he admits that no proof of God may satisfy her. Rather, the wise priest advises she must "love [her] neighbor actively and indefatigably":

> Insofar as you advance in love you will grow surer of the reality of God and of the immortality of your soul. If you attain to perfect self-forgetfulness in the love of your neighbor, then you will believe without doubt, and no doubt can possibly enter your soul. (*Brothers Karamazov* 48)

In his brief consolation of the woman, Zosima explains the mystery of faith: it begins in action, not thought. He instructs her to love in order to remove the doubt about the "reality of God and immortality of your soul," tying the two beliefs together. Moreover, he defines love as "self-forgetfulness" and unites this active love with a belief in God. When Frank describes the function of the catastrophe in *Notes from Underground,* he contrasts the Underground Man's "self-indulgent, self-glorifying, sentimental Social Romanticism" with "love springing from the total forgetfulness of self that had now become Dostoevsky's highest value."[21] If Binx is to overcome his romanticism and to find life outside the *merde* of scientific humanism, he needs to begin with self-forgetting love.

At the conclusion of the novel, Binx forgets himself by loving Kate. He waits for her, then spies her at the bus stop, her "looking sideways at the children and not seeing, she could be I myself" (*Moviegoer* 231). Terrye Newkirk pinpoints this moment as Binx's "moment of grace": "seeing her miss the obvious ('looking sideways at the children and not seeing'), he is at once made aware that he, too, has missed the obvious."[22] Earlier in the novel, when Binx explained his search to Kate, she warned him, "It is possible, you know, that you are overlooking something, the most obvious thing" (*Moviegoer* 83). Although she does not explain what she means in words, she "becomes gay and affectionate," kisses him, and "watches [him] with brown eyes gone to discs" (ibid.). She is observing him the way he observes everyone else, trying to see if he will see the "most obvious thing"—her. At the end of the novel, when Binx sees himself in Kate, he wonders, "Is it possible that— . . . Is it possible that—it is not too late?" (*Moviegoer* 231). The phrase regarding possibility recalls Kate's earlier suggestion that "it is possible" he may be overlooking her.

In other instances in *The Moviegoer,* Binx has used phrases of "possibility" concerning not Kate but God. He reluctantly writes in his journal, "Yet it is impossible to rule God out" (*Moviegoer* 146). Later, sitting in his car with

---
21. Frank, *Writer,* 435.
22. Newkirk, "Via Negativa," 193.

Kate, Binx watches a man exit a church with ashes on his forehead, and the phrase "it is impossible" is repeated three times: "It is impossible to be sure that he received the ashes. . . . It is impossible to say why he is here. . . . It is impossible to say" (235). The "possibility" connects Binx's vision of Kate as the answer to his search with the earlier indication of a search for God. In a discussion of Dostoevsky's Trinitarian theology, David Cunningham discusses the Russian author's "subsistent relationality," his contention that through love of one's neighbor, one participates in the divine, the God who is Love. Binx unwittingly follows Zosima's advice to the lady of little faith, and his decision to love Kate will convince him of the existence of an unprovable God. As a lady of little faith may become a believer, so may an underground man.

The ultimate effect of reading *The Moviegoer* alongside *Notes from Underground* is that the reader can suddenly see the bread crumbs that Percy is dropping along the way, hints that there is hope for Binx. Percy attempted to leave clues throughout *The Moviegoer* that would foreshadow the hope Binx finds in the end. Passages from Dostoevsky's novels are like spotlights on the clues of hopefulness within *The Moviegoer*. For instance, in the epilogue, off-stage, Lonnie tells Binx that "he had conquered an habitual disposition" (*Moviegoer* 239), which Binx does not elucidate further to Kate. This strange remark to Binx may easily be passed over, but by remembering Dostoevsky's ending to *The Brothers Karamazov*, the reader realizes that Lonnie's comment assures readers not only of Binx's conversion but also indicates how this conversion has occurred.

When Lonnie informs Binx that he has conquered his habitual disposition, he refers to the sin of envy, his sin against his brother Duval who has already died. In this same conversation, he reminds Binx, "I am still offering my communion for you" (*Moviegoer* 165). According to Binx, Lonnie possesses "the gift of believing that he can offer his sufferings in reparation for men's indifference to the pierced heart of Jesus Christ" (136). By offering communion on behalf of Binx, one whom is indifferent, Lonnie hopes Binx will receive the gift of faith. Percy does not attempt to explain this mystery, but affirms conclusively, "The sacraments work nevertheless."[23] Binx seems to have reaped the benefits of Lonnie's Eucharist. In the same manner that the practice of fasting seems to have conquered Lonnie's envy, so his dedication of the Eucharist seems to have changed Binx.

Furthermore, as a "gloss" on *The Brothers Karamazov*, *The Moviegoer* elucidates the significance of the strange pancake supper that follows Ilyusha's funeral, tying this event to the Eucharist. Kolya protests this tradition: "It's all

---

23. Percy, *Conversations*, 12.

so strange, Karamazov, such sorrow and then pancakes after it, it all seems so unnatural in our religion" (*Brothers Karamazov* 733). Since Kolya does not believe in their religion, he cannot understand the ritual practice. Alyosha does not explain, only laughingly responds, "Don't be put out at our eating pancakes—it's a very old custom and there's something nice in that!" (735). In between Kolya's remarks and Alyosha's answer, though, the devout Karamazov offers his reflections on the power of memory, which may offer a clue to the meaning of the "old custom."

Earlier in the novel, Alyosha received a revelation while listening to the story of Jesus' miracle at the wedding at Cana of Galilee in which Jesus transforms water into wine. This first miracle is often connected with Jesus' later insistence that taking wine "in remembrance" of him will be drinking his blood, as will taking the bread be ingesting his body. Alyosha exclaims, "It was not men's grief, but their joy Christ visited. He worked his first miracle to help men's gladness" (*Brothers Karamazov* 338). By making this connection between the miracle of the wine and joy, Alyosha affirms the mystery that the Eucharist too helps "men's gladness." Rather than commemorating a solely sorrowful event, the Eucharist allows believers to remember the resurrection that followed the passion. The pancakes take on this sacramental significance following the funeral of Ilyusha: sharing the bread, the children participate in an old custom in which they remember both Ilyusha's death and resurrection.

In an interview, Percy switches the identity of Dostoevsky's characters, substituting Kolya for Ilyusha, which suggests to Lewis Lawson "that Walker Percy, like the rest of us, remembered not the concrete particulars of a scene but the significance that scene had for him."[24] Instead of taking his brothers and sisters for pancakes, Binx takes them for a train ride. Although the Eucharist is only mentioned in the earlier conversation between Binx and Lonnie, the "mystery of the Eucharist is at the heart of *The Moviegoer*," as Newkirk attests.[25] Binx's participation in the sacraments affirms his belief in a paradoxical vision in which the world is both good and evil, humans are heroes and villains, and reality is both immanent and transcendent.

The fundamental importance of the sacraments is that they suggest the truth about resurrection. When Binx avows to the children that Lonnie will rise in a new body after death, he believes what he says. Because Percy intended to salute Dostoevsky in this final passage, he compares Binx to Alyosha to elucidate this final moment: "Like Alyosha he tells the truth. He wouldn't have said, 'Yeah' if he didn't mean it."[26] Kate assumes that Binx merely

---

24. Lawson, "From Tolstoy to Dostoyevsky," 419.
25. Newkirk, "Via Negativa," 200.
26. Percy, *Conversations*, 66.

wants to assuage the children's fears and sorrows, but Percy thinks she misses it. Whereas *Notes*, as a parody of confession, ends with an unsatisfied antihero still living underground and still rambling with no one listening, Percy's hero commits to a community, one that allegorically represents the church. In contrast to the confusion and isolation still persistent at the end of *Notes*, Binx joins, in the final words of the novel, "his brothers and sisters [who] call out behind [him]" (*Moviegoer* 241). Such an image resembles that toward which, Bakhtin suggests, all of Dostoevsky's world gravitates, "the church as a communion of unmerged souls, where sinners and the righteous come together."[27]

What does this reading of *The Moviegoer* in light of Dostoevsky mean for the scholarly understanding of Percy's work more broadly? Hopefully, this analysis of Dostoevsky's influence on *The Moviegoer* has shown how, during Percy's very act of writing, he came to realize that the central influence on his work would be the Russian novelist Dostoevsky. By remembering and re-membering Dostoevsky in his first published novel, Percy brings his forerunner into his present, midcentury America. Harold Bloom contends "that one cannot write a novel without remembering another novel," but he claims that such a memory causes anxiety.[28] Instead, after Percy realized his debt to Dostoevsky, he made it explicit in his epilogue by writing an intentional salute to his forerunner. This analysis of Dostoevsky's influence on Percy demonstrates that influence, whether intentional or not, is not equivalent to derivation, and that therefore it need not be stigmatized. Certainly Percy was inspired by the work of Dostoevsky, and yet in modeling his work after the Russian's, Percy still retained, or perhaps discovered, his own voice. As T. S. Eliot suggests, "We shall often find that not only the best but the most individual parts of [a poet's] work may be those in which the dead poets, his ancestors, assert their immortality most vigorously."[29] The words of Eliot remind us that artistic influence is not to be denied or sneered at, but rather to be honed and celebrated.

---

27. Bakhtin, *Problems*, 141.
28. Bloom, *Anxiety*, 55.
29. Eliot, "Tradition," 38.

CHAPTER 3

Modeling a Holy Fool in *The Last Gentleman*

"SHELBY, IT'S *The Idiot*, that's what I've written," said Walker Percy to his friend Shelby Foote upon completing his second published novel, *The Last Gentleman*.[1] Foote would assume that Percy had only seen the connection in hindsight; however, as this chapter makes clear, a trove of notes that have been buried in Percy's archives for decades proves that *The Last Gentleman* grew out of Percy's conscious attempt to reconstitute Dostoevsky's *The Idiot* in a twentieth-century Southern setting.[2] Caroline Gordon intuited as much in a letter to Percy's editor, Robert Giroux (Mar. 11, 1966), calling the novel "the Odyssey of a Southern Prince Myshkin [protagonist of *The Idiot*] through regions as strange as Odysseus." Gordon adds, "The events which, at times are almost incredible, take on the Dostoyevskyean [*sic*] stage of the modern novel."[3]

---

1. Recounted in Robert Coles's introduction to the 1997 printing of Percy's second published novel, *The Last Gentleman*, xvi.
2. Foote informs Coles, "There are differences between the two novels, of course, but I can see why Walker would *look back* and suddenly realize the important similarities" (ibid., xvii, emphasis mine).
3. Gordon writes, "Fr. Charles found the key to it in the Dostoyevskyean [*sic*] inspiration. Walker said he was right and expressed pleasure at his discernment. . . . I felt that Walker's book is quite important" [Vanderbilt University. Special Collections. Lytle papers. 2.17]. This conversation probably affected her initial reading of the manuscript. When Gordon returned to the Northeast, she read Percy's novel for herself in conjunction with a syllabus of reading focused on Dostoevsky. She explains to Percy why the first reading took longer than expected (May 13,

Although Percy's first published novel, *The Moviegoer*, had achieved critical success, laudatory reviews, and strong sales, Percy felt the novel had failed to achieve its purpose. Just as Dostoevsky had been adopted (some would say misread) by the Beat poets and British modernists, Percy felt that his first novel was embraced by modern readers for all the wrong reasons. Percy's intention in *The Moviegoer* had been to reveal hope to an unbelieving audience, yet many read the novel as affirmation of modern despair.[4] For his second novel, Percy wanted to be more forthright in communicating his purpose without preaching directly at readers or producing artless propaganda. His desire was to write a novel that addressed the root of Americans' despair; that would make readers question their facile answers to big questions about good, evil, love, and death; and that would show human beings nothing less than how to live in the world. However, Percy did not feel confident in his ability to write such a grandly polemical novel without preaching. In a letter to Gordon, the same letter in which Percy decries readers' responses to *The Moviegoer*, he phrases the problem thus: "How does a Catholic fiction writer handle the Catholic Faith in his novel?"[5] Percy adds quickly that he does not expect Gordon to solve his problem for him; rather, he believes that he has already found an appropriate model: "(Actually the only reason I can raise the question now is that I see the glimmerings of an answer.) Dostoevsky knew the answer."[6]

It would not have been *en vogue* for Percy to claim a literary influence, especially not after his recent success as the National Book Award winner. After all, critics view influence as a passive process, as Harold Bloom claims, "Strong writers do not choose their prime precursors; they are chosen by them."[7] For Percy to seek intentionally to follow another writer's example would be to admit, in Bloom's and other's esteem, that he was a weak writer. In contrast to Bloom's argument, scholars such as Maria Bloshteyn, who primarily studies Dostoevsky's influence on American writers, asserts:

1966): "The delay was caused mainly by trying to read *The Idiot* and since it was a first reading for me, and an experience, I could not skim through it." Princeton University, Firestone Library (PFL), Gordon papers 35.24.

4. Percy complains about the reception of *The Moviegoer* to Caroline Gordon in 1962: "Its most enthusiastic supporters were precisely those people who misunderstood it worst. It was received as a novel of 'despair'—not a novel about despair but as a novel ending in despair. Even though I left broad hints that such was not at all the case" (quoted in Samway, *Walker Percy: A Life*, 224).

5. Ibid. Cited also in chapter one.

6. Ibid., 223–24.

7. Bloom, *Western Canon*, 11.

> The American adoption of Dostoevsky shows that . . . the choice of a literary ancestor is frequently the outcome of a host of practical decisions that have little to do with an anxiety of influence but a lot more with the pragmatics of how to attract attention and gain acknowledgement and respect for one's own work.[8]

In Percy's case, Dostoevsky was the right choice of a literary progenitor because only he modeled how to ask ultimate questions from a Christian perspective to secular readers. And Percy intended his second novel to be "an ass-kicking for Jesus' sake."[9]

Percy chose to model one Dostoevsky novel in particular: *The Idiot*. But why did Percy deem Dostoevsky's *The Idiot* to be the most apropos novel to imitate? Why did he consider this work the best example for showing modern audiences how to live? On its surface, *The Idiot* seems a dubious choice. It is a dark novel with a bumbling protagonist who interferes in an adoptive family, messes up marriages, idly watches a sick young man attempt to take his own life, and indirectly promotes the murder of his one true love by his "brother." Yet in Percy's reimagination of *The Idiot*, complete with altered tone and an ambiguously "happier" ending, Percy creates a satirical version of *The Idiot* that attests to the philosophical core of Dostoevsky's novel while offering more hope than its predecessor. Percy's epigraph, drawn from Romano Guardini's *The End of the Modern World*, hints at the hopeful tone of *The Last Gentleman*: "Love will disappear from the face of the public world, but the more precious will be that love that flows from one lonely person to another."[10]

As this chapter will show, *The Last Gentleman* represents Percy's most direct and intentional copy of a Dostoevsky novel. Percy undertook a similar practice of glossing to that of medieval Christians. Like a monastic scribe transcribing an ancient manuscript, Percy pored over *The Idiot*. Of all of Dostoevsky's novels in Percy's library, only *The Idiot* receives twenty-six pages of notes, carefully handwritten during an intimate study of Dostoevsky's novel, tracing its structure, theme, and character development almost page by page.[11] Although Percy accessed *The Idiot* in translation, his method of writing *The*

---

8. Bloshteyn, *Henry Miller's Dostoevsky*, 179.
9. Letter to Caroline Gordon, Apr. 6, 1962. Private papers of Ashley Brown (cited in Tolson, *Pilgrim in the Ruins*, 301).
10. *The Essential Guardini*, 58.
11. Percy has two copies of *The Idiot* in his collection. His 1935 Modern Library edition is translated by Constance Garnett and illustrated by Boardman Robinson, with some haunting black-and-white depictions of the most melodramatic scenes in the text; Percy used this edition for his handwritten notes. Also, he has a copy of David Magarshack's translation from Penguin, 1958, in which the introduction says much about Dostoevsky's process in composing *The Idiot*.

Last Gentleman is itself a *translation* of the Russian novel into the American twentieth-century culture. In their description of the process of medieval translation of Greek and Latin literature, L. D. Reynold and N. G. Wilson extend the concept of translation to include the creation of new texts: "Translation is primarily designed to make a work available to those who cannot read the original; but if the translation is freely executed and the opportunity is taken to correct, bring up to date, or otherwise modify the original, then a new version comes into being."[12] This creation of new texts in the process of translating the old ones caused no problems for the medieval scribes, who were not concerned with the autonomy of the authors nor had any notion of plagiarism. Instead the focus was on the truth of what was written, so these scribes would correct the work, clarify it for accessibility, or even baptize certain meanings and ideas with Christian glosses and marginalia.

The very texts that medieval monks translated and transcribed would have been developed on a mode of imitative instruction. In classical education, Greek and Latin rhetors trained by imitating other writers with the final step in imitation to compose a new piece. This educational technique is "paraphrasis," from which we draw our word "paraphrase." Marko Juvan explains, "It is the retelling of some known, usually classical verse or prose text, in which the original sense must be preserved, although expressed in other words; interpretation was often involved in such a new formulation of an older text's contents."[13] Paraphrasing, in the classical context, would begin with dissecting another writer's form, interpreting the pieces, and then creating a competitive new work. Juvan explains that this new piece would "surpass [the first piece] with [the student's] own inventive spirit (*aemulatio*) and apply its meaning to the needs of his [piece]."[14] Juvan gives an example of modern types of *paraphrasis,* including the Russian romantic Pushkin's imitation of Horace's ode, in which the poet "channels Horace's semantics into his own historical *hic et nunc*" and connects the classical writer's poem with Pushkin's "political resistance to tsarist absolutism."[15] Other modern examples of this type of translation or adaptation include Charles Lamb's tales for young readers, which he drew from Shakespeare's plays. The goal was to recompose the "source's shape and content to a new function and another target audience."[16] When Percy writes *The Last Gentleman,* he follows suit, translating and adapting *The Idiot*

---

12. Reynolds and Wilson, *Scribes and Scholars,* 236.
13. Juvan, *History and Poetics of Intertextuality,* 30.
14. Ibid., 31.
15. Ibid., 31–32.
16. Ibid., 32.

in a manner that retains the meaning of the original in a way that contemporary American readers can understand.

In this chapter, I undertake a close reading of both texts to show not only how Percy drew from Dostoevsky but also how Percy's version reveals meaning to us in *The Idiot*. Juvan notes how "pre-texts evoked or rewritten in post-texts often figure as interpretants of the latter and vice versa."[17] Through close examination of the parallels between Percy's novel and Dostoevsky's *The Idiot*—including the two protagonists' "strangeness," their journeys from orphanhood to adoption, and their abstracted "angelic" love of idealized women—I demonstrate that Percy learned from Dostoevsky how to create novels that could make Christianity palatable to a modern audience. I also show how both Dostoevsky and Percy draw from a shared inspiration, *Don Quixote*, in constructing their romantically inclined protagonists. Audiences' responses to Percy's previous novel, *The Moviegoer*, had convinced Percy that he had heretofore failed as a novelist by leaving readers with the sense that he was writing about existential despair.[18] Thus in his second novel for publication, Percy was determined to elevate his readers with affirmations of Christianity, albeit couched in satire. As closely as *The Last Gentleman* parallels *The Idiot*, the two novels diverge in their conclusions. Dostoevsky's novel is a tragedy, in which the false unity of two brothers erupts into deadly violence, while Percy's is a comedy, in which two become brothers.

PARALLELS BETWEEN *THE LAST GENTLEMAN* AND *THE IDIOT*

At first glance, the plot differences between the two novels belie their profound likeness. *The Idiot* revolves around two love triangles, with Prince Myshkin at the center of both, while *The Last Gentleman* follows Will Barrett's trek from New York to Alabama to Santa Fe. Storylines that were peripheral in *The Idiot*

---

17. Ibid., 184. Although Juvan states this as part of his conclusion that literature is an "autopoetic system, living on cultural memory" (217), with which I heartily disagree, I do consent to this initial premise. To make such a claim, Juvan removes the role of the author from the process. My study instead emphasizes the author's role.

18. In chapter six, I will address Kieran Quinlan's claim that Percy "imposed" his "philosophical and theological views" on *The Moviegoer*. Quinlan writes, "Walker Percy's reference to Dostoevsky helps, perhaps, to clarify what is being enacted in *The Moviegoer*. Recent interpretations of the Russian novelist have focused interest on the tension between that author's well-known Christian dogmatism and what is actually achieved in his great novels" (*Last Catholic*, 97). According to Quinlan, Percy's allusion to Dostoevsky solidifies Quinlan's assessment of Percy as an ideologue following in the footsteps of another ideologue.

take center stage in *The Last Gentleman*: The Epanchin family becomes the basis for the Vaught family, and Ippolit's charismatic performance as a dying adolescent inspires the more prominent role of the character Jamie in Percy's novel. Despite the superficial alterations that Percy makes to *The Idiot*'s storyline, though, he retains many familiar elements. In *The Last Gentleman*, Dostoevsky's bumbling idiot reappears, as do the wealthy and silly family, the sick young man, the ideal lover, and the foil character. Both novels end with death and with the bonding of the foil characters. Most importantly, the two novels share profoundly similar protagonists who follow essentially the same journey and ask the same questions.[19] Central to both works is the question of how to be not just good, but completely innocent.

When Dostoevsky began writing *The Idiot*, he desired to "portray a positively beautiful man," an ideal human being modeled on the "only one positively beautiful figure in the world—Christ."[20] His goal was to embody the ideal of Christ within the real world of nineteenth-century Russia. For the Christians writing the fiction, such a question should anticipate its own answer, for the doctrines of the Christian faith assert the sinfulness of human beings and the necessity of the grace of Jesus Christ for any goodness from within a person. Dostoevsky encountered this problem in the drafting of his novel; he could only create an imperfect hero. Indeed, what Dostoevsky creates is a tragic satire of an innocent man attempting to be good in an immoral world. In his monograph on Dostoevsky, Rowan Williams writes, "It may not be possible to represent the historical Christ in a real novel . . . and the sheer particularity of the figure means that creating a Christ *figure* will always be a doomed enterprise."[21] Yet the experiment to create such a figure proffers truth about the imperfect nature of human beings as well as the perfect nature of Christ.

---

19. Admittedly, the initial introductions of these protagonists are not so alike; *The Idiot* begins with Prince Myshkin meeting his foil character Parfyon Semyonovich Rogozhin in a railway carriage, while *The Last Gentleman* opens with Will Barrett thinking, alone, in New York. The similarities between the narratives do not proceed much further than a solitary man thinking. *Crime and Punishment* begins, "At the beginning of July, during an extremely hot spell, a young man left the closet he rented" (1). *The Last Gentleman* opens with, "One fine day in early summer a young man lay thinking in Central Park" (3). Gordon finds these introductions less effective than that of *The Idiot*, which involves other characters, dialogue, and action. After Gordon first read *The Last Gentleman*, she chides Percy for beginning his novel in this way rather than emulating the opening of *The Idiot* (May 7, 1966): "Your novel starts more like *Crime and Punishment* than *The Idiot*. It takes a genius to triumph over a start like that: *a young man alone, thinking!* . . . I know the way *Crime and Punishment* begins—but why follow Dostoyevsky in his weaker moments when he is such a superb architect when he is at his best?" (PFL 35.24).

20. Cited in Frank, *Writer*, 562.

21. Williams, *Dostoevsky*, 48.

Both Dostoevsky and Percy faced difficulties in creating their ideal characters, including others' hesitancy to accept such a figure, the question of whether such an ideal could function without divinity, and the problem of whether goodness could be sustained amidst immorality. The protagonist whom Dostoevsky invents, Prince Myshkin, is like Christ in that he is incongruent with his culture, existing more out of the world than in it. When Percy sets out to emulate Dostoevsky's protagonist, this characteristic interests him. Like other characters and situations that Percy borrowed directly from Dostoevsky's *The Idiot*, Percy's protagonist, "Williston Bibb Barrett or Will Barrett or Billy Barrett" (*Last Gentleman* 17), also known as "the engineer," among other denominations, shares many peculiarities with Dostoevsky's hero Prince Myshkin.[22] The defining feature of both protagonists, Myshkin and Barrett, is their strangeness.

One way to describe the two characters' strangeness is to say that they are seemingly not of this world. Other characters recognize their peculiarity and comment on it. Over three dozen times, Myshkin is called an "idiot," a moniker Percy uses a couple of times for Barrett (*Last Gentleman* 89, 277). In his first note on Dostoevsky's novel, Percy observes, "the arrival of a strange young man"[23] in reference to Myshkin. Then Percy uses a similar phrase in the opening paragraphs of *The Last Gentleman* to introduce his protagonist: "He was an unusual young man" (3). The two protagonists are both young men in their mid-twenties of pleasant appearance despite their pale complexions (*Last Gentleman* 8, *Idiot* 4).[24] To some, Myshkin looks like an Orthodox icon of Christ with his blue eyes and yellow, pointed beard, distinctions that Barrett lacks. Percy deems Myshkin a "poor fellow" in his notes,[25] a descriptor that Barrett employs twice for himself (*Last Gentleman* 22). The phrase "poor fellow" occurs in a self-interrogation after he voluntarily leaps into a "brierpatch like a saint of old" (ibid.). When Barrett finds himself conforming to a group of Ohioans on a vacation to Bear Mountain, he briefly acts like an old saint, or what might be called a holy fool in Russian Orthodoxy. Like Prince Myshkin, Barrett seems more out of the world than in it.

---

22. According to Paul Elie, "Percy later said he modeled Barrett on the saintly hero of Dostoevsky's *The Idiot*, and he spoke of the difficulty of making a good character come to life in fiction" (*Life You Save May Be Your Own*, 384). Tolson concurs that Percy set out to model Dostoevsky's *The Idiot*, "although Percy envisioned a character even worse off than the epileptic holy fool, Prince Myshkin" (*Pilgrim in the Ruins*, 305). *The Last Gentleman* by Walker Percy will be cited in text throughout the book.

23. Percy, SHC 257.2.

24. *The Idiot* by Dostoevsky will be cited in text throughout the book. Percy owned two different translations of *The Idiot*, but I cite from Garnett.

25. Percy, SHC 247.2.

Both heroes are able to offer an extraordinary perspective on the world because of medical conditions that provide them clearer visions of the world. When Myshkin suffers an epileptic seizure—as did Dostoevsky himself—it grants him supernatural revelations. The narrator describes a "quickening of self-consciousness" that precedes "the very last conscious moment before the fit" (*Idiot* 214), in which Myshkin thinks to himself, "For this moment one might give one's whole life!" (Ibid.). Myshkin also compares himself to Mahomet the prophet, and these two connections mark his moment of clarity with religious significance (215). In similar fashion, Barrett undergoes sporadic amnesic episodes. Barrett's psychiatrist reminds him, "You also recall that this great thirst for the 'answer,' the key which will unlock everything, always overtakes you just before the onset of one of your fugue states?" (*Last Gentleman* 38). The answer is undefined in *The Last Gentleman*, but it makes everything clear, similar to Myshkin's epileptic insights.

In many ways, neither hero subscribes to the values of their respective cultures, one striking example being their indifference to money. At the opening of *The Idiot,* for instance, Myshkin receives an inheritance, a scene that catches Percy's attention. Admiring Dostoevsky's craft, Percy describes the "sudden inheritance" scene "*good!*,"[26] and he underlines the page in which Nastasya burns the money, calling it a "melodramatic act with terrific effect."[27] Although the inciting incident of the novel hinges for most of the characters on who has the most money—each making bids for Nastasya—the Prince values his inheritance as little as Nastasya does. This frame of reference should highlight the passages concerning money in *The Last Gentleman*. In the opening chapters, Barrett receives an inheritance (much smaller than Myshkin's) of $17,500. According to his analyst, Barrett spends extravagantly before one of his fugue episodes: "The last time it was a Corvette" (*Last Gentleman* 38) and this time, a telescope. The purchases matter no more to the engineer than the money itself: he gives his telescope to Jamie as a birthday gift.

Another aspect of the two protagonists' strangeness is their seeming to exist outside of time. Both characters have visions that remove them from the particularities of temporal existence. Myshkin, speaking to his friend and rival Rogozhin, characterizes the moment before his seizure in terms of the book of Revelation: "I seem somehow to understand the extraordinary saying that *there shall be no more time*" (*Idiot* 214). The character has no history of his own and does not acknowledge the history of others. Moreover, he absorbs future utopian visions into the present without an eternal context. While his illness seems to grant him a clearer vision of the world, it omits the physi-

---

26. Ibid., 257.8.
27. Ibid., 257.8–9.

cal realities of space and time. In a 1967 interview with Ashley Brown, Percy explains how he models Barrett on Myshkin:

> He bears a conscious kinship to Prince Myshkin. He is a device with considerable potentialities. . . . His amnesia allows him to be a blank tablet. [Also,] Barrett's amnesia suggests a post-Christian shakiness about historic time.[28]

A hero drowning in possibilities, Barrett has no direction at the beginning of the novel. He feels as insecure in his time and place as Myshkin does, perhaps more, for he often forgets who he even is.

KNIGHTS-ERRANT

Dostoevsky, foreseeing that such a strangely good character may be unpalatable to his audience, chose to make his Christ figure ridiculous.[29] Just as Percy would look to Dostoevsky for inspiration in creating such a character, so Dostoevsky turned to Miguel de Cervantes, the author of *Don Quixote*.[30] Don Quixote's goodness succeeds in the novel because the reader sees it as comical and therefore nonthreatening. The mockable protagonist is generally the most loveable one. In *The Idiot*, Dostoevsky embeds a hint that Don Quixote is the source of Myshkin's character. In part two, when Myshkin writes to one of the women with whom he is in love, Aglaia, she places his letter into a book, and a week later, she notices the title of that book—"Don Quixote de la Mancha"—a revelation which causes her to "burst out laughing for some unknown reason" (*Idiot* 178). The author may expect that readers will discern the reason for her laughter, but the narrator feigns obtuseness. Like that good and noble knight of Cervantes, Myshkin lives in a fantasy world. His virtues seem unfitting, even laughable, in an immoral world. In Percy's study of Dostoevsky, he takes note of a second moment in which Dostoevsky connects Myshkin with Quixote: Aglaia's recitation of Pushkin's "Poor Knight." Percy calls Aglaia's behavior "bold faced" and underlines the page reference.[31] In this scene, Aglaia alters the original poem by changing the initials "A. M. D." to "N. F. B." to connect the "poor and simple knight" with Myshkin himself.

---

28. Percy, *Conversations*, 13.

29. He writes in his notebooks for *The Idiot*: "Compassion for the beautiful man who is ridiculed and who is unaware of his own worth generates sympathy in the reader. And this ability to arouse compassion is the very secret of humor" (cited in Frank, *Writer*, 563).

30. Dostoevsky writes: "Of the most beautiful figures in Christian literature, the most complete is that of Don Quixote. But he is only good because at the same time he is ridiculous" (cited in Frank, *Writer*, 562–63).

31. Percy, SHC 257.12.

Percy would read *Don Quixote* while writing *The Last Gentleman*, just as Dostoevsky would be engrossed in it while writing *The Idiot*. Within Percy's manuscript notes for *The Last Gentleman*, Percy jots down the phrase, "BACK TO DON QUIXOTE." Several times he calls his engineer character "INGENUOUS," likely referring to the full title of Cervantes's novel: *The Ingenious Gentleman Don Quixote of La Mancha*. Of course the similarly spelled words "ingenuous" and "ingenious" have different meanings; Cervantes's gentleman is clever while Percy's is "frank," a word Percy repeats half a dozen times in his observations of the idiot.[32] The character of Don Quixote bore a profound influence on both Dostoevsky and Percy in constructing the characters of Myshkin and Barrett, respectively. Quixote is the quintessential example of a character who does not live in reality; instead he lives in his version of reality He paints over the dark and ugly in his mind, refusing to acknowledge anything but what is good, true, or beautiful. The last gentleman in Percy's novel does not resemble the "positively beautiful man" of Dostoevsky's intentions but rather the parody of Don Quixote that Dostoevsky constructed.

The protagonists of Dostoevsky and Percy are alike in so many ways: their strangeness, their medical conditions, their comical purity of heart. Another parallel, one that drives the plot of both narratives, is that the idiot and the last gentleman are orphans. Myshkin lost his parents when he was young; he informs Lebedyev and Rogozhin, "There are no Prince Myshkins now except me; I believe I am the last of them" (*Idiot* 6). Like Myshkin, Barrett is "the last of his line" (*Last Gentleman* 10), descending from a line of men who become "ironical" and fight to live normal lives. Through the course of the narrative he exhibits curiosity about his history, the full details of which are not exhumed until the sequel to this novel, *The Second Coming*. When Percy observed that Myshkin was the last of his line, he noted that the character "is inevitably curious about his history."[33] During the course of their narratives, both men are homeless, and they journey back to a place that had been home only to find that it is no longer home. When Myshkin and Barrett return to Russia and the

---

32. Gordon admits that to understand Percy's *The Last Gentleman*, in addition to reading Dostoevsky's *The Idiot, Possessed*, and *Crime and Punishment*, she had to reread *Don Quixote*. In antebellum South and even later, Cervantes's novel was popular with Southern readers, such as Percy, because of the chivalry it seemed to extol. According to Eugene and Elizabeth Fox Genovese in *The Mind of the Master Class*, "The southern gentleman is the outgrowth of Chivalry and Christianity—the *knight-errant*, civilized and softened down" (336, emphasis mine). While Southerners uplift conventions of medieval romances and chivalry, the sixteenth-century poet Cervantes parodied these ideals. In *The Waning of the Middle Ages*, Johan Huizinga indicates why chivalry becomes ridiculous in a Christian context: "Its earthly origin draws it down. For the source of the chivalrous idea is pride aspiring to beauty" (58).

33. Percy, SHC 257.2.

American South, respectively, they find that these places are not the homes they remembered. In their orphaned, homeless state, neither possesses much in the way of material possessions; at one point, Myshkin has a bundle and Barrett only seven dollars to his name. Socially, economically, and personally these men stand aloof from their societies. Throughout the course of their narratives, they will journey from orphanhood to adoption, involvement in society, and a kind of disembodied romantic love.

In the absence of their own familial ties, the two characters are adopted by the Epanchins and the Vaughts, respectively. For the character of Mr. Vaught, Percy chose to reconfigure General Ivolgin instead of General Epanchin for the head of the family. The former old man is something of a buffoon, innocent and delightful, who pretends to experience stories he reads in newspaper accounts and falsifies connections with those he first encounters. When Myshkin meets him, the General imagines a history between himself and the Prince's parents. Percy underlines the page number on which this scene occurs and jots notes to "create a character," which are difficult to decipher but appear to allude to General Ivolgin.[34] A similar moment occurs when Barrett meets Mr. Vaught, who insists that he knew his father: "'We used to hunt together down at Lake Arthur,' he cried as if he were launching into a reminiscence but immediately fell silent. The engineer guessed that either he did not really know his father or they were on different sides of the political fence" (*Last Gentleman* 52). The political divide is not brought up again, but the former reason for his silence coordinates with Ivolgin. Their personalities are also similar; Percy writes of Vaught, "His cordiality was excessive and perfunctory" (53). Because Ivolgin is a more comic character than Epanchin, Percy's choice to emulate him reveals his intention to enhance the comedy of his novel.

Both the idiot and the last gentleman engender natural affection from others, either despite or because of their unusualness. Both are talkative, yet shy; and both evince a candor that signifies the congruence between their inner and outer selves. For example, early in *The Idiot*, Myshkin attempts to befriend the Epanchins because of the possibility that Madame Epanchin has a distant relational connection to the Myshkin line. When Myshkin first meets the family, Mme. Epanchin demands, "Come, tell me something" (*Idiot* 50), and Myshkin begins to tell stories on cue. The girls cannot stop laughing at his seeming gregariousness. While reading *The Idiot*, Percy makes the note, "M[yshkin] talkative at the beginning,"[35] and indeed he borrows this charac-

---

34. Ibid., 257.5.
35. Ibid., 257.25.

teristic for his "talkative engineer" (*Last Gentleman* 58). Upon Barrett's introduction to the Vaught family, the narrator observes, "It was understood that it was open to him at that moment to spin just such a yarn, half-serious and curious" (57). Like Myshkin's tale, Barrett's story causes "laughter" that startles him. The two ridiculous lone wanderers are drawn into the families as though they have always been a part of them.

While both characters are talkative, they are ironically shy. Percy notes throughout his study of *The Idiot* how "painfully shy" Myshkin is and how often he blushes.[36] In an early draft of the scene in which Barrett meets the Vaughts, the engineer "blushes" twice, an allusion to Myshkin:

> "What wonderful men!" he cried, turning to the others, his eyes shining. "You must excuse me for expressing myself this way," he added, *blushing*, "but I feel that I am among friends and that I am free to speak—really, I feel perfectly free and comfortable." The others gaze at him until he *blushes* again.[37]

The sentences have the cadence of Dostoevsky's style, and any reader familiar with Dostoevsky can recognize his features in this passage: the exclamatory observation, the shining eyes and elated physical response, such as the blushing, the rambling dialogue riddled with unnecessary adverbs, and the self-consciousness about one's own expressions. In the published version, Barrett does not blush, but he refers to himself as "shy": "Yes, it's true. I was shy! I don't know why I'm not shy now" (*Last Gentleman* 57). Throughout the novel, Barrett is unable to explain why he is talkative amidst the Vaughts despite his accustomed shyness. If Barrett is read as having been modeled on Myshkin, however, Barrett's talkativeness can be seen as a sign of his honesty, of the congruence between his inner and outer self.

For Percy reading *The Idiot*, he certainly saw the talkativeness of the Prince as stemming from his candidness. When Myshkin converses with Ganya about Agalaia, Percy observes that Myshkin "keeps no secrets."[38] Romano Guardini, from whom Percy drew the epigraph to the novel, notes, "Myshkin confides in everyone so much so that people think he is a chatterbox."[39] In his notes on the scene between Myshkin and Ganya, Percy seems to admire this characteristic of the Prince. He scribbles his thoughts:

> The oppressiveness of our dealings with enemies and unpleasant people—our lack of frankness—what if we should speak our feelings to them ... → the

---

36. Ibid., 257.6–7.
37. Ibid., 17.80.
38. Ibid., 257.4.
39. Guardini, "Dostoevsky's Idiot, A Symbol of Christ," 362.

worst that could happen is a physical assault . . . not a bad thing, not nearly as bad as silence.[40]

Percy interprets the Prince's lack of discretion as genuineness, for Myshkin does not have an interior self concealed behind a false presentation. At this point in the novel, Ganya does not physically assault the Prince, but Percy intuits such tension beneath their first quarrel here. Although Percy makes Ganya the enemy in this scene, labeling him a "villain," he is surprised that Ganya "believes M."[41] The only pages that Percy dog-ears are these, in which Myshkin divulges Aglaia's rejection without hesitation, and Ganya calls him an idiot for telling the truth. Ganya's response illustrates how disconcerting other characters find the idiot's proclivity to tell the truth. In sum, Percy's Barrett is closely modeled on Dostoevsky's Myshkin, both biographically and psychologically.

THE DOUBLES

As pure as Barrett and Myshkin are, it seems inevitable that both characters should have dark doubles. In Dostoevsky's early drafts of Myshkin's character, he wonders whether the character is good or evil: "Who is he? A fearful scoundrel or a mysterious ideal?" Dostoevsky writes the question to himself in his notebooks, and then answers himself, "Prince, innocent."[42] As Dostoevsky develops the Prince's innocent nature, he subsumes the sinister aspects into another character, Rogozhin. When the two meet in a railway carriage, they "take" to each other without understanding the affinity, and they call each other "brothers" throughout the novel. Steiner would call Rogozhin "Myshkin's original sin,"[43] and indeed Myshkin does seem complicit in Rogozhin's violence. In *The Last Gentleman*, Barrett too has his double, Sutter. In *The Message in the Bottle*, Percy describes a "monstrous bifurcation of man into angelic and bestial components" (113), a discovery he seems to have made in the study of Dostoevsky's *The Idiot* and through the writing of *The Last Gentleman*.

Both the angelism of Myshkin and Barrett and the bestialism of Rogozhin and Sutter are deeply problematic. The former disconnect from reality by living in denial of their flesh and abstracted from time and space. Their "angelism" is, in the words of Gordon, quoting Jacques Maritain to Percy, "the

---

40. Percy, SHC 257.4.
41. Ibid.
42. Quoted in Steiner, *Tolstoy or Dostoevsky*, 151.
43. Ibid., 152.

sin of the age."[44] If Myshkin and Barrett embody an abstracted angelism, their doubles represent its reverse. Rogozhin and Sutter, the bestial doubles of Myshkin and Barrett, respectively, are wedded to concrete, physical reality. Rogozhin is robust, whereas Sutter is unusually thin; and yet the characters are similar in that both are overtly sexual and violent, and they oppose the Christian faith for the same reason, namely that they believe only in the physical present. Sutter writes in his notebooks:

> Man who falls victim to transcendence as the spirit of abstraction, i.e., elevates self to posture over and against the world . . . has no choice but to seek reentry into immanent world *qua* immanence. But since no avenue of reentry remains save genital . . . post-orgasmic despair without remedy. (*Last Gentleman* 344)

While Sutter wants to triumph over the angelism, or "spirit of abstraction," that haunts Myshkin and Barrett unbeknownst to them, he finds sex an inadequate solution. For the angelist, the physical reentry that sex provides loses its hold after orgasm; the present elation disappears into a future despair.

To return again to Myshkin's and Barrett's angelic natures, we find a crucial illustration of these natures in the way in which these knight-errants fail to woo their damsels. In a 1952 letter responding to Percy's first unpublished novel *The Charterhouse*, Gordon instructs Percy:

> A novel, any novel, in the first place, must be about love. There is no other subject. It is a *romance*. . . . Human love—the love between man and woman, is the proper and only subject, as an analogue for Divine Love.[45]

The immanent human love between a man and a woman should lead to a transcendent divine love. Within the human romance, the participators learn to identify divine love. For Gordon, novels should narrate the story of divine love through a human love story. She states explicitly, "The proper subject of a novel then, is love, and it must be incarnated, as Christ was."[46] Gordon's explanation about the nature of love reveals why Myshkin's and Barrett's love flounders. They love abstractly, without understanding the embodied nature of love, which is why they fear sex and misunderstand marriage.

Both Dostoevsky and Percy show two very different concepts that both go by the name of love. In *The Idiot*, both Myshkin and Rogozhin claim to love

---

44. Percy, SHC 387.2.
45. Percy, SHC 387.3.
46. Ibid.

Nastasya, yet they use the word differently. Rogozhin has a sexual fascination with her, whereas Myshkin feels pity for her. Nastasya is a beautiful woman, but her beauty may be of either "the ideal of Madonna" or "the ideal of Sodom" to use the terms of Dmitri in *The Brothers Karamazov*. Dmitri is in love with two different women who represent both ideals, and he quotes Schiller's "Ode to Joy," which concludes with "To angels—vision of God's throne, / To insects—sensual lust" (*Brothers Karamazov* 96). According to Dmitri, he may choose to be an angel and pursue the Madonna or an insect and succumb to Sodom. However, because Nastasya embodies the contrasts within her, she appeals in different ways to both Myshkin and Rogozhin. In Percy's South, the two different kinds of love were reserved for two different kinds of women, those labeled "lady" and those labeled "whore." Barrett, when he begins "courting" Kitty Vaught, recalls his father's advice: "Don't treat a lady like a whore or a whore like a lady" (*Last Gentleman* 100). Barrett confesses, "I've never really got the straight of this lady-and-whore business" (180). Kitty, too, acknowledges feeling torn between the two ideals, offering to be his whore in one moment or asking in the next to be loved like a lady. Although the narrator seems to acknowledge the Dostoevskian lens, which would make this choice one between angel or insect, love or lust, those categories seem diminished: "neither Christian nor pagan nor proper lusty gentleman" (ibid.). Similar to Binx's inability to properly "sin" with Katy, Barrett cannot get "the straight of it." The problem is that Barrett's ideals have supplied him with a false either-or view of women as pristine ladies made to marry or whores made to be used.

Despite the pressure of this choice for how to love Kitty, Barrett is, like Prince Myshkin, impotent. Although Myshkin is "*surrounded* by beautiful girls," as Percy observes,[47] he does not desire them sexually. In contrast with his usual frankness, Myshkin talks circuitously about his impotence. Rogozhin asks him directly, "And, women, Prince, are you keen on them?" to which he responds, "I know nothing of women" (*Idiot* 13). A similar conversation occurs between Sutter Vaught and Barrett in which Sutter attempts to diagnose him and asks, "Do you like girls?" (*Last Gentleman* 220). In contrast with Myshkin, Barrett answers in the affirmative, "Very much." Yet when Sutter pries into his sexual history, the background is empty. The engineer remains silent, insisting that he never even informed his psychiatrist of whether he had intercourse with women. When Percy revises his manuscript, he makes a note to himself: "revisions 1) Make E[ngineer] shy sexually."[48] Despite Barrett's attraction to

---

47. Ibid., 257.4.
48. Ibid., 19.784.

Kitty and confession that he likes women, Percy intended that the engineer, like Myshkin, would be sexually withdrawn.

For both protagonists, their pull toward sexual purity—or disinterest, or discomfort—is a sign of their abstraction, their distance from the world. Although neither Dostoevsky nor Percy considered sexuality oppositional to spiritual goodness, they both wanted to emphasize their protagonists' disassociation from this world. While the sexual purity of the protagonists connects them with Christ, who (notwithstanding the imaginings of Dan Brown) was holy and blameless, the authors seem to have Don Quixote more in mind. In Cervantes's novel, his hero invents an ideal love for whom to fight and serve, Dulcinea. According to Don Quixote, "She is my queen and lady, and her beauty superhuman, for in her all the impossible and chimerical attributes of loveliness that poets ascribe to their ladies are become reality" (*Quixote* 100).[49] As would a chivalric knight-errant, Quixote extols her merits with poetic descriptors, applauds her before strangers, and dedicates all his successes to her name. His squire Sancho Panza knows the real Aldonza Lorenzo, on whom Quixote bases his fantasy, and he describes her actual nature as "hale and hearty," calling her a "lusty lass" who "isn't at all priggish [and] enjoys a joke with everyone and turns everything into a good laugh" (214–15). Through his imagination, Quixote has cast a "whore" as a "lady."

Like Cervantes's hero, Myshkin and Barrett both idealize the women they love. Myshkin paints Nastasya as a Dulcinea, seeing her as the ideal he desires and not her in reality. Though Totsky has used her as a kept woman and the men surrounding her all speak of buying and trading her, Myshkin refuses to see her as such. His primary rival, Rogozhin, views her as the ideal of Sodom, a whore, and he offers a hundred thousand to purchase her. However, like the gallant Don Quixote, Myshkin casts Nastasya as a saint and proposes to her: "I'm going to marry an honest woman, Nastasya Filippovna, not Rogozhin's woman" (*Idiot* 143). Whether the Prince desires to see her as such or not, Nastasya is Rogozhin's kind of woman. Even though she has been victimized, Nastasya has too much pride to live as an honest woman. The Prince cannot see her sin or acknowledge the stains of her past. He tells her, "Everything is perfection in you" (121), which she knows to be false. She has not nor can she attain perfection, especially in terms of chastity.

These two predecessors, Quixote and Myshkin, are the inspiration for Barrett's strange relationship with Kitty. In their first intimate moments, he thinks, "She was his sweetheart, his certain someone" (*Last Gentleman* 71). Barrett uses clichéd phrases, monikers that recall romance novels, classic

---

49. *Don Quixote* will be cited in text throughout the book.

films, or Hallmark cards. However, when she speaks, he finds himself disenchanted by her jokes and gags because "she was his sweetheart and ought to know better" (73–74). His fantasy about Kitty's identity is incongruent with her reality, and Barrett wavers between seeing her through the eyes of Quixote and those of Sancho. Barrett fears that Kitty has transformed from the girl he met in the North to this new perplexing creature in the South: "No longer was she the solitary girl on the park bench as inward and watchful as he.... No, she was Miss Katherine Gibbs Vaught and the next thing he knew she'd have her picture in the *Commercial Appeal*" (259–60). In reality she probably has not changed, only his view of her has. Barrett fell in love with Kitty from a distance, but when he knows her up close, she fails to fit his imaginary ideal. Not that Kitty is anything like Nastasya, but both are transformed by the imaginations of the heroes into ideals.

Marriage remains, for Barrett, an abstract reality; and yet when he holds Kitty naked in his arms, he glimpses how love in the flesh might lead to a transcendent knowledge: "The astounding immediacy of her. She was more present, more here, than he could ever have calculated" (*Last Gentleman* 109). In this moment, Barrett almost overcomes his abstractness. He recalls his colleague Perlmutter from Macy's: "Making love to his wife, Perlmutter said, was like 'being in heaven'" (ibid.). Before holding Kitty in his arms, the engineer could not understand how the physical marriage could invoke a spiritual experience, but now, holding this woman whom he loves awakens in him an awareness, by analogy, of the Divine love.

The angelic/bestial duality, as embodied in the pairings of Myshkin/Rogozhin and Barrett/Sutter, drives both Dostoyevsky's and Percy's novels. But the tension between the two reaches a very different culmination in *The Last Gentleman* than in *The Idiot*. To understand how Percy departed from Dostoevsky in his resolution of the angel/beast duality, it is helpful to refer to Sigmund Freud's theory of the two ego impulses: Eros, the sex drive or life drive, and Thanatos, the compulsion towards death. In the characters of Rogozhin and Sutter, these two drives are so powerful as to destroy them. Dostoevsky determined these drives based on his observations of human nature, but Percy may have garnered them from his extensive reading of psychology articles and textbooks. In Percy's notes on *The Idiot*, he scribbles, "with the glib answers in Freud."[50] When Percy begins sketching Sutter (sometimes called Sadler in the notes), he uses phrases reminiscent of the dual impulses: "Sadler search for death/life," "Sadler is carnal," and "Sutter killed himself."[51] Before his first draft

---

50. Percy, SHC 257.6.
51. Ibid., 15.100–101.

of the novel, Percy knew Sutter would be characterized by both his carnal sexuality and suicidal death drive.[52] Sutter outlines these two drives as ways of recovering the immanent from feeling "transcendent": after fornication fails as "the sole channel to the real," then comes "the certain availability of death" (*Last Gentleman* 372). For mortal beings without eternal future, every impulse, whether sexual or destructive, is a death drive.

As an emblem of the two drives, Rogozhin, like Sutter, is characterized by violent destructiveness. From Rogozhin's first encounters with the idiot, Myshkin concludes that he will probably put a knife into Nastasya, which he does by the conclusion of the story. In a climatic conversation between the Prince and Rogozhin, Myshkin twice absentmindedly handles a knife belonging to Rogozhin, who explains that Nastasya is marrying him "because she expects to be murdered!" (*Idiot* 187). Although both characters recognize the truth behind his words, they treat the idea as a joke. Rogozhin is a physically destructive character: he drinks to drunkenness, treats Nastasya as a prostitute, abuses her physically, threatens her life as well as Myshkin's, and in the end, commits murder. In *The Last Gentleman*, Sutter is all too similar to Rogozhin. Rita tells Sutter that he should not be with Jamie, "because of your deliberate cultivation of destructiveness, of your death-wish, not to mention your outhouse sexuality" (*Last Gentleman* 242). Rita rightly connects Sutter's sexual behavior (his *eros* drive) with his death-wish (his *thanatos* drive). For a twentieth-century readership, Percy has intensified Sutter's suppressed violence by placing a loaded gun in his hand. When Barrett first observes Sutter, he is shooting at a wall without care for the trajectory of the bullet. Later in the novel, during a quarrel with his ex-wife Rita, she exclaims, "Put up your knife, you bastard" (243). She is speaking figuratively, but the sentence ties Sutter with his antecedent Rogozhin. He enjoys playing with instruments of death, with increasing the tension between life and death. In the manuscript notes, Percy writes of the Sutter character: "I WANT DEATH—I LOVE DEATH."[53] Like Rogozhin who fiddles with a knife as he speaks with Myshkin and jokes about killing Nastasya, Sutter amuses himself with tools of violence. However, in *The Last Gentleman* the weapons are directed against himself.

---

52. According to Havi Carel in *Life and Death in Freud and Heidegger*, Freud draws his theory from the Darwinian assumption that the human being is only an organism like any other "despite its intellectual and emotional sophistication" and "is ultimately motivated by the search for pleasure and governed by bodily need and environmental demands" (44). As a purely physical being, in Freud's view, humans succumb to the drive for life or death. Carel explains that although Freud wanted to distinguish two separate drives, "Eros and Thanatos repeatedly collapse into one another" (41). Because both drives lead to nothing beyond—the pleasure of Eros dissipating quickly—Thanatos is simply desexualized Eros.

53. Percy, SHC 15.19.

These two competing desires, the Eros and Thanatos drives, stem from the same source, a misconception about the nature of reality. Neither Rogozhin nor Sutter believes in a spiritual realm. They each ask their angelic counterparts, "Do you believe in God?" (*Idiot* 219, *Last Gentleman* 221). These conversations engage the reader in Dostoevsky's and Percy's ultimate concern: for these authors, the existence of God determines the nature of human beings and how those beings should live. In his study of Dostoevsky, Nicolas Berdyaev asserts, "Dostoevsky devoted the whole of his creative energy to one single theme, man and man's destiny. The problem of man was his absorbing passion."[54] According to Berdyaev, "To solve the question of man is to solve the question of God."[55] In 1966, the year that Percy publishes *The Last Gentleman*, he writes, "What began to interest me was not so much a different question as a larger question . . . the problem of man himself, the nature and destiny of man" (*Signposts* 188). In Dostoevsky's novel, Percy recognizes how his predecessor engages readers in the question of God through the nature of "man."

The despiritualized world of Rogozhin and Sutter is a flat one. At one point, Rogozhin queries Myshkin's faith as they stare at a painting by Hans Holbein entitled *Christ's Body in the Tomb*. The painting is horizontal, roughly six feet long, and one foot high: "The picture represented Christ just taken down from the cross" (*Idiot* 280). The lack of physical vertical dimension corresponds to the artists' intent to drain the world of its spiritual element. The picture hangs in Rogozhin's hallway. Neither the narrator, Rogozhin, nor Myshkin describe the painting further, but it is horrifying in its realism. Christ lies dead with eyes and mouth part open, hair frayed and spread out, fingers crooked with one pointing down; he is pale and gaunt with blood smears on his hand and ribcage. In 1867 Dostoevsky visited the Basel Museum with the intention of viewing the painting. He told his wife the same thing that Myshkin exclaims to Rogozhin: "That picture might make some people lose their faith"[56] (*Idiot* 190). The reality of the death in Holbein's depiction would make even the most devout believer in spiritual life doubt the resurrection. Rogozhin concurs with Myshkin, admitting his atheism, "That's what it's doing" (ibid.). Rogozhin views reality as devoid of any spiritual realm: like Holbein's painting, the world is only horizontal and all ends in death.[57] Dos-

---

54. Berdyaev, *Dostoievsky: An Interpretation*, 39.
55. Ibid.
56. Cited in Frank, *Writer*, 549.
57. Describing the biographical episode in which Dostoevsky encountered Holbein's *Dead Christ*, Joseph Frank acknowledges the significance of this painting to the meaning of *The Idiot*. He writes, "No greater challenge could be offered to Dostoevsky's own faith in Christ the Godman than such a vision of a tortured and decaying human being, whose face bore not a trace of the 'extraordinary beauty'" (*Writer*, 549).

toevsky's aim in *The Idiot* was to create the beautiful ideal, which for him was Christ. The beauty and truth of Christ is in the incarnation of God becoming human, which the painting negates. Through his resurrection, the natural order becomes subject to the supernatural will, but, as Frank notes, this painting "expresses the subjection of the supernatural Christ to the physical order of nature."[58] This painting questions Christ's divinity. It symbolizes for the reader the question of the novel, whether God exists and if so, what then is a human being?

Initially Myshkin does not answer Rogozhin's question about God's existence, only to respond a few moments later with four stories threaded together by the question itself. Episodes of Myshkin's life, including the execution story and his reaction to Holbein, have resembled Dostoevsky's autobiography, and the anecdotes he relates to Rogozhin are drawn from newspaper accounts that Dostoevsky has read. Like Dostoevsky himself, Myshkin does not think that he may give a rational argument to satisfy the question of God's existence. Myshkin answers Rogozhin: "The essence of religious feeling does not come under any sort of reasoning" (*Idiot* 192). If read in line with Dostoevsky's biography, then, such a statement sounds reminiscent of Dostoevsky's assertion: "If someone proved to me that Christ is outside the truth, and that *in reality*, the truth were outside of Christ, then I would prefer to remain with Christ rather than with the truth."[59] Scholars have debated the meaning of his assertion, but it seems the Russian word for truth here, *istina*, pertains more to rational and theoretical than spiritually experienced truth. Dostoevsky calls Christ, "the ideal of Beauty in Himself" (*Brothers Karamazov* 754), registering how the person of Christ shows beauty, or reveals truth, that must be experienced rather than reduced to a reasonable principle or syllogism.

In a sense, Myshkin answers by placing himself before Rogozhin as another story revealing truth. Frank contends, "The values of Christian love and religious faith that Myshkin embodies are too deep a necessity of the Russian spirit to be negated by his practical failure, any more than they are negated by reason, murder, or sacrilege."[60] While Christian ideals should not be invalidated by "practical failure," Myshkin does not embody these values as his author originally intended. In *Dostoevsky and the Christian Tradition*, Diane Oenning Thompson argues, "Christian virtues cannot function in *The Idiot* because they lack adequate embodiment and an adequate spokesperson."[61] It is when Myshkin establishes himself as a Christ figure that he truly becomes

---

58. Ibid.
59. Quoted in ibid., 913.
60. Ibid., 582.
61. Thompson, "Problems of Biblical Word," 75.

insane. Many of the characters in *The Idiot* seem to intuit this conundrum: they want Myshkin to save them, yet they find him an inadequate savior.

Although superficially Myshkin appears as a character who functions according to "love," he does not understand the word itself. Reading the anecdote Myshkin relates about the mistreated soul Marie, Percy notes, "only resource is love—he loves in the most miserable of all."[62] When living in a small village in Switzerland, the Prince encounters Marie, a vagabond cruelly treated by the townspeople. Out of pity, he kisses the girl; he admits, "I kissed her not because I was in love with her but because I felt very sorry for her, and that I had never from the very beginning thought of her as guilty but only as unhappy" (*Idiot* 48). In this anecdote, he connects his pity with his view of Marie as an innocent. He pities her because others condemn her, and he ignores her guilt. Later when he attempts to love Nastasya, his pity compels him to insist on her purity rather than her need for forgiveness. Though she mocks him and laughs at his proposal, as do the others in the room, Myshkin continues, "I expressed myself very absurdly and have been absurd myself . . . but you are not to blame for anything" (147). In making this speech in which he disregards Nastasya's impurity, the Prince does not understand others' laughter. Through Myshkin's assertion that others find him funny, Dostoevsky highlights Myshkin's ridiculousness. Nastasya wants love, not pity; forgiveness, not ignorance.[63] By denying the existence of sin, Myshkin fails to be a Christ figure and instead becomes a ridiculous caricature of innocence.

TRAGEDY VS. COMEDY

Like *Don Quixote*, both novels end in death, but what makes one a tragedy marks the other as a comedy. In Cervantes's seventeenth-century novel, Don Quixote regains his senses, takes the sacraments, and dies a converted, sensible hero. Perhaps seeing what Dostoevsky saw in the Spanish protagonist, W. H. Auden called Quixote a "Christian saint." He did so for at least two reasons that are pertinent to understanding the divergent endings between *The Idiot* and *The Last Gentleman*: (1) Quixote loved his neighbor, Sancho Panza, and (2) he understood suffering as a blessing. Auden is quoted in Arthur Kirsch's *Auden and Christianity*: "Without Sancho Panza [Don Quixote] would not be Christian. For his madness to be Christian, he must have a neighbor, someone other than himself about whom he has no delusions but

---

62. Percy, SHC 257.2.
63. Louise Cowan made this point in teaching a course on Russian literature at the University of Dallas, which I took in 2006.

loves as himself."[64] And in his writing on "The Christian Saint," Auden clarifies the difference between the tragic, comic, and Christian heroes: "For the tragic hero suffering is real and destructive; for the comic hero it is unreal or temporary or curative; for both it is a sign that they are not in the truth: both suffer with misunderstanding. The saint, on the other hand, is ironically related to suffering; it is real, nevertheless he understands that it is a blessing, a sign that he is in the truth."[65] Neither Dostoevsky nor Percy create Christian saints in these novels; however, they share Auden's assumptions about what such characters and their novels' endings must look like in order to do so. The former writes a tragedy and the latter, a comedy: Dostoevsky shows how Myshkin's inability to love leads to tragic destruction, and Percy displays a hero who begins to love his neighbor though he cannot understand the suffering his witnesses.

The Idiot ends with a horrific scene of violence: Nastasya's murdered corpse lies still in the bedroom, all but her bare foot covered by a sheet and a fly buzzes over the bed. Dostoevsky stresses the ugliness of concrete reality in this scene: death, mortality, even her stench. Both Rogozhin and Myshkin comment repeatedly on her smell. In the final description of Nastasya Fillipovna's body, Dostoevsky recalls Holbein's depiction of Christ's corpse in order to emphasize how the heresy symbolized in the earlier image prompted the violent reality. In Russian, Nastasya Fillipovna's name translates roughly as "resurrected lamb." Just as Holbein did not portray the reality of Christ as the resurrected lamb in his painting, so Rogozhin and Prince Myshkin only recognize Nastasya's fleshly existence, not her potential immorality. When people discover them, Rogozhin shouts and raves. The onlookers declare him an "idiot." Here the idiot has engendered another idiot; his pity has produced nothing but violence. Although Myshkin did not commit the murder, his inactivity makes him complicit. Williams notes, "The gulf between him and Christ is to do with the fact that the Prince makes no adult choices."[66] In his innocence, Myshkin is a prefallen Adam who does not know how to choose between good and evil. Because he evades adult responsibility and plays the part of the naïve child, he fails to be anyone's savior. At the conclusion of the novel, Myshkin returns to the care of his psychologist abroad. Myshkin had the potential to be a positively beautiful man, but his ignorance of his own imperfection and distance from reality reduces him to a tragic parody of a hero.

When Percy writes *The Last Gentleman*, he has the advantage of learning from Dostoevsky's exploration. In his manuscript notes, Percy writes,

---

64. Kirsch, *Auden and Christianity*, 101.
65. Auden, *Complete Works*, 379.
66. Williams, *Dostoevsky*, 48.

"E[ngineer]'s faith? Non-violent→ *violence*."[67] He recalls how Prince Myshkin's heretical faith led to violence. However, rather than a violent tragedy, Percy chooses to create a more comedic and hopeful story. Like the innocence of Don Quixote, that of Prince Myshkin and Will Barrett should be read ironically, not as exemplary ideals but as satirical caricatures. Percy writes in his notes, "SATIRE AND IRONY ALL THE WAY."[68] Percy defines satire as that which "attacks one thing in order to affirm another. It assaults the fake and the phony in order to affirm another. It ridicules the inhuman in order to affirm the human. *Satire is always launched in the mode of hope*" (*Signposts* 188). Although *The Idiot* accomplishes such an attack by revealing the impossibility of a perfect human being apart from Christ, the characters in the novel miss the truth and end tragically. In opposition to this conclusion, Percy allows Barrett an encounter with the truth—with a reality that he cannot paint over or remake with fantasy.

Both Myshkin and Barrett have observed, at critical distance, that death brings one closer to a truthful vision of the world. At the start of the novel, Myshkin describes an execution that he witnessed. As though he is the man himself, Myshkin imagines, "I fancy there is a continual throbbing of ideas of all sorts . . . 'That man is looking at me. He has a wart on his forehead. One of the executioner's buttons is rusty'" (*Idiot* 60). With death quickly approaching, the criminal has a heightened ability to see things around him, a vision that Myshkin envies because he intuits the truthfulness of such sight. Yet Myshkin's observation is a "fancy" only. Similarly Barrett discovers that the nearness of death enlightens one's vision of reality. Watching people in a museum, Barrett notices how they cannot see the paintings well: "In they came, smiling, and out they went, their eyes glazed over" (*Last Gentleman* 27). However, when a chandelier crashes and almost kills a family, suddenly Velazquez "was glowing like a jewel!" (28). The almost-fatal disaster transforms his vision: "The paintings could be seen" (ibid.). Moreover, Barrett connects clearer vision with happiness. Whereas before the cataclysm, the visitors of the museum "were afflicted in their happiness" (27), the trial fills them with real mirth and tears of joy at their survival. As in Myshkin's anecdote, Barrett is an observer and not a participant.

At the conclusion of *The Last Gentleman*, Jamie's impending death provides the impetus for a change in his own vision. The character of Ippolit from *The Idiot* inspires Percy's creation of Jamie. In his notes on Ippolit's diatribe against his suffering, Percy writes "a man with 2 months to live."[69] Both Ippolit

---
67. Percy, SHC 22.10.
68. Ibid., 15.4.
69. Ibid., 257.22.

and Jamie are adolescents dying of illness. Later Percy makes a note to himself: "Don't be afraid to use ordinary human crisis i.e. proposal, death, marriage."[70] Percy seems to follow his own advice when he situates Jamie's death at the climax of the novel. In *The Idiot*, Ippolit rejects resurrection, denouncing the stories of Lazarus and Jairus's daughter as false. He desires to commit suicide: while no one reaches out a hand to help him, the gun misfires and chance saves him. In *The Last Gentleman*, suicide is one option in the face of suffering. All of the characters offer Jamie options on how to die that reveal their worldviews. His looming death brings the question of God and immortality to the forefront.

Although both *The Idiot* and *The Last Gentleman* end with death, in the former, the physical world overpowers any sense of the unseen: Nastasya's rotting corpse tempts readers to lose their faith as much as the Holbein painting prodded Myshkin to do so. For *The Last Gentleman*, the physical disturbance of death seems overpowering but is ultimately defeated by Jamie's acceptance of his own sin, Christ's salvation, and his immortal resurrection. Before Jamie loses consciousness in the hospital, he asks enigmatically for Barrett to call his sister Val, who then insists that Barrett take responsibility for Jamie's baptism. Barrett hesitates, so Val tries to reason with him: "Would you deny him penicillin if it would save his life? . . . I think you can tell when someone is deadly serious about something, can't you?" (*Last Gentleman* 392–93). Val uses the analogy of physical aid to explain the life or death importance of baptism. If baptism only occurs in the concrete realm, then it matters not. However, if it signifies spiritual cleansing that secures salvation and resurrection, then Jamie must receive it before his physical body dies. Although Barrett fears that the baptism will occur against the unconscious youth's will, he complies with Val's request and calls a priest.

The book climaxes at this death scene and the dilemma over Jamie's baptism. Here Jamie confesses Christ, and his implicit resurrection triumphs over the ignobility of death. While the priest is insisting that he cannot baptize the unconscious Jamie, the youth rises miraculously from his bed, eyes still shut, like a zombie, as the boy's body seeks to use the restroom. Though he defecates on the wall and then returns to bed, the priest takes this opportunity to administer the sacrament. The "last gentleman" watches in horror for this scene defies his notions of propriety and honor. As in *The Idiot*, death has a mortal stench, yet here Jamie and the priest transcend the ignoble circumstances of death and converse about his baptism. In the brief moments of consciousness left to him, Jamie answers that he believes in God and that his

---

70. Ibid., 257.25.

faith will bring him "life everlasting" (*Last Gentleman* 405). With this confession, the priest baptizes him and holds his hand until he passes.

Even more triumphant than the content of the moment is the form of its presentation. Percy had attempted to show a deathbed conversion in *The Gramercy Winner*, but the scene lacked conviction. It's related from an outsider perspective, that of the nurse, who overhears hushed debates between a Roman Catholic, Dr. Scanlon, and Will (the protagonist). The former then baptizes him with a glass of water before he passes into a coma. Not only is the reader unprepared for the conversion, the moment itself has no more transcendence than it does immanence. All is found wanting. However, in this scene with Jamie, what works is the stench of excrement, the apathy of the overworked priest, Will's jaw dropping, the pistol invisibly hid in Sutter's pocket, Jamie's bruised forehead with fried dusty hair and thick Vaught eyebrows, and the sound of the holy words themselves—"I baptize you in the name of the Father, and the Son and the Holy Spirit"—echoing in the sterile room. Comparing the two is like reading the work of an amateur compared with a master.

The transition has occurred, in part, because of Percy's tutelage under Dostoevsky. In a 1943 essay, "The Hovering Fly," Allen Tate (one of Percy's aesthetic mentors alongside Gordon and Foote) reads the final image in Dostoevsky's *The Idiot* as a poetic rendering of the truth that poets must locate their ideas in this sensible world. Instead of the Holy Spirit hovering—beneficent but abstract—Dostoevsky reverberates the buzzing of a nasty insect associated with death and decay as it whirls around Nastasya's corpse. Such an instance is not only notable for its particularity and high realism but also for its implementation of contrasts. The disparity between Nastasya's pure white foot and the disgusting insect synthesize into an unforgettable image of death in all its disparate reality. For Dostoevsky and Percy, death is a combination of loss and gain, for in the biblical accounts, it was introduced by sin but redeemed by Christ. Thus death is the detested gateway to resurrection.

In his analysis of Percy's connection between the obscene and the divine, critic Frank Arthur Wilson notes that although such a scandalous pairing as emptied bowels and baptism "contradicts normal religious sentiment," the scene "suggests a sacred presence amid the obscenely foul."[71] Percy's scene imitates the Incarnation in which God becomes human—or more particularly the Son of God is born into the stench of the manger. Wilson lists out places where Percy creates similar purposeful disparities, such as the dung beetle in *The Moviegoer*, "to express the sacramental presence of God in the often

---

71. Wilson, "Bible Notes," 204.

traumatic mess of human existence."[72] Instead of Dostoevsky, Wilson credits Percy's Bible reading. Whether Percy first discovered this method through reading scripture, he absorbed Dostoevsky's fictional rendering of it. Ultimately what Percy learned was an aesthetic guided by the Incarnation.[73]

Before Jamie dies, Sutter admits that he plans to kill himself following his brother's death. Neither Sutter nor Barrett can articulate what they witnessed, yet both seem strangely affected by the baptism. When Sutter first questioned Barrett, "Do you believe that [God loves us]? . . . Do you believe that God entered history?" Barrett responds, "I haven't really thought about it" (*Last Gentleman* 221). However, like those in the museum who could better see the paintings after the chandelier nearly took their lives, the death of Jamie has heightened Barrett's vision. Although he has not discovered the God that Jamie claims in his deathbed confession, Barrett refuses the nihilistic alternative that Sutter devises. We'll see in *The Second Coming* that Barrett reconsiders Sutter's idea; whatever insight he has is brief and ineffective for himself. However, at least he hinders Sutter from committing suicide.

In contrast to Myshkin who allows Ippolit to attempt suicide in front of him as well as for Rogozhin to commit murder, Barrett intercedes; he stops Sutter. He states, "Dr. Vaught, I need you. I, Will Barrett—' and he actually pointed to himself lest there be a mistake, '—need you and want you to come back. I need you more than Jamie needed you'" (*Last Gentleman* 409). In this declaration, Barrett calls them both by name. He lovingly affirms, "I see you, Sutter." In addition to seeing Sutter, Barrett sees himself more clearly. The "idiot" who did not know himself has remembered his name. Over the course of the novel, Percy calls him the "engineer" or other monikers, to emphasize that he does not know who he is. However, when Barrett calls himself by name, he claims his identity. Whereas Myshkin was impotent, Barrett acts. He refuses to let either himself or Sutter continue in isolation. After the loss of his brother, Sutter intends to take his own life. However, Barrett substitutes himself as a new brother when he claims that he needs Sutter more than Jamie did. The motif of "brothers" was misemployed by Myshkin and Rogozhin; although they called one another "brothers," they were rivals. In Dostoevsky's novel, Percy noted the theme of "the loss of the meanings in words!"[74] Percy saw that without an acknowledgement of the world in its dirty and beautiful,

---

72. Ibid., 197.

73. In an annotation of John 9, in which Jesus spits on the dirt before him and makes clay to heal a blind man's eyes, Percy has written "*Sensible*" and "Power, obsenity, belief" (ibid., 198). Coincidentally this gospel was the favorite of both Dostoevsky and Percy. Percy even chose "John" as his saint's name when he converted.

74. Percy, SHC 257.23.

painful and joyful, sin-stained but redeemable reality, the characters in *The Idiot* could not be brothers, could not love or know truth or see themselves clearly. By contrast in *The Last Gentleman,* Barrett's decision to love Sutter overcomes the loneliness that Guardini alludes to in the epigraph: "Love will disappear from the face of the public world, but the more precious will be the love that flows from one lonely person to another."

CHAPTER 4

Borrowed Critiques in *Love in the Ruins*

ALMOST ONE HUNDRED years before the assassination of President John F. Kennedy occurred the first attempt to assassinate Czar Alexander II. As much bedlam of moral confusion and unnecessary violence occurred in the 1860s in Russia as in the 1960s in America. Amid the respective national turmoil, Percy and Dostoevsky saw signs of the end of the world. Rather than excuse current events as merely political activity, these authors place the assassinations and social uprisings of their times in a spiritual context. A century apart, Dostoevsky and Percy wrote their novels in fits of disgust and frustration in the aftermath of these attacks on their governments' leaders. Percy first tried to integrate his distress over Kennedy's assassination into *The Last Gentleman*: "The assassination affected me so strongly it caused me to lose a year of work.... I got off on the wrong track, wrote a long thing about Kennedy, brought Kennedy into the book, and I actually wasted a year."[1] When Percy read *The Possessed*, he noticed how powerfully Dostoevsky transformed his frustration with the world at large into literary fiction. As Percy tells one interviewer in 1973, "Dostoevski [sic] reads one news story, gets angry[,] and this triggers a creative process."[2] Percy admires how Dostoevsky was able to "get below the

---

1. Interview with Carlton Cremeens, 1968. Percy, *Conversations*, 19.
2. Ibid., 83.

surface of current events."[3] Like a modern Dante, Dostoevsky diagnosed the societal problems around him as symptomatic of the maladies of individuals' souls, and Percy emulates this creative endeavor in *Love in the Ruins*.

Percy never seems to have claimed that his third novel, *Love in the Ruins*, was modeled on a work by Dostoevsky, as *The Moviegoer* and *The Last Gentleman* had been. Still correspondence and annotations that I recently discovered in Percy's archives indicate that, in writing his third novel, Percy did emulate Dostoevsky's creative process for *The Possessed* (1872). Like his predecessor, Percy pored over newspaper articles for inspiration, and he also availed himself of more modern news sources such as television and radio reports.[4] The significance of Percy's using Dostoevsky's technique is that it enabled Percy to follow Dostoevsky in creating a novel that swept grandly over a secular contemporary world and pronounced a diagnosis upon the souls of its inhabitants. Unlike Percy's first two novels, which explored the inner life of single alienated individuals, *Love in the Ruins* attempts a Dostoevskian scope, taking on the spiritual sickness of an entire nation. Just as the journey of Dostoevsky's protagonist in *The Possessed*, his "Great Sinner" Nikolai Stavrogin, can only be comprehended within the context of the whole city of man, the same is true of Percy's hero in *Love in the Ruins*, his "Bad Catholic" Tom More.[5]

Even though *Love in the Ruins* is not a direct imitation of Dostoevsky's *The Possessed*, the former resulted from Percy's quest to discover how to unite his ultimate questions about the existence of God, suffering, and evil with broader concerns about politics and social ills. In his critique of Percy's intentions, Kieran Quinlan argues that the desire to be a propagandist overcame Percy's artistry. Quinlan claims that Percy's desire to write novels that would offer a specific worldview and cause changes in his audience created the "so-called philosophical or religious novel" that Percy feared, one "which simply used

---

3. Ibid.

4. In his critical companion to *The Devils*, William J. Leatherbarrow includes a handful of Dostoevsky's letters that are pertinent to understanding the text. Dostoevsky explains that he intends to touch "directly on the most important contemporary issues," so he reads "*three* Russian newspapers from cover to cover, and [he] receives two journals" to keep his finger on the pulse of Russia while he is in exile in Dresden (137, 140). Similarly, in the folders of preparation for *Love in the Ruins*, Percy has collected news clippings on current events whose topics appear in the novel (SHC Box 42). For instance, Percy has underlined an article from *The New York Times* on "The Use of Drugs on College Campuses," which is one in a collection of articles on drugs, as well as clippings on sex, with titles such as "Research on Sex made public" and "The Sex Buffs." He uses this information for his Love Clinic in *Love in the Ruins*.

5. Dostoevsky's intended title was originally *The Life of a Great Sinner*, which correlates with part of Percy's subtitle, "The Adventures of a Bad Catholic" (Quoted in Leatherbarrow, *Dostoyevsky's* The Devils, 141).

a story and a plot and characters in order to get over a certain idea."[6] Percy does have didactic purposes. He envies Russian novelists (like Aleksandr Solzhenitsyn) who "can so irritate the state that the state will go to a great deal of trouble to get rid of him" (*Signposts* 171). However, Dostoevsky shares Percy's intentions to have an agenda and his fears about aesthetics. In a letter to his friend Strakhov, he insists, "I wish to speak out about several matters even though my artistry goes to smash!"[7] Yet Dostoevsky maintains his novelistic prowess, and thus he shows Percy a way out of writing poor fiction with an overbearing message.

Both *The Possessed* and *Love in the Ruins* are moralistic texts. Both novels are driven by the diagnosis of social problems, although Percy's treatment of society's sins is more comic than Dostoevsky's. Both follow wayward protagonists, struggling in apocalyptic settings with the existential question of whether to commit suicide, locked in conflict with sinister characters that function as their demonic foils. Both are set in the future, at the end of the world. Percy attempts the same panoramic scale of Dostoevsky, although he does not quite succeed. At the end of his essay on apocalyptic novels, Percy defends his use of the genre: "Perhaps it is only through the conjuring up of catastrophe, the destruction of all Exxon signs, and the sprouting of vines in the church pews, that the novelist can make vicarious use of catastrophe in order that he and his reader may come to themselves" (*Signposts* 118). By zeroing in on flesh-and-blood protagonists in concrete settings with vivid and unforgettable images, Dostoevsky and Percy create more than "pamphlets" about their concerns over contemporary politics but rather narratives with the force of glowering warning signs.[8] The mode of literary influence that is exemplified in *Love in the Ruins*—borrowing one writer's critiques and applying them to one's own time—is possible because the ills that plague one society are all too often the result of universal spiritual sickness rather than isolated contingencies. In *The Possessed* Dostoevsky observes that the problems of his nineteenth-century Russia stem from demonic possession, a diagnosis Percy assumes for twentieth-century America at the start of *Love in the Ruins*. His protagonist claims, "Most people nowadays are possessed, harboring as they do all manner of demonic hatred and terrors and lusts and envies, [and] prin-

---

6. Percy, *Conversations*, 89.
7. Cited in Frank, *Miraculous Years*, 403.
8. In the aforementioned letter to Strakhov, Dostoevsky continues, "What attracts me is what has piled up in my mind and heart; let it give only a pamphlet, but I shall speak out" (Cited in Frank, *Miraculous Years*, 403). For Dostoevsky, the present troubles in Russia demanded a response, whether or not his novel suffered artistically for the sake of his message.

cipalities and powers are nearly everywhere victorious" (*Love in the Ruins* 31).[9] Under this description, the social problems of Dostoevsky's Russia become the same ones of Percy's America. Thus the ills written about in one society can appear in another society in similar form, so that a writer in the latter society (Percy) can construct a novel that critiques his own society by modeling it on the work of a writer (Dostoevsky) from the former society. Critiques can be borrowed and reapplied through literary influence because one writer's milieu may resemble another's.

Percy wrote *Love in the Ruins* in a world that bore striking similarity to the Russia of the mid-nineteenth century, where Dostoevsky wrote *The Possessed*. In both Percy's mid-twentieth-century American South and Dostoevsky's Russia, the divinity of Christ had been rejected, and materialism was exalted above spirituality. In Dostoevsky's lifetime, he watched as growing Socialist groups touted political agendas that were nominally linked to Christianity but that, at their core, denied Christ's divinity. Dostoevsky himself had once been a Christian socialist, but he had come to see this view as heretical and as "the first step in the European process of secularization, which . . . he saw as his calling to oppose."[10] Two examples of the secularization that so disgusted Dostoevsky were D. F. Strauss's *The Life of Jesus* (1835) and Ludwig Feuerbach's *The Essence of Christianity* (1841). Strauss and Feuerbach both demoted Jesus from God-man to mere mortal. Strauss's biography of the historical personage of Jesus made him seem weak and easily deposable, whereas Feuerbach, following Strauss, asserted that God had been made by man and in man's image, rather than the other way around. Such a god is worse than deposable; he is disposable, a ruse. Within *The Possessed*, which features the despicable character Stavrogin, Dostoevsky blamed the existence of such vicious people upon the philosophy of Christian socialism and the cult of Arianism. Indeed, the suicidal engineer in *The Possessed*, Kirillov, regularly spouts Feuerbachian language such as the line, "Man has done nothing but invent God" (*Possessed* 356).[11] Kirillov retells the story of Christ's death on the cross as "a great idea" that is only a lie (ibid.). In Dostoevsky's Russia, with transcendent reality having been denounced as delusion, the empirical world alone seemed worthwhile.

A century later and a continent to the west, American Christians in the 1960s and 1970s similarly appended their theology onto "the political and social activism of the era," using Jesus as the "model for responsible service to

---

9. *Love in the Ruins* by Walker Percy will be cited in text throughout the book.
10. Frank, *Miraculous Years*, 101.
11. *The Possessed* by Dostoevsky will be cited in text throughout the book, using Percy's edition.

the neighbor in a profane world."[12] In this theology, which was so pervasive in Percy's lifetime, Jesus was a good person who performed the decent duty of showing Americans how to be nice to one another. In Ross Douthat's *Bad Religion*, he offers several reasons for this shift "in American spiritual ecology," including the aforementioned political polarization and the sexual revolution, both of which concerned Percy in *Love in the Ruins*.[13] According to Douthat, as church leaders and public theologians took sides in the Civil Rights movement, the Vietnam War protests, and other political controversies, American institutions of faith became lobby houses with partisan identities. Douthat also explains how, in the concurrent sexual revolution, the birth control pill levied "the most direct blow to the faith's appeal since the publication of *On the Origin of Species* a century earlier."[14] Percy's world, like Dostoevsky's, was one in which the immanent was all-important, and politics and sex were the new religions of the age. The mid-twentieth-century discussion of humanism—both atheist and Christian—was fanned by a group called the death-of-God theologians. Religion professor Ronald Bruce Flowers summarizes their theology: "Since modern people work in the realm of empirical verification, as secular/scientific humans, God has become dead to us because there is no way to verify empirically a supernatural, miraculous deity."[15] Following in the century-old footsteps of Strauss and Feuerbach, death-of-God theologians considered their work to be a necessary adaptation to the times. Instead of depending upon a God whose very existence was up for debate, humans could, through the advancements of science, become capable of solving their own problems.

Percy began writing *Love in the Ruins* in 1967, when he was fifty-one years old and in a state of "melancholy and depression," as he confesses to his friend Shelby Foote, to whom he dedicates this novel.[16] At this point, the maturing novelist was learning how to appropriate his political discouragement into his art. The Dostoevsky novel that interested him most at this moment was *The Possessed*, which Percy had probably first encountered when at the Trudeau Sanatorium in the 1940s.[17] The novel is certainly on his mind when he writes *Love in the Ruins* (1971). He mentions *The Possessed* in a handful of interviews in the years preceding and following publication of his novel, 1967–74, and

---

12. Flowers, *Religion in Strange Times*, 19.
13. Douthat, *Bad Religion*, 62.
14. Ibid., 70.
15. Flowers, *Religion in Strange Times*, 19.
16. Percy, *Correspondence*, 128.
17. Ibid., 126.

he annotated approximately twenty pages of his edition, underlining various statements and writing marginal notes. In addition to his annotated edition of Dostoevsky's novel, Percy tucked a couple of pages of handwritten notes on *The Possessed* into a folder entitled "Save for Book." Unfortunately, his notes on the text are undated;[18] but what they make clear is that Percy saw in Dostoevsky that most political problems stem from theological roots, and that when Christianity assumes a political agenda, the religion usually takes on a frighteningly heretical quality.

The setting that Percy depicts is all too similar to the twenty-first-century American landscape that Percy did not live to see: what he referred to as the "victorious secular city,"[19] borrowing a phrase from theologian Harvey Cox's popular 1966 book *The Secular City*, in which Cox argued that the city of man is a disenchanted, despiritualized version of God's kingdom, wherein God accomplishes his purposes through national politics and human will.[20] In *The Moviegoer*, Percy had labeled this state of despair "malaise," a word that Charles Taylor adopts in his book *A Secular Age*. Taylor concludes with Percy that this "disenchanted world lacks meaning," and thus people "suffer from a lack of strong purposes in their lives."[21] Without a transcendent cohesive worldview, the human being is bifurcated and alienated, forced to choose from among experts' conflicting accounts about how the world ought to be viewed. A human being in this world knows not whether he is an angel or merely a biological organism, and therefore does not know the purpose of life or its origin. Percy writes, "Such a man could not take account of God, the devil, and the angels if they were standing before him" (*Message in the Bottle* 113).[22] Living in this secular city, blind to religious realities, and unable to create meaning for his life, the problem for this postmodern man is "how to keep from blowing his brains out" (112) Indeed the question of suicide is the central dilemma of Tom More in *Love in the Ruins*, as it is for Stavrogin (and Kirillov) in *The Possessed*.

---

18. Percy, SHC 275.
19. Percy uses the term in his essay "Notes for a Novel About the End of the World."
20. In his copy of Cox's book, Percy has underlined the conclusion, "In the epoch of the secular city, politics replaces metaphysics as the language of theology" (*Secular City*, 255). Although Percy borrows the phrase, he questions Cox's conclusions. In Percy's essay "Notes for a Novel About the End of the World," he expresses the belief that the substitution of politics for metaphysics will increase the despair that he observes around him.
21. Taylor, *Secular Age*, 303.
22. *The Message in a Bottle* by Walker Percy will be cited in text throughout the book.

TOM MORE AS AN AMERICAN STAVROGIN

The plot of *The Possessed* was inspired by the true story of the murder of I. I. Ivanov by S. G. Nechaev, his revolutionary leader.[23] Dostoevsky followed the newspaper headlines upon returning to Russia at the time of Nechaev's trial and was horrified at the nihilist propositions of the unabashed murderer.[24] In his manifesto, *Catechism of a Revolutionary,* Nechaev justifies any means to accomplish the goals of anarchism: "Make use of the Devil himself if the Revolution requires it."[25] For Dostoevsky, the demonic alliance of politics and nihilism may have been horrifying, but it was also unsurprising, and he makes it the central motif of his novelistic account of the story. As Dostoevsky saw it, the ideological battle against these revolutionaries could not be fought only in civil trials, for the war was spiritual and apocalyptic. Dostoevsky discerned that the heresy at these reformers' roots would sprout into the eventual destruction of Russia. Indeed, in hindsight critics would read *The Possessed* as a prophetic narrative that foretells the Russian Revolution of 1917. In Percy's copy of *The Possessed,* he underlines the foreword, in which Avrahm Yarmolinksy describes the upheaval as "a transformation ruled by a violent intransigent spirit, and going beyond mere political and economic change."[26] For Dostoevsky the conflict is between the Christian faithful, of whom Dostoevsky depicts only minor portraits, and the antichrist with his accompanying posse of demons; the goal is either the city of God or the city of man, the means will be sacrifice or violence, and the outcome is possibly the end of the world.

The fundamental similarity between *Love in the Ruins* and *The Possessed* is the character of the protagonist: a lost wanderer, tempted by the possibility of suicide, a sort of messiah figure complete with a demonic counterpart, concerned with the antiquated question of "am I saved or damned?" That question appears in Charles Taylor's *A Secular Age,* where Taylor points out that this question has in the modern world been replaced by the question "what is my purpose?" Taylor remarks, "You couldn't even have explained this problem

---

23. In *Dostoievsky: An Interpretation,* Berdyaev asserts, "The Netchaev affair, which suggested the plot of *The Possessed,* did not actually resemble the book at all, for Dostoievsky was not interested in surface things: inner depths and final principles were his concern" (134).

24. When Dostoevsky began writing *The Possessed,* he was living in exile in Dresden and admits to reading "*three* Russian newspapers from cover to cover, and I receive two journals" to keep up with Russian life (From his letter to A. N. Maikov, 25 March [April 6] 1870, in Leatherbarrow, *Dostoevsky's* The Devils, 140).

25. Cited in Radzinsky, *Stalin: The First In-depth Biography Based on Explosive New Documents from Russia's Secret Archives,* 97.

26. Yarmolinsky, foreword to *The Possessed,* vii.

[of discovering the meaning of one's individual life] to people in Luther's age. What worried them was, if anything, an excess of 'meaning,' the sense of one over-bearing issue—am I saved or damned?"[27] Because Tom More and Nikolai Stavrogin are haunted by this antiquated question of their salvation, they are set in contrast to their secular cities. At first glance, More may not seem to bear much similarity to the tragic and possessed villain of Dostoevsky's *The Possessed*, yet Percy drew unlikely inspiration from Dostoevsky.

In Percy's notes for his future book, he reduces Stavrogin's character to a description that suggests the genesis of More's character. Percy writes:

> THE MAN Who is not at home in an ordinary society (~Stavrogin, he is capable of seizing a [gentleman] by his nose)—He envisions himself capable of anything—he looks upon conventional society as a straight and perilous path with yawning abysses of weird behavior on either side.[28]

Filtered from all the despicable aspects of his story, Stavrogin here looks like Percy's "stranger in a strange land where the signposts are enigmatic," as he writes in "Notes for a Novel About the End of the World" (*Message in a Bottle* 102).

In Percy's reading of *The Possessed*, he would have seen that Stavrogin initially appears as a harmless ruffian, rebelling against customs and not living up to the expectations of his mother and guardian. His tutor Stepan Trofimovich chalks his wild behavior up to youth and consoles his mother, Varvara Stavrogina, with the thought that like Shakespeare's Henry IV, Stavrogin is merely going through a "Prince Harry" stage. In the early pages of the novel, at his mother's request, Stavrogin has returned to his hometown, where he commits a series of unexplainable insults to the community. In Percy's preparatory notes for *Love in the Ruins*, he alludes to the first outrage: the "seizing" of an elderly man "by his nose." When Stavrogin hears an old man exclaim, "No, you can't lead me by the nose!" (*Possessed* 21), he responds to the cliché by grabbing the man by his nostrils and dragging him around the bar. The narrator observes, "The devil knows why, for no reason at all."[29] In Dostoevsky, any reference to the devil, even in a seemingly disposable phrase, has purpose. In this instance, Dostoevsky revitalizes the clichés with meaning: the devil knows why Stavrogin behaved as he did—*because* there was no good reason.

---

27. Taylor, *Secular Age*, 303.
28. Percy, SHC 275.4.
29. The actual Russian is "черт знает для чего," which means "the devil knows why," but Garnett sanitizes it: "utterly silly and mischievous" (21). The Russian text is available online at http://www.ilibrary.ru/text/1544/p.11/index.html.

When Percy created Tom More, he was emulating Dostoevsky. The way that Percy read the character of Stavrogin, he was a man who refused to conform to the expectations of the inauthentic, banal fellow human beings parading around him. Like the Underground Man, Stavrogin rejects the life of an ant in the anthill, and he sees through the façades that he encounters. In Percy's fashioning of More, he imitates this aspect of Stavrogin's character, who "find[s] the world a madhouse and a madhouse home" (*Love in the Ruins* 106). More observes, "People look and talk and smile and are nice and the abyss yawns" (107). The latter phrase of that observation—"abyss yawns"—is derived from Percy's notes for a future character, notes in which he insinuates that such a character will draw on Stavrogin's example. Although not as young as Stavrogin—so perhaps with less excuse—More responds to the empty world in a similar way: he too is a womanizer and an alcoholic.

Tom More, lives in a world that is on the brink of destruction but fixated on pleasure. More resides in the aptly named "Paradise Estates," a land of golf courses, new homes, and television, but the larger action is set in Fedville, a collection of scientific laboratories where scientists investigate how to make human beings happy. In one lab, a Love Clinic, scientists study sexual behavior using vaginal computers. Fedville is a sort of twentieth-century Crystal Palace, wherein people seek sources of happiness in the material world, constructing a would-be utopia to showcase human accomplishment.[30] But More, like another Underground Man, opposes this Crystal Palace. He insists on the unseen reality of the human soul, which cannot be dissected or programmed by the Fedville experiments.[31] More creates a lapsometer with which he declares that he will save the world, improving mankind by making all people happy. For More, "happiness" is emotional satisfaction, and he plans on scientifically stimulating people into this state. Whereas in *The Moviegoer* and *The Last Gentleman,* Binx and Barrett sensed the malaise, in *Love in the*

---

30. In 1851, the Crystal Palace in London (which Dostoevsky visited in 1862) housed the Great Exhibition of the Works of Industry of All Nations. According to Philip Landon, the Crystal Palace represents "industrial society as the utopian product of a teleological process" ("Great Exhibitions," 30).

31. De Lubac coined the label "Crystal Palace" heresy, which he proposes "often go[es] hand in hand" with the building of Babel (*Drama,* 339). Landon cites Dostoevsky's *Winter Notes on Summer Impressions* where he attacks the Crystal Palace: "Yes, the exposition is striking. [Y]ou become aware of a gigantic idea; you feel that here something has already been achieved, that here there is Victory and triumph" (quoted in "Great Exhibitions," 44). Dostoevsky worries that such an edifice presents a false victory for human glorification. In *Notes from Underground* the antihero attacks the Crystal Palace as that which removes human freedom by masquerading as the provider of human happiness where suffering and doubt are inadmissible. In his critique of *Love in the Ruins,* Martin Luschei calls Fedville "the latter-day Crystal Palace to which Tom is destined to play the Underground Man" (*Sovereign Wayfarer,* 177).

Ruins, Tom More represents the universal blindness of the world, the millions who are unaware of their despair.

Among More's fellow scientists, he is anomalous because, unlike them, he believes in a soul. He cannot assent to their classification of the human being as merely material. Just as, in *Notes from Underground,* the antihero protests that he is neither an insect nor a hero, so too Percy has Tom More make a similar declaration that human beings are "not pigs, nor angels" (*Love in the Ruins* 109). This either-or, the status of being either body or soul, is the lot of a human being in the absence of the God whose mysterious incarnation reveals how human beings are both body and soul. More, as a hesitant humanist, assumes that his lapsometer will bridge this chasm "that has rent the soul of Western man ever since the famous philosopher Descartes ripped body loose from mind and turned the very soul into a ghost that haunts its own house" (191). More blames science for the Cartesian divide but he also plans to utilize science to reunite the two halves of the human being.

Notwithstanding the evident similarity between More and Stavrogin, Dostoevsky's character is more extreme and intense. In his analysis of *The Possessed,* Romano Guardini explains how "a demoniacal force urges him, despite everything, to exercise influence, to drive home an idea, to unleash a movement."[32] Through their hero worship, the young students around Stavrogin exalt him as a savior. Rather than renouncing the position in which they have placed him, Stavrogin allows the exaltation. Geir Kjetsaa calls him a "false prophet" like the one from Revelation and faults his religious rebellion for his tragic fall: "His downward progress from being the servant of God to being the servant of Satan appears in the book as a result of the great apostasy."[33] At the core of Stavrogin's rebellion is pride, the same instrument that clipped Lucifer's wings and unraveled his angelic halo. In his attempt to be godlike, Stavrogin abrogates the place of God, and thus falls. The evil that possesses Stavrogin nibbles at the soul of More.

More, like Stavrogin, ends up unwittingly siding with the devil. He follows Stavrogin in viewing himself as the savior of the world, an impulse which de Lubac argues is spurred on by the demonic: "If it is not God who helps [human beings], then it must be devils. It will be the work of those who are really 'possessed.'"[34] Dostoevsky entitles his novel *The Possessed* because he recognizes that once human beings have dislocated the soul from the body, a devil will seize its place. His epigraph to the novel comes from Luke 8:32–35, in which devils depart one man and enter a herd of swine only to rush off a cliff

---

32. Cited in de Lubac, *Drama,* 315.
33. Kjetsaa, *Dostoevsky and the New Testament,* 108.
34. De Lubac, *Drama,* 320.

into a lake. In a letter to his friend Valerian Maikov, Dostoevsky explains how he draws the plot of *The Possessed* from contemporary Russia: "That's exactly like our Russia, those devils that come out of the sick man and enter into the swine" (*Possessed* 376–77). From the earliest stages of *Love in the Ruins,* Percy also intended to employ the devil as a cast member in his drama. He scribbles "Devil's proposition," "pact with devil," and "Devil's machine in action" on initial pages of his notes for the novel.[35]

Percy constructed the protagonist Tom More to exemplify the dominant worldview that he, Percy, found so troubling. The novel begins with the forecast of an apocalypse, couched in terms such as "Christ-forgetting Christ-haunted death-dealing," and More waiting idly by (*Love in the Ruins* 1). More, with all the pride of his Dostoevskian predecessor, delineates the atheist creed with which he rejects orthodox faith: "I believe in God and the whole business but I love women best, music and science next, whiskey next, God fourth, and my fellowman hardly at all. Generally, I do as I please" (6). The humorous tone obscures the horror of such a list. With a mere few words, More has rejected Jesus Christ's two greatest commandments, to love God and one's neighbor. He chooses instead to love himself first and foremost. Not only does More admit to idolatry but he also deceives himself in this litany of loves. He continues by offhandedly quoting St. John: "A man . . . who says he believes in God and does not keep his commandments is a liar. If John is right, then I am a liar" (ibid.). The line should raise a tingle on the spine of anyone versed in scripture, for Jesus Christ warned that the devil is the father of liars—so that, implicitly, More has chosen the devil's side.

When the novel begins, More presents himself to his reader as the savior of the ending world. He has invented the Qualitative-Quantitative Ontological Lapsometer, an instrument that he can use to "diagnose and treat" people's unhappiness (*Love in the Ruins* 20). More makes the audacious claim that "in fact it could save the U.S.A. if we can get through the next hour or so" (ibid.). More describes his machine as a "stethoscope of the spirit" that can reunite the sundered spirit and body (62). Although More professes a desire to save the world, he inadvertently exposes the pride that motivates his rescue mission: when More thinks of saving the world, he does not picture those he loves living happily ever after. Rather, he imagines receiving the Nobel Prize, and he hopes this occurs before the world ends. More prays:

> Lord, grant that my discovery may increase knowledge and help other men. Failing that, Lord, grant that it will not lead to man's destruction. Failing

---

35. Percy, SHC 47.3–5.

that, Lord, grant that my article in *Brain* be published before the destruction takes place. (7–8)

In his prayer to "save the world," More intimates his real desire for his own glorification. Rather than pray to an omnipotent creator, More prays to his own reflection, to a "Lord" who will make him into a savior. Later in the novel, More encounters a picture of a "new Christ": "a dim hollow-eyed Spanish Christ. The pox is spreading on his face. . . . It is the new Christ, the spotted Christ, the maculate Christ, the sinful Christ" (153). This image is a merely human figure robbed of his divinity, the Arian Christ that Dostoevsky had worried lay at the root of the socialist agenda. According to Gary Ciuba, "If More's Lord is nothing more than a glorified version of his own wretchedness, this new Christ is no Christ but the Antichrist."[36] More himself may not be an Antichrist, but he produces such a figure when he devalues the Incarnation to the level of his own reflection. By diminishing God and augmenting his own image, More enacts a Stavrogian venture. Given the trajectory that his predecessor had followed, More's messianic ambitions take on a significance that is less comical and more terrifying.

Notwithstanding the influence of Dostoevsky on the character of More, Percy is also drawing from the view of Aleksandr Solzhenitsyn, the Russian author to be credited for exposing the Communist Gulags, who writes, "If humanism were right in declaring that man is born to be happy, he would not be born to die."[37] In the twentieth century, Solzhenitsyn survived a government that tried to force happiness upon its citizens. In the Russian Revolution of 1917, the Communists came to power in Russia. In their efforts to create a society of happy individuals, the Communists systematically disposed of those who did not submit to their vision. Dostoevsky foresaw the death of hundreds as the necessary corollary of such utopian schemes. When in *The Possessed* one revolutionary, Shigalyov, proposes "paradise on earth," another character, Lymashin, responds, "Instead of paradise . . . take nine-tenths of humanity and, if there's no place to put them, I'd blow them up and leave only a few handfuls of educated people who'd begin to live their lives in a scientific manner" (*Possessed* 428). Shigalyov instantly agrees because the two plans are congruous. Paradise on earth may only be accomplished with perfect human beings, and the elite will determine whom to select.

---

36. Ciuba, *Books of Revelation*, 143.
37. Solzhenitsyn, "World Split Apart." Percy would have more likely read Solzhenitsyn's speeches than have had access to Dostoevsky's letters. However, Dostoevsky agrees with Solzhenitsyn that Christianity (his "Orthodox point of view") opposes happiness as a human goal: "Man is not born for happiness" but rather for "suffering" (quoted in Frank, *Writer's*, 598).

For Tom More, as for Percy, the construction of a utopia is impossible because of original sin. In *Utopia* Tom More's namesake, Sir Thomas More, sardonically asserts that utopia will not be possible until human beings are perfect, which will not be for a long time yet. Indeed, the author's understanding of the impossibility of human perfection is evident in the Greek etymology of the word utopia (*ou-topos*): "no place." In *Love in the Ruins*, even as Tom More worries about the approaching catastrophe, he does not fully acknowledge the doctrine of original sin. He buys into the idea rationally, but he does not experience it. In a conversation with his psychiatrist and friend Max, More admits that he wants to feel guilty but does not. More clarifies, "The problem is that if there is no guilt, contrition, and a purpose of amendment, the sin cannot be forgiven [which] means that you don't have life in you" (*Love in the Ruins* 117). Because More cannot acknowledge his sin and suffer proper guilt, he cannot repent, and thus despite all the pleasures in which he indulges, he feels lifeless.[38]

Percy draws a link between the ambition for a perfect world and the increasing secularization of his culture. A perfect world requires perfect human beings, so there must be no notion of a perfect god with whom to compare people. In *The Drama of Atheist Humanism*, de Lubac puts it like this: "Henceforth nothing about [people] must recall a transcendent origin and sacred destiny."[39] People must forget their origins, ignore their sinful state, and reorient their destiny to an earthly and limited *telos*. Although socialism in Russia began as "Christian socialism," the liberal idealists soon realized how incongruent "Christianity" and their form of "socialism" truly was. The former projected a future kingdom of God, while the latter attempted to construct a present utopia on earth. As if to underline the absurdity of such an enterprise, Percy shows the character Father Kev Kevin—a priest who has renounced the faith—"reading a book, *Christianity Without God*" (*Love in the Ruins* 195).

Both Percy and Dostoevsky recognized that such secularization was actually a myth, for humans will still worship.[40] They will simply replace God with a new god; in *The Possessed* and *Love in the Ruins*, this god is science. After Stavrogin has preached about the new society to be pursued, one of his followers, Shatov, recites his message back to him: "Socialism by its very nature

---

38. In "Notes for a Novel" Percy calls the novelist "one of the few remaining witnesses to the doctrine of original sin, the imminence of catastrophe in paradise" (*Message in a Bottle*, 106).

39. De Lubac, *Drama*, 323.

40. Percy admits to being a former science devotee: "It was a religion for me; I believed that any problem, anything wrong, could be solved by one or another of the sciences" (quoted by Robert Coles in *Walker Percy: An American Search*). He understood the lure to make other systems into a religion.

must be atheism, because it has from the very beginning proclaimed itself an atheistic organization which intends to establish itself exclusively on principles of science and reason" (*Devils* 264). For these nineteenth-century revolutionaries, science allows them to conquer sickness, disprove the existence of God, and achieve their utilitarian aims. De Lubac cites Dostoevsky's preparatory notes for *The Possessed*, where he expresses his concern about science replacing God: "Christianity is neither a necessity for mankind nor a source of living life . . . but that it is science that will be able to vitalize life and set up a perfect ideal."[41] Having exchanged God for science, the socialists of *The Possessed* build their "Tower of Babel" upon this human foundation. However, this foundation falters when the great theorists resort to killing one another to accomplish their victory. Ironically, Shatov becomes the primary victim of the theory that he here espouses.

In *Love in the Ruins*, Percy uses euthanasia as a twentieth-century example of how the theoretical idolization of science may lead to death. Midway through the novel, More debates with another doctor about the fate of an elderly man, Mr. Ives, and whether or not to throw the "Euphoric Switch," a euphemism for carrying out euthanasia. According to their scientific experiments, the local doctors have diagnosed "the subject" Mr. Ives as a stroke victim. Yet More sees in the patient an older version of himself, a man who does not want to conform to society's category for him, and who, in protest, disrupts those around him. More gains ground in the debate when he uses honest—though loaded—vocabulary such as "funeral" and "executioner" instead of euphemistic terms. Although More fights for the life of Mr. Ives, he does so using the lapsometer, his scientific invention for curing divided selfhood. In More's world, unlike Stavrogin's, science has reigned as god for the previous century; thus he can employ it without irony. More's colleague Art Immelmann calls "scientific knowledge": "neutral morally, abstractive, and godlike" (*Love in the Ruins* 214). However, even as More refutes the other doctors' diagnosis of Mr. Ives, he still feigns a godlike perspective on the situation. He simultaneously enjoys and feels discomfited by the elevation of science to a godlike role.

While More desires to both serve the God of his former faith as well as the science in which he trusts, his fellow scientists disapprove of what they deem his religious and metaphysical assumptions. For instance, when More discusses belief, souls, or truth, he makes his colleague Max nervous: "Well now. The soul of Western man, that's a large order, Tom. Besides being rather uh metaphysical" (*Love in the Ruins* 115). His colleague trusts his science but

---

41. De Lubac, *Drama*, 304.

not his religion. Before their debate in the pit, his interlocutor Buddy Brown accuses him, "You have allowed nonscientific considerations to affect your judgment," by which he means "religious considerations" (197). In fact, Brown mocks his use of metaphysics as though it is magic or superstition: "How is my metaphysical ontology? Or is it my ontological metaphysics?" (226). For these scientists, any mystery that cannot be calculated by science must not exist. Amidst his notes on *The Possessed*, Percy wrote, "How discretely the name Christ is avoided in radio, newspaper, movies too (even religious movies)."[42] Percy's observation is concretized and exaggerated in *Love in the Ruins*. Not only is the name of Christ avoided but so is any mention of God, religion, or the soul of man.

ART IMMELMANN AS DEMONIC FOIL

As I have shown, *The Brothers Karamazov* looms large over Percy's oeuvre. Thus in addition to *The Possessed*, it is unsurprising to find its influence in Percy's third novel. *The Brothers Karamazov* showcases as much demonic activity as the novel that alludes to demons in its title: Fyodor Karamazov tells stories of devils; Father Ferapont is plagued by devils; and most significantly, Ivan Karamazov has an infamous meeting with a little demon. Since the publication of *Love in the Ruins*, critics have seen More's counterpart Art Immelmann as a descendent of Ivan Karamazov's demonic foil. When Foote first read *Love in the Ruins*, he congratulated Percy on creating "the best devil figure since Ivan Karamazov's."[43]

Like the detailed depiction of Ivan's devil, Percy spends time describing Immelmann's appearance:

> He's an odd-looking fellow, curiously old-fashioned. Indeed, with his old-style flat-top haircut, white shirt with short sleeves, which even have vestigial cuff buttons, and neat dark trousers, he looks like a small-town businessman in the old Auto Age. . . . His face is both youthful and lined. (*Love in the Ruins* 166)

While his facial features lend a supernatural aura to the mundane man, his old-fashioned dress alludes to Ivan's devil, who is donned in dated attire. Percy describes one item of clothing as "a tight gabardine 'bi-swing' jacket, a style popular many years ago" (209), echoing Dostoevsky's description of

---
42. Percy, SHC 275.1.
43. *Correspondence*, 151.

a "reefer jacket . . . of a fashion at least three years old" (*Brothers Karamazov* 602). Dostoevsky writes that such a person holds "the position of a toady, a sponger of the best class" (ibid.), monikers that seem appropriate for Immelmann.

In the introduction of Immelmann, a scene that is comic rather than foreboding, Percy parodies the entrance of Dr. Faust's Mephistopheles. As Dr. More sits wishing that his "lapsometer could treat as well as diagnose," Immelmann appears to fulfill his desires (*Love in the Ruins* 165). Percy exaggerates the appearance of this demon with light and sound effects: "The tape rolls. Don Giovanni begins his descent into hell. A bolt of lightning strikes a transformer with a great crack. Sparks fly" (ibid.). With the power out, the man's face is only lit up by the occasional flash of lightning. Thomas LeClair elucidates the sources of Percy's devil: "Percy's devil is a modern avatar of the Faust and Don Juan myths so prominently alluded to in the novel, but the details of Immelmann's appearance and method also owe much to the devil in Dostoevsky's *The Brothers Karamazov*."[44] The lightning alludes to a joke from Ivan's devil who mocks is interlocutor: "You are really angry with me for not having appeared to you in a red glow, with thunder and lightning, . . . but have shown myself in such a modest form" (*Brothers Karamazov* 614). Despite the flashy meteorological accoutrements, Immelmann emerges as an unthreatening drug salesman.

In *The Brothers Karamazov* readers only see the devil on one occasion (although Ivan implies that the devil has visited before). Immelmann, on the other hand, turns up sporadically throughout Percy's novel. Both characters reflect their "host" protagonist, conforming to the Augustinian notion of parasitic evil. Since evil is nothing, then it must feed off goodness to exist. Ivan continuously challenges the devil to prove his existence and tries to catch him in moments where he repeats Ivan's own thoughts. Unfortunately, More is less observant than Ivan and willingly overlooks the cues that he himself has produced Immelmann. For instance, More rationalizes Immelmann's uncanny knowledge of the lapsometer by a news leak (*Love in the Ruins* 168), and he disregards his awareness that Immelmann's "every movement makes itself known" to him (227). Although Immelmann always materializes out of nowhere, in flashes, and is acquainted with information accessible only to More, the protagonist does not recognize Immelmann's demonic nature until the end of the novel.

Because Dostoevsky's audience—not to mention Percy's—would doubt the identity of supernatural evil, both authors create ambivalent demons. Percy

---

44. LeClair, "Walker Percy's Devil," 157–58.

and Dostoyevsky's literary forerunners could rely on their religious audiences to read a demonic encounter with dramatic irony, waiting for the saint to recognize the devil. However, as Simon Franklin observes, "For Dostoevsky's demon the change of cultural environments has literary consequences, and the structures of deception implicate the reader."[45] In other words, the modern reader suffers the oscillation between belief and unbelief right alongside Ivan. Likewise, in *Love in the Ruins*, the nature of Immelmann is suspect to the reader. While More's secretary Ellen interacts with him as though he is an embodied reality, he materializes and dissipates in and out of More's consciousness. Immelmann does not conduct himself like a material being, but he exaggerates his humanness by hawking, spitting, and patting himself in "standard fashion," as More observes (*Love in the Ruins* 200). More also notices, "In the mirror, which reverses things, there was nothing amiss" (ibid.). These small "oddities," as More refers to them, unnerve the reader without resolving into a clear interpretation.

While Percy does ask the reader to be skeptical of Immelmann's identity, he also preserves conventional dramatic irony. Within their first conversation, More twice questions, "What in hell" (*Love in the Ruins* 166, 168), references the reader should recognize as more accurate than More intends. After More exclaims "goddamn," Art pales and falters, to which More responds, "Art must be a Holy Name man or a hard-shell Baptist" (170), a conclusion humorous to any reader aware of Art's demonic nature. In one of the most obvious moments of detection, More says offhandedly, "Speak of the devil" when Immelmann arrives (200). These small witticisms shrink Immelmann from any resemblance to Satan; he becomes more like Dostoevsky's "*chert*" or a "little devil."[46] Despite the seriousness of the potential tragedies that these demons incite, Percy appreciates Dostoevsky's example to create a more comic devil.[47]

Like Ivan's devil, Immelmann desires to exploit his host's utopian dreams and abstract love of humanity. The devil concludes his lengthy dialogue with an uplifting speech about the possibility of the future, which appears in snippets again in Immelmann's conversation with More:

---

45. Franklin, "Nostalgia for Hell," 48.
46. Dostoevsky, *Selected Letters*, 508.
47. It's notable that More and Art interact similarly to the way in which Ivan and his devil do. While Art and Ivan's devil are always amiable, More and Ivan respond with name calling and curses. The devil advises Ivan: "It would be better to be a bit more polite, even with me. Fool, lackey—what sort of talk is that?" (*Brothers Karamazov*, 638). Similarly, after More calls Art an "evil-minded son of a bitch," Art responds, "I can't understand why he calls me those extraordinary names" (*Love in the Ruins*, 376). Both devil's respond with incredulity at their host's disdain.

And for the good of mankind! *Science* to help all men and a *happy joyous love* to help women. We are speaking here of *happiness, joy,* music, spontaneity. . . . This love has its counterpart in *scientific knowledge*: it is neutral morally, abstractive, and *godlike.* (*Love in the Ruins* 213–14, emphasis mine)

Ivan's devil delivers a similar speech that bears comparison:

Men will unite to take from life all it can give, but only for *joy and happiness* in the present world. Man will be lifted up with a spirit of divine Titanic pride and the *man-god* will appear. From hour to hour extending his conquest of nature infinitely by his will and *his science,* man will feel such *lofty joy.* . . . Love will be sufficient only for a moment of life. (*Brothers Karamazov* 616, emphasis mine)

Both speeches emphasize that human happiness is derived from this world, namely from love, though love defined as fleeting and romantic; they also exalt the trajectory of human beings to become like gods through their scientific power over nature.

Although Ivan's devil acts primarily within his mind, Immelmann participates in More's reality. Immelmann unleashes More's lapsometer into the hands of unsuspecting scientists at the pit. When he does so, More cautions the director that his invention has the power to cause "severe angelism, abstraction of the self from itself," which he calls "the Lucifer syndrome: that is, envy of the incarnate condition and a resulting caricature of the bodily appetites" (*Love in the Ruins* 236). Hidden—or not so hidden—in More's warning is his theology of the devil "Lucifer." Without subscribing to the doctrines of his Church in word or action, More has assumed Catholic knowledge of demonic evil. The division between soul and body would have two demonic consequences—angelism and bestialism—both which will render the self in two and cause its eventual destruction. Suffering from the Lucifer syndrome, a human being would lose his or her humanity and either exalt the self as a god or surrender to the lower animalistic impulses. Once the Lucifer syndrome has begun, it acts as a contagion: the choice for escape is between suicide or salvation. In this episode, Immelmann is the propagator of the Lucifer syndrome; a not-so-subtle hint at his demonic nature.

LIFE AS AN EX-SUICIDE

The dichotomy More draws between suicide and salvation is particularly pertinent, for after the death of his daughter and the departure of his wife, More slit his wrists. More chose suicide because he could not contend with his own suffering, but more than that, because he felt—and still feels throughout the novel—lost. In *Lost in the Cosmos,* Percy's nonfiction satirical self-help book, Percy wonders whether the suicidal impulse stems from a lost identity. He addresses his reader with the problem, "You live in a deranged age—more deranged than usual, because despite great scientific and technological advances, man has not the faintest idea of who he is or what he is doing" (*Lost in the Cosmos* 76). While Percy writes "despite" human advances, he may also have indicted them, for they may have contributed to the problem. John Desmond writes, "For Percy, the suicidal culture of despair emerged through a complex intertwining of forces that included the redefining and devaluation of the self, the decline of religious belief, and the dominance of the ideology of scientism and technology."[48] This triad of twentieth-century ills confront Percy's antagonist across his fiction, especially in *Love in the Ruins.* In response to such a deranged world, Percy presents suicide as the potential escape route intended by Ivan Karamazov: "As Ivan said to God in *The Brothers Karamazov*: If you exist, I respectfully return my ticket" (*Lost in the Cosmos* 77).

Whereas Ivan does proffer a philosophical rebellion for which suicide will be his culminating act, other Dostoevskian heroes both profess and carry out their suicidal designs, two of which occur in *The Possessed.* Perhaps the most famous suicide in recent literary history is Kirillov, a character who fascinated the existentialists of Percy's era as much as Percy himself. In his copy of Albert Camus's *The Myth of Sisyphus,* Percy has bracketed and marginally lined the opening paragraph that begins, "There is but one truly serious philosophical problem and that is suicide" (3). Camus prizes Kirillov as the example of an absurd victor, a modern hero. He validates his suicide as pedagogical instruction used to teach human beings that God does not exist, a notion directly opposed to Dostoevsky's intention. Camus's argument, drawn from Kirillov's rationale, is that because one can unmake his life by a force of will, he is god unto himself. Thus, an external God does not exist.

Although Dostoevsky sympathized with Kirillov's fervor, he pitied him for missing the reality of God. Kirillov determines to kill himself because his suicide will induct the "new man":

> Life is pain. . . . Now all is pain and terror. . . . Now man is not yet what he will be. There will be a new man, happy and proud. For whom it will be the

---

48. Desmond, "Walker Percy and Suicide," 60.

same to live or not to live, he will be the new man. He who will conquer pain and terror will himself be a god. And this God will not be. (*Possessed* 114)

Percy underlined this section, as well as marking squiggles and doodles on the page. Indeed, in Percy's edition of *The Possessed,* most of the notes concern Kirillov. For Kirillov, suicide overcomes the pain of life and the terror of death; it exalts "man" to the status of god. Kirillov is the "Man-god," as he proclaims to Stavrogin, the new man who may achieve godhood apart from God.

Through Kirillov, Dostoevsky warns his readers about the false sense of control for which human beings are striving. Although Tom More does not even appear to be a distant relative to Kirillov, the two easily could have drunk bourbon or vodka together while criticizing others for believing in a god of one's own invention. Both men's problem, however, is that they want God to exist. Stavrogin too wants God to exist, and he is troubled by the possibility of damnation. At the end of the novel, unable to cope with the secular city, he chooses what Percy insists is the only alternative and takes his own life. If More is to survive, he must stop resembling Stavrogin. He needs a new model (perhaps St. Thomas More?) and he must discover the other choice, a life in submission to a transcendent God.

Tom More discovers the alternative to suicide only after attempting it. During the week between Christmas and New Year's Day, More suffers "simultaneous depressions and exaltations, assaulted at night by longings, succubi, and hideous shellfire of Verdun, and in the morning by terror of unknown origin" (*Love in the Ruins* 97). Manic and alone, More attempts to take his own life. While recovering in the hospital, he experiences "the best months of [his] life" (105) and compares his experience with "Dostoevsky" who did his "best work in prison" (106). He realizes that the world *outside* of the madhouse is actually mad because those outside cannot see clearly. From the moment he commits suicide, More decides that he wants to live: "Seeing the blood, I came to myself, saw myself as itself and the world for what it is and began to love life" (97). He ventures to his friend Max's home, who sews him up, then he commits himself to a mental hospital. More's revelation correlates with Percy's discussion of suicide in *Lost in the Cosmos.* Percy details the advantage to such a serious consideration of suicide—minus the action: "As soon as suicide is taken as a serious alternative, . . . you are dispensed. . . . You are like a prisoner released from the cell of his life" (*Lost in the Cosmos* 76–77). While the free man takes freedom for granted, the newly released prisoner celebrates his freedom as gift. Similarly, the "ex-suicide," as Percy labels it, has a new appreciation for the gift of life after almost losing it.

For Percy when death comes closer, life becomes clearer, a necessary attribute for his protagonist. In his essay on apocalyptic novel writing, Percy describes the historical Thomas More as "most cheerful with Brother Death in the neighborhood" (*Message in a Bottle* 109). However, Percy's protagonist suffers from an inability to hold on to the revelations that he receives, to act on the grandiose dreams he posits. When More returns to the outside world, he regresses to loving the earthly goods in and of themselves, falling to the temptation of the devil. Recalling Immelmann's advice, he wonders, "What does a man live for but to have a girl, use his mind, practice his trade, drink a drink, read a book, and watch the martins wing it for the Amazon and the three-fingered sassafras turn red in October?" (*Love in the Ruins* 336–37). The temptation sounds good; it *sounds* as though More is quoting Ecclesiastes about the necessity to live according to the seasons of time. However, the devil perverts the good in More's mind. More loves the things of this world apart from God, yet they cannot be loved adequately as such. In the hospital he prays, "Dear God, I can see it now, why can't I see it other times, that it is you I love in the beauty of the world and in all the lovely girls" (109). Although More appreciates the gift of this life, his time in the world jades his revelation about the source of the good.

Unable to act as the saint in his own story, More refrains from acting at all. Only when his secretary and potential wife, Ellen, is threatened to be taken by Immelmann does More admit his weakness and call on his namesake for help. Immelmann advances on Ellen, and More feels powerless to stop him. Since he "can't seem to move," More prays, "Sir Thomas More, kinsman, saint, best dearest, merriest of Englishmen, pray for us and drive this son of a bitch hence" (*Love in the Ruins* 376). The man who tried to be the savior of the world discovers that he needs saving. By rescinding his claims as messiah, More is freed from the demon that haunted him. Ellen hears his prayer and asks, "Do you think you're a saint?" (377). Although the question applies to the literal situation, it demands that More diagnose his own soul. When More answers in the negative, he reveals how he has changed. By calling on a saint, the false messiah has begun the journey to sainthood.

However, the novel does not end with More's victory; the narrator tries to zoom out from the trajectory of the hero and reexamine the larger stage. While the action of the novel began on July 4, a national holiday, it concludes with Christmas Eve, a Christian celebration. This transition turns focus away from political identifications and toward religious realities. Outside of Mass, as More "eat[s] Christ, drink[s] his blood," children shoot off firecrackers and cry, "Hurrah for Jesus Christ!" simultaneously with, "Hurrah for the United States!" (*Love in the Ruins* 400). Joseph Schwartz contends that these cries hail back to those at the conclusion of *The Brothers Karamazov*. He credits Dostoevsky for Percy's affirmative ending: "The Mass of Resurrection in the Dostoevsky novel resonates quite nicely with Christmas mass in *Love in the Ruins*, for both celebrate birth."[49] Yet paired with shouts for the nation, the joyous acclamation for the birth of Jesus Christ sounds hollow. The satirical equality between the two phrases underscores the problem that More identified at the start of the novel, a confusion between the role of theology and politics.

The warning that More foresaw in the political and religious turmoil did not bring the apocalypse, and five years after the major events of the novel, not much has changed. More still believes his "lapsometer can save the world," that the world is "broken," and that human beings are "ghosts locked in its own machinery" (*Love in the Ruins* 382–83). He summarizes the state of society five years after the potential apocalypse, and the synopsis sounds similar to the opening of the novel; in fact, it also seems partially to describe our world fifty years later: "Learning and wisdom are receding nowadays. The young, who already know everything, hate science, bomb laboratories, kill professors, burn libraries" (383). At the end of this lamentation over society, More adds a line of hope: "Already the monks are beginning to collect books again" (ibid.). The elliptical statement alludes to Walter Miller's *A Canticle for Leibowitz*, a book Percy read "several times" and reviewed in the same year that he published *Love in the Ruins*.[50]

Miller's novel starts in AD 2600 and documents three different time periods, approximately five hundred years apart. It begins after an apocalypse has wiped out much of the human race, and the monks of the Abbey of Leibowitz are collecting any written works they find for illumination and study. Through the setting and separate epochs, Miller shows the cyclical nature of time. Moreover, his novel confirms More's reflection near the conclusion of the novel, that each time period has its own apocalypse. More contemplates the previous five years:

> I thought of Christ coming again at the end of the world and how it is that in every age there is the temptation to see signs of the end and that, even knowing this, there is nevertheless some reason, what with the spirit of the

---

49. Schwartz, "Will Barret Redux?," 45–46.
50. In *Lost in the Cosmos*, Percy's "Space Odyssey II" begins with a footnote: "The adventures recounted here owe something to Walter Miller's extraordinary novel, *A Canticle for Leibowitz*, from which I have borrowed Leibowitz and the state of Utah." Percy should add that he also "borrows" the handicapped and malformed children. This note is indicative of Percy's unabashed use of other's works.

new age being the spirit of watching and waiting to believe that—. (*Love in the Ruins* 387)

More leaves the musing unfinished, yet that is the point. So many times throughout history, the world has appeared to be ending. When Rome fell to the barbarians, the Black Death killed much of Europe's population, or when the whole world went to war twice in the same century, these moments seem to presage apocalypse.

Unlike the ending of *The Possessed,* Percy's *Love in the Ruins* is a comedy, ending with the potential salvation of the protagonist, the survival of the world, and order somewhat restored. Yet the comedy is not unqualified; the world remains dichotomous, with good and evil intermingled. From the beginning of the novel, More has circled around the antidote to the dichotomous world he inhabits. For example, when More recalls a discussion with his ex-wife Doris about what occurs in church, he reflects on the Eucharist: "It took religion to save me from the spirit world, from orbiting the earth like Lucifer and the angels, [it took] eating Christ himself to make me mortal man and let me inhabit my own flesh" (*Love in the Ruins* 254). By attending church and participating in the Eucharist, the division between spirit and flesh that More experiences in his world is overcome. He himself does not triumph, but he receives reprieve. Thus despite its pretense of a happy ending and seeming closure for Tom More, the conclusion of *Love in the Ruins* still protests spiritual reality. More ends the novel waiting at a bus stop, contemplating the unfulfilled prophecy with which the novel began.[51]

As he was five years before, More continues watching and waiting; however, now he knows more. When More describes how the mornings remain difficult for him, he asserts, "What has changed is my way of dealing with it" (*Love in the Ruins* 384), and this observation applies to all of his life. The apocalypse—political or religious—may be perpetually approaching, yet More thinks that he knows how to live through it all. He follows the advice that Father Smith gave him in the confessional, counsel in which the priest includes himself: "doing our jobs . . . showing a bit of ordinary kindness to people, particularly our own families [and] doing what we can for our poor unhappy country" (399). Unfortunately, Smith's recommendation sounds weak, too much like the atheist humanism that de Lubac describes. Where is the transcendent reality? Where is Jesus Christ? By following Smith's guidance, More can stave off suicide, but there is no embrace of life.

---

51. The setting evokes Samuel Beckett's *Waiting for Godot* in which two men wait on a mound for Godot/God who never arrives.

THE IMPORTANCE OF THE INFLUENCE

In *Love in the Ruins,* Percy attempts a novel of Dostoevskian scope, depicting the spiritual sickness of an entire nation. Although political and contemporary on its surface, the core of Dostoevsky's novel, its very theme, is spiritual. The epigraph for *The Possessed* from Luke indicates its spiritual source and thus larger implications. For Dostoevsky, when a man "loses his people and his nationality [he] loses also his faith in his fatherland and his god."[52] This was the universal theme that Percy picks up in *Love in the Ruins.* "Is it," Tom More wonders in his opening narration, "that God has at last removed his blessing from the beloved U.S.A?" (*Love in the Ruins* 3). Tongue-in-cheek, this passage reveals a lack of faith from Percy in any national salvation, such as what Dostoevsky mistakenly believed about his own Mother Russia. More himself sees through such messianic national fervor: "And as for the Russia and the Russian Christ who was going to save Europe from itself: ha" (57). However, More's question indicates a larger question about whether there is any God, any blessing, any hope. Percy's ambitious replica culminated in a novel of modest scope, focused on a single protagonist. Reading *Love in the Ruins* in light of Dostoevsky's *The Possessed* intensifies the spiritual import of Percy's comedy and suggests aesthetic merit for his potentially heavy-handed narrative. By seeing Stavrogin and Kirillov as ancestors of Tom More, his situation, however comic, becomes weighted with latent peril. Although his prophecy of violence and destruction sounds laughable, when interpreted against the backdrop of *The Possessed* and the 1917 Russian Revolution, it is recast as seriously terrifying. Percy may have been catching his twentieth-century readers' attention with his humor, but his fears contain the gravitas of Dostoevsky's earlier novel. And while critics have accused *Love in the Ruins* of propaganda, perhaps a look at Percy's novel through a Dostoevskian lens validates not only its concerns but also its artistry. My close reading of the two artists flies in the face of critics who think that truth is relative, that imitation leads to weak writing, and that any relation to a predecessor must be antagonistic. In the conclusion of his book on Percy, for example, Kieran Quinlan asserts, "[Because] the notion of 'absolute' truth has shown itself to be culturally and historically bound, it is unlikely [after Percy] that there can be any more 'Catholic' novelists: there is no such goal toward which an intellectually informed and honest human being can now aspire."[53] Yet an examination of Dostoevsky's and Percy's ideas from their two novels reveals universal truths and intellectually rigorous faiths.

---

52. Cited in Leatherbarrow, *Dostoevsky's* The Devils, 146.
53. Quinlan, *Last Catholic,* 226.

Moreover, when you compare the two novels, you witness the freedom of the artists. In his essay on Herman Melville, in which he also refers to Dostoevsky, Percy explains how Melville wrote in response to Hawthorne. He uses the example as evidence that all writers are responding to others, and that artistic "happiness comes from the ineffable sociabilities when they succeed, when the writing works and somebody knows it" (*Signposts* 199). For Percy, *Moby Dick* becomes an instance of "the artist discovering, breaking through into the freedom of his art" (ibid.), a freedom that is paradoxically the result of Melville's writing for, to, and against Hawthorne. Similarly, Percy writes for Dostoevsky, and while their novels both respond to contemporary situations, the products are profoundly different. The process by which they created was similar—reading newspaper accounts alongside their reading of Scripture—but their outcomes vary. Some of their tropes and figures align, but the characters are free with unwritten futures (with the exception of the suicides). While Dostoevsky writes a tragedy, Percy writes a satire. Reading the two in tandem illustrates their artistic liberty and personal voices while also showing the universal and absolute truth at the core of their disparate narratives.

Finally, Percy does not draw upon Dostoevsky in order to correct his work or replace him in the canon. In *Retelling Dostoevsky: Literary Responses and Other Observations*, Gary Adelman assumes a Bloomian paradigm for those who retell Dostoevsky's stories. He shows how Camus, Coetzee, and others employ Bloom's strategies, such as *clinamen, tessera,* or *askesis,* in order to improve upon Dostoevsky. Adelman asks rhetorically, "Where else does the impulse to retell a work of literature come from, but from dissatisfaction and a need to argue with some aspect of the author's worldview?"[54] Applauding such a stance, Adelman has charted a host of modern novelists who have chosen to retell Dostoevsky in order to argue with him. "Dostoyevsky can no longer be read naively," Adelman claims, "as a champion of Christian love, post-Holocaust, because . . . he was a rabid anti-Semite."[55] Writers like Percy who chose to imitate (and not argue) with Dostoevsky's worldview are cast out of Adelman's purview because of their Christian naivete.

Although Dostoevsky biographically had major moral failings, anti-Semitism and problematic beliefs in national superiority among them, his novels do not forward such racist ire. Rather, his art overcomes his authorial weaknesses, and their arguments are prophetic. Percy imitated Dostoevsky for the very reason that Adelman casts as unacceptable—because Percy saw Dosto-

---

54. Adelman, *Retelling Dostoevsky,* 12.
55. Ibid., 12.

evsky as a "champion of Christian love." He found universal truth at the core of Dostoevsky's novel and wanted to replicate that in his own style of narrative. *The Possessed* may have prophesied the 1917 Russian Revolution, but even more prophetically, it shows the demonic stimulus of pride and violence. By following in Dostoevsky's footsteps, Percy could not speak more truly in *Love in the Ruins* about those same predicaments in our own culture and that same temptation for our own souls.

CHAPTER 5

"Outdostoevskying Dostoevsky" in *Lancelot*

"OUTDOSTOEVSKYING DOSTOEVSKY" is a phrase that Shelby Foote uses that describes Walker Percy's accomplishment in his fourth novel, *Lancelot*.[1] The novel features coarser language, raunchier sex, and bloodier violence than any other novel by either Percy or Dostoevsky. In it, the idols that Dostoevsky denounced in his nineteenth-century Russia are recast as Hollywood icons, drugs, and loose sexual mores. The eponymous antihero of *Lancelot*, a failed N.A.A.C.P lawyer residing in an antebellum mansion on Belle Isle, is an amalgam of three Dostoevskian characters: The Underground Man from *Notes from Underground*; the philosophical murderer Raskolnikov from *Crime and Punishment*; and Ivan Karamazov's Grand Inquisitor from *The Brothers Karamazov*. Although rooted in a nineteenth-century inspiration, *Lancelot* is nevertheless very much of the twentieth century. The protagonist Lancelot passes his days in a haze of alcohol, narcotics, and sexual voyeurism—which he masks as investigation—while a Hollywood film is being produced around him. He is very much a man of his times.

In bringing Dostoevsky into the twentieth century, Percy pushes the Russian novelist's signature themes—violence, sexuality, tortured conscience—further than Dostoevsky himself ever did. In each of Percy's other novels,

---

1. O'Gorman, "Confessing the Horrors," 119.

he revises Dostoevsky by lightening the tone and infusing the ending with hope. In *Lancelot* though, Percy departs from this method by darkening the characters, the plot, and the universe in which they exist. It is in this way that, in *Lancelot*, Percy "outdostoevskys" the Russian—if we take Dostoevsky to be synonymous with dark dramas of the human soul. In this fourth novel, Percy situates the Russian's characters and themes within a twentieth-century universe that is amoral, where people can exchange sexual partners without flinching, and God is a distant, antiquated memory. In doing so, Percy critiques the problems of his era through an invocation of Dostoevsky. This work is Percy's darkest, but even it offers a glimmer of hope reminiscent of *The Brothers Karamazov*.

Although the text itself through the maniacal ruminations of its monologic protagonist appears to argue for absolute autonomy, the nature of the narrative—both its confessional genre and its connection to Dostoevsky's previous novels—belies the claims of the central character. In other words, no matter how convincing Lancelot Lamar sounds, no matter how much control Percy appears to give his antihero in this story, the fact that the text itself is thickly intertextual denies Lancelot's radical individualism. In his article "Confessing the Horrors of Radical Individualism in *Lancelot*," Farrell O'Gorman calls *Lancelot* Percy's "most substantively allusive" novel.[2] He suggests that *Lancelot* was written "as if to highlight T. S. Eliot's argument in 'Tradition and the Individual Talent' that great works of literature, like individual human beings, necessarily come into being only in relationship to a constellation of predecessors," of which O'Gorman cites Dostoevsky and Edgar Allan Poe as the strongest influences on *Lancelot*.[3] O'Gorman argues that *Lancelot*, in line with the two aforementioned writers, reveals the danger of radical individualism and focuses on Lancelot's confessional mode as the character's necessary antidote. However, I would like to press O'Gorman's claims further and suggest that Percy not only refutes his protagonist's claims in the narrative mode but more so in Percy's unintentional responses to Dostoevsky's previous works.

A close reading of *Lancelot* reveals that the text bears the distinct influence of three different works by Dostoevsky. First the form of an incoherent, one-sided dialogue, spoken by an unreliable narrator to a largely silent interlocutor, comes from *Notes from Underground*. Both two narrators jabber incoherently, their sentences ragged in structure and ridden with colloquialisms,

---

2. Ibid.

3. They echo Edgar Allan Poe's narrator from *The Tell-Tale Heart* who opens his narrative with the sentence, "True!—nervous—very, very dreadfully nervous I had been and am; but why will you say that I am mad?" http://xroads.virginia.edu/~hyper/poe/telltale.html.

fragments, and dissembling;[4] in addition, both narrators are questionable in their honesty and their sanity.[5] Second, *Lancelot*'s plot is inspired by *Crime and Punishment*: a nihilist turned murderer. Finally, the conclusion of *Lancelot* bears the influence of *The Brothers Karamazov*. A demon resembling that of Ivan Karamazov had briefly appeared in *Love in the Ruins*, but in *Lancelot* the demonic waxes at great length about his profane worldview, as the main character echoes the philosophy espoused by the Grand Inquisitor. In these three ways, *Lancelot* bears the influence of Dostoevsky. Yet Percy would do something different with this influence than he did in any other novel, depicting a universe that is amoral and a protagonist who seems to lack any moral compass. This would be Percy's only instance of adapting Dostoevsky not into a comedy, but into dark tragedy.

EVIDENCE OF DOSTOEVSKY IN PERCY'S WRITING PROCESS

In 1972 as Percy begins writing *Lancelot*, he receives a letter of encouragement from Foote that opens, "Did you know Dostoevsky was 56 when he sat down to write The Brothers?"[6] At the time, Percy too was fifty-six. Having drawn attention to the parallel between Percy and his favorite Russian novelist, Foote lays out some advice about what and how Percy should write next.[7] "I think [it] should either be a *short, highly experimental novel* marking a new direction, or else the really big novel you are headed for." He adds, "Good for you rereading C&P," implying that *Crime and Punishment* is a worthy inspiration for Percy's next novel.[8] A few weeks after this letter, Percy follows Foote's

---

4. Within a few pages, the Underground Man admits, "And I lied about myself just now. . . . I lied out of wickedness" (*Notes*, 4). Similarly, before chapter two begins, Lancelot confesses to Percival, "I was not quite honest yesterday when I pretended not to notice you" (*Lancelot*, 9). Lancelot continues, "You still look doubtful. About my sanity? Well yes, after all, here I am in the nuthouse" (9).

5. Differences: The Underground Man speaks directly to the reader, while Lancelot does not. The Underground Man frankly admits to being sick and wicked, however, Lancelot's state is more ambiguous.

6. The letter reads more fully, "Youve [sic] got three books behind you, essentially preparatory work (which even *Notes from Underground* was) for what comes next, which I think should either be a *short, highly experimental novel* marking a new direction, or else the really big novel you are headed for. . . . Good for you rereading C&P. While you are at it, go to the short novels and give *The Eternal Husband* another run-through. He writes much like you in that one" (*Correspondence*, 164, emphasis mine).

7. Ibid., emphasis mine.

8. Ibid., 168.

advice and begins writing "something experimental"[9]—the novel *Lancelot*, which would combine features from three different Dostoevsky novels, including *Crime and Punishment*.

Throughout the writing process for *Lancelot*, from 1972 to 1977, Percy is plagued by devils. In his letters of this period, he admits several times to depression and *acedia*, what monks call the "noon-time demon" or the sin of sloth. In a letter to Brainard Cheney, Percy writes (Nov. 14, 1973):

> I am into one [novel] which is about to kill me—suffering depression and other symptoms—It's a rotten profession—God help us both. Truthfully I don't know whether I've been overtaken by a virus or male menopause or the *devil*—who I am quite willing to believe does indeed roam about the world seeking whom he may devour. Anyhow it takes the form in my case of disinterest, accidie, little or no use for the things of God and the old virtues. I'd rather chase women (not that I do). . . . I think it has something to do with laziness or the inability to give birth to a 2-year-old fetus of a novel. (cited in Tolson, *Pilgrim in the Ruins* 393, emphasis mine)

Percy hopes this whipping from the demonic "might even help with the novel," as he writes Caroline Gordon.[10] Percy himself attributes his apathy and unhappiness to "old virtues," his yearning for women, and the stalling of his novel to the pressure of the devil, not mere neurosis. In any case, Percy's depression during this period could explain why *Lancelot* is so much darker than Percy's other novels.

Also in these years, Percy was burrowing deeply into Dostoevsky's works, which may have been either a cause or an effect of his darkening imagination. Percy chose to put the Russian author at the center of American literature courses he taught at Loyola University, New Orleans, beginning in 1967. In that year, the chair of the English department at Loyola, Bill Corrington, invited Percy to teach a course on American literature. Percy accepted, and his response letter of April 10, 1967, reads in part,

> It will, in any case, be unlike any English course ever taught anywhere. It will be a medical-pathological-psychiatric-anthropological approach to modern fiction which will probably set out with *Notes from Underground* and have nothing to do with Hemingway and Faulkner.[11]

---

9. Letter from Percy to Cheney, Box 14, Folder 21, Brainard Cheney Papers, Vanderbilt University, Special Collections (Summer 2010).
10. Percy, SHC 374.
11. Cited in Tolson, *Pilgrim in the Ruins*, 394.

As this letter makes clear, before Percy had even ascertained the trajectory of the course, he had selected Dostoevsky's short novel as the core of the syllabus. Percy would teach Dostoevsky's *Notes from Underground* again in the fall of 1974 and for Louisiana State University in the spring of 1975. Lewis Simpson speculates, "Percy's experience at LSU during the 1974–1975 academic year had a decisive influence on the writing of *Lancelot*."[12] Simpson does not elaborate on his point, like so many other Percy scholars who mention influences in passing without delving into the nature and significance of the influence.

Why Dostoevsky at this moment in Percy's teaching and writing career? Archival evidence enables us to reconstruct Percy's close, sustained interest in the Russian novelist at this time. Percy's library contains five copies of *Notes from Underground*, two of which are unmarked, but three of which are "teaching" copies containing ample notes in Percy's hand. In addition, Percy's archive includes almost thirty pages of notes on the novel, in which one can see him grappling with the novel's meaning. Taken together, the notes in all three copies and on loose-leaf pages reveal how Percy taught the novel, what he considered valuable in each semester's rereading, and which questions he pursued each time he reread the work. His deep contemplation of Dostoevsky while teaching the novelist in 1974–75 doubtless influenced the shape of the novel *Lancelot*, which he wrote in 1972–77.

Of all his protagonists, Percy claims to share the closest resemblance to the character of Lancelot. He considered *Lancelot* to have come from what was going on in his life and not from any outside sources. In *The Moviegoer*, he recognized his draw from Dostoevsky in hindsight; in *The Last Gentleman*, he realized that he was inspired by Dostoevsky and Cervantes, and in *Love in the Ruins*, he knew that he was basing the novel on Dostoevsky and the contemporary political situation. Yet in this work—his most Dostoevskian—the only inspiration Percy speaks of in letters and interviews is his own dark soul. Even still, the very first line of *Lancelot* sounds like an echo from *Notes*, which Percy was teaching as he worked on writing his own novel. This chapter demonstrates how profound influence can occur unintentionally. We see in *Lancelot* an instance of George Steiner's model of influence, in which a writer reads and digests another's work, so that the other's work unconsciously becomes part of oneself and one's own work. In a sense, *Lancelot* represents how Percy so fully absorbed Dostoevsky that he performs Dostoevsky without even realizing it.

Each of Percy's novels centers on a wayfarer who undertakes a journey: Binx Bolling goes on a search for an unidentified end, Will Barrett undertakes a geographical odyssey from New York to New Mexico, and in *Lancelot*,

---

12. *Lancelot* by Walker Percy will be cited in text throughout the book.

Percy's fourth novel, Lancelot Andrewes Lamar, the self-proclaimed "Knight of the Unholy Grail," is on a quest to discover evil (*Lancelot* 138). The main trajectory is the degeneration of the atheist Lancelot; he is the Underground Man or Raskolnikov or the Grand Inquisitor a century later. Yet Lance also has a double, his largely silent interlocutor, a priest named Percival. Percival's quest is never defined or even actively pursued. (His name alludes to the Arthurian hero "who found the Grail and brought life to a dead land" [10],[13] as Lancelot phrases it, referring not to his Unholy but to the Holy Grail.) Like Percy's previous heroes, Lancelot is an outsider who is able to perceive what is wrong with the world by standing aloof from it. However, unlike Percy's other wayfarers, what makes Lancelot an outsider is his criminal insanity. He is not quirky, endearing, or religious, but rather immoral and sinister. This antihero does not suffer from mere malaise or sporadic amnesia; he murdered his friends and family and burned down his ancestral home without any apparent guilt or regret.

The journey of Lance is a movement from disillusionment with his "happy" life to a cold recognition of the pervasiveness of evil, and Percival's journey is a movement from disillusionment to a return to God as the only counter against evil. Although both characters are drawn from Percy, they become two completely separate personalities. Instead of a Jekyll and Hyde, Percival and Lancelot are more like Father Tikhon and Nikolai Stavrogin from *The Possessed*, or Alyosha and Ivan Karamazov from *The Brothers Karamazov*. Percy had observed of Dostoevsky early in his writing notes, "Dostoievski's [sic] way of creating characters from his own complexity. The Brothers. He is all three. Priest, atheist, worldling."[14] So too Percy draws from the complexity of his own inner self to create the atheist Lancelot and the priest Percival.

In recounting the tale to Percival about how he ended up locked away in the cell, Lancelot reveals a journey of moral deterioration. What began as slovenliness and apathy degenerates into sadistic sexuality, murderous rage, and ultimately cold-hearted nihilism. Lancelot's decline over the course of the novel can be illuminated by reading his journey in conjunction with three works by Dostoevsky. As this chapter will show, Percy depicts the various stages of Lancelot's dehumanization in terms of Dostoevsky's Underground Man, Raskolnikov from *Crime and Punishment*, and the Grand Inquisitor from *The Brothers Karamazov*. The first begins the slip toward inhumanity, the second recedes further, and the third embraces his rebellion. In *Lancelot*, a novel set in a wholly amoral universe, Percy creates an atheist who surpasses

---

13. Percy, SHC 164.19.
14. Percy, *Conversations*, 146.

them all. The proceeding sections will discuss each of these stages of Lancelot's degeneration in turn: first *Notes from Underground*, from which Percy draws his style of narration; then *Crime and Punishment*, on which Percy modeled his murderous prisoner, and finally *The Brothers Karamazov*, which inspired both Lancelot's deranged utopic visions as well as Percival's concluding "yes" of hope.

NOTES FROM UNDERGROUND AND THE ANTIHERO NARRATOR

The narrator and style of narration in *Lancelot* shows Dostoevsky's most significant contribution to this novel. Percy spent a considerable amount of time devising the opening line, "Come into my cell," which sounds as though it has been borrowed from Dostoevsky's *Notes from Underground*. In Dostoevsky's novella, the narrator, the proclaimed antihero of the work, resides in a cell of his own making. Not only does Percy's narrator echo this character but also the point of view that Percy employs points back to *Notes*. While Percy did not intentionally imitate these choices from one of his favorite texts, *Lancelot* employs the form of *Notes from Underground*, and its narrator sounds awfully similar to the Underground Man.

The form of *Lancelot* is of a lengthy, one-sided monologue, with Lancelot speaking to his silent interlocutor, Percival. Percy's decision to structure *Lancelot* in this way came relatively late in the writing process. In the original manuscripts, both Lancelot and Percival are speaking characters. Percy claims in a 1977 interview that his inspiration for the technique in which "one man talked to another man"[15] came from Camus, primarily from his novel *The Fall*,[16] which Percy also taught in his course on alienation in the novel. According to Ray Davison in his exploration of Dostoevsky's influence on Camus, "*La Chute* [*The Fall*] must unquestionably be seen as Camus's most Dostoevskian work," a similar claim to the one I make regarding *Lancelot*.[17] Davison describes how Camus's novel engages "very self-consciously in an extensive intertextual dialogue with Dostoevsky's world and work,"[18] by which he specifies *Crime and Punishment, Notes from Underground,* and "The Grand Inquisitor," the same works that Percy draws on in *Lancelot*. However, Percy

---

15. For more on the connection with *The Fall*, read John F. Desmond, "Revisioning *The Fall*, 619.
16. Davidson, *Camus: The Challenge of Dostoevsky*, 161.
17. Ibid.
18. Kobre, *Voices*, 162.

alters Camus's *The Fall* by silencing the second character Percival throughout nearly the entire the narrative, and thus the novel stylistically more closely resembles *Notes from Underground*.

Despite its one controlling voice, critics debate whether *Notes* or *Lancelot* are monologic or polyphonic narratives. In his study of *Walker Percy's Voices*, Michael Kobre asserts that in *Lancelot* "monologue, rather, has been transformed into the kind of dialogic encounter that Bakhtin finds so often in Dostoevsky's work."[19] Kobre refers to Mikhail Bakhtin's *Problems of Dostoevsky's Poetics*, in which the Russian critic establishes his theory of polyphonic discourse based on Dostoevsky's fiction. Drawing from this acclaimed critical work, Kobre shows how *Notes* is a multi-voiced text—despite the one narrator—and how *Lancelot* emulates the method of creating many voices within a one-voiced narrative. By drawing on *Notes from Underground* in addition to other stories, such as "Tell-Tale Heart," as O'Gorman claims, the text enters conversation with others. Moreover, while Percival does not speak until the end, his affirmative word is the final word of the novel. Quantitatively imbalanced, the two voices are, however, qualitatively weighted, for Percival's side is stronger than all of Lancelot's "long-winded rant."[20]

Lancelot is a novel of extremes: the antihero divides the world into dichotomous categories of lady or whore, master or slave, black or white, and eventually God or the Devil. He lives within a bifurcated deconstruction of the universe, which he dares his interlocutor to repudiate: "Tell me if I'm right or wrong" (*Lancelot* 256). His entire narrative is a query for which side of the either-or is "right," and he engages Percival in conversation to uncover the answer. In Percy's notes for teaching Dostoevsky's *Notes from Underground*, he comments, "D[ostoevsky]'s moral world is dialectical. Every choice man makes is a free choice between self and God—there is no middle good of reason and humanism."[21] *Lancelot* presents a similar dialectical world in which the "middle good" has been removed, leaving the question, what would happen if an argument is drawn out to its furthest ends and if one must decide between either self or God? Lancelot presents this question to Percival several times and receives an answer at the conclusion of the novel.

---

19. Tolson defends Percy's choice of one voice, claiming that "he could not give these opposing voices equal time in the way that Dostoevsky had; the age would not tolerate such preaching. But he could transform the dialogue into a monologue, allow the darkness to talk itself out in one long-winded rant, and by subtlest hints imply a response" (*Pilgrim in the Ruins*, 404). The "preaching" that Tolson references here may have referred to Zosima's life story from *The Brothers Karamazov*, which Dostoevsky considered his answer to Ivan's "The Grand Inquisitor."

20. Percy, SHC 44.12.

21. O'Gorman, "Confessing the Horrors," 136.

When Lancelot first describes himself to his interlocutor, Percival, he begins with who he was before he committed his crimes. In his portrayal, Lancelot sounds like an average, middle-class Southerner:

> Gentleman and even bit of a scholar (Civil War, of course), married to a beautiful rich loving (I thought) wife, and father (I thought) to a lovely little girl; a moderate reader, moderate liberal, moderate drinker (I thought), moderate music lover, moderate hunter and fisherman, and past president of the United Way. (*Lancelot* 24)

The parenthetical statements "I thought" indicate the distance between the way Lancelot perceived his life before the discovery of his wife's unfaithfulness and the awakening that he undergoes afterward. By repeating the adjective "moderate" five times, Lancelot underscores the monotony of his life at the time. Here the passage appears monologic, but, as in *Notes,* there are two narrators—the past and present self.

Like the Underground Man who looked back on his former life, Lancelot recognizes that his previous self was not as happy as he seemed. He admits to Percival that he read Raymond Chandler novels frequently because it was his only happiness: "The only way I could stand my life in Louisiana where I had everything, was to read about crummy lonesome Los Angeles in the 1930s" (*Lancelot* 25). His happiness was superficial, a disguise even from himself of his own empty existence. The conclusion of *Notes from Underground* clarifies Lancelot's state. In a section underlined by Percy, the Underground Man strikes out at his readers for living only "halfway" or moderately living: "We regard real 'living life' almost as labor, almost as service, and we all agree in ourselves that it's better from a book" (*Notes* 129). Rather than live with our freedom, according to the Underground Man, we choose to depend on the realities created in fiction. Earlier in the narrative, the Underground Man professes that his earlier self dreamed of living out romantic fictions, which may have been drawn from Lermontov's *A Hero of Our Time* or Chateaubriand's *René,* solitary heroes with adventurous lives. O'Gorman indicates an American complement to these fantasies—that of the lone frontiersman like Daniel Boone or the solitary investigator of Lancelot's Chandler novels.[22] Dostoevsky's and Percy's antiheroes prefer to live vicariously through these literary characters and their exciting worlds, choosing fantasy living to real life.

Lancelot shares more than the Underground Man's disenchanted view of life; he is also as apathetic and noncommittal as his nineteenth-century counterpart. In Percy's notes for future novels, he references a passage from *Notes*

---

22. Percy, SHC 275.3.

from Underground in which the narrator describes himself as a "sluggard," an apt description of Lancelot. Percy titles the page in all capital letters "NOTES FROM UNDERGROUND" and stars a passage from page 141 of his text:

> Question: what is he? Answer: a sluggard; how very pleasant it would have been to hear that of oneself! It would mean . . . that there was something to say about me. 'Sluggard'—why, it is a calling and a vocation, it is a career.[23]

Next to this quote Percy boxes the word "USE" as though intending either to create a figure that is this self-titled "sluggard" or to mimic this quote stylistically or thematically. Lancelot fits the description of a "sluggard": he has retreated to his pigeonnier, withdrawing from the bed of his wife, his responsibility to his family, and his role as master of his ancestral home. As Lancelot confesses to Percival, "Do you know what happened to me during the past twenty years? A gradual, ever so gradual, slipping away of my life into a kind of dream state in which finally I could not be sure anything was happening at all" (*Lancelot* 57). Considering himself incapable of or uninterested in action, Lancelot is a "sluggard." The line suggests Percy's own acedia, which he confessed in his letters of the period.

Within Lancelot's confession, Percy alludes to the quote from *Notes from Underground*: "Categories made sense—now it is impossible to complete the sentence: I am a—what?" (*Lancelot* 58). Syntactically, the phrases reflect one another, though Lancelot is speaking about political alliances. In Percy's 1973 introduction to William Alexander Percy's *Lanterns on the Levee*, which he published concurrent with his writing of *Lancelot*, he explains how "current categories and names, liberal and conservative are all past thinking of" (*Signposts* 58). The old ideological labels have lost their meanings. Just as the Underground Man pleads for a self-label, so Lancelot appeals to Percival for a meaningful category. While these rants may appear harmless, Lancelot carries his lethargy and world-weariness to another level. Both characters mistakenly categorize other people, but in Lancelot's case, this stance toward human beings leads to objectification and then to murder.

SUPERSEDING THE VIOLENCE OF *CRIME AND PUNISHMENT*

Of all the violence in Dostoevsky's novels, his most famous murderer is probably that of Rodion Romanovich Raskolnikov, the young philosopher who

---

23. *Correspondence*, 162.

kills a pawnbroker to prove his nihilism. Percy regarded this murder, like the other violence in Dostoevsky, as instances of evil at work. Around the time Percy began writing *Lancelot* in 1972, he wrote a brief summary of *Lancelot*'s plot that included a parenthetical reference to Dostoevsky: "a horrendous crime committed by a fellow who doesn't believe in sin (just re-read *Crime and Punishment* for edification)."[24] Moreover on the first page of his notes for *Lancelot,* Percy jots down, "~Raskolnikov,"[25] reflecting his intention to create a similar protagonist. The two novels are undeniably similar. Joseph Schwartz traces several connections between the two protagonists:

> We have the same prison window through which Lance and Raskolnikov view the outside world, the similarity of Sonya and Anna, the sacramental and Eucharistic images that haunt both heroes in spite of the terrible "dream" of reality both have.[26]

The likeness between the two characters goes far beyond what Schwartz observes, and the contrast indicts the twentieth century as a godless society.

First the protagonists appear similar because of their animal-like descriptions. In the opening of *Crime and Punishment,* Dostoevsky writes, "[Raskolnikov] had decidedly withdrawn from everyone, like a turtle into its shell. . . . This happens with certain monomaniacs when they concentrate too hard on one thing" (28).[27] Dostoevsky here connects Raskolnikov's hermit living with a "turtle," emphasizing the animal nature and thus his hero's dehumanization. Of course the "one thing" that concerns Raskolnikov is the crime he is going to commit, whereas for Lancelot it is his wife's unfaithfulness. Following his discovery of her adultery, Lancelot also withdraws, like a turtle, and becomes less of a husband and father than he already was, even less of a person. Confining himself to his pigeonnier, Lancelot wonders, "Why is it that shelters for animals now seem more habitable than ordinary houses?" (*Lancelot* 252). Dostoevsky's description of Raskolnikov clarifies Lancelot's choice to withdraw from his human home.

Moreover both characters undertake theoretical searches for evil, which lead them to commit murder. Neither murderer kills in a rage or fury, rather each plots in cold blood and then, paradoxically, carries out the act almost absentmindedly. In *Crime and Punishment,* Dostoevsky describes Raskolnikov

---

24. Percy, SHC 70.1.
25. Schwartz, "Will Barrett Redux?," 46.
26. Ibid.
27. Even in *The Brothers Karamazov,* Dostoevsky foretells this increasing coldness, when the prosecutor asserts, "What's so horrible [is] that such dark deeds have ceased to horrify us" (659).

as acting "mechanically": "He took the axe all the way out, swung it with both hands, scarcely aware of himself, and almost without effort, almost mechanically, brought the butt-end down on her head" (76). The woman has become merely a head that Raskolnikov must cut through. Lancelot recalls his first murder rather absentmindedly: "I was cutting his throat, I think. No, I'm sure" (*Lancelot* 242). Again the victim has become simply a body part in relation to the murderer's action. The portrayal of the murders conveys how the murderers have objectified their victims.

Yet there is a crucial difference between Raskolnikov's murder of Alyona and Lizaveta and Lancelot's murders of his wife and houseguests. In order for Percy to horrify jaded twentieth-century readers, Percy knew that he had to make the murder colder, more violent, and more despicable. Lancelot outdoes Raskolnikov because, unlike his Russian predecessor, he shows no guilt or despair following his violent deeds. While the senseless killing of Alyona and Lizaveta should scandalize any reader, Percy realized that not even the combination of sexual violence, bloodbath, and arson would disturb his twentieth-century readers.[28] Indeed Lancelot expresses the twentieth-century immunity to horror when he asks Percival, "When was the last time you saw anybody horrified?" (*Lancelot* 23). Following Percy's note that Lancelot will resemble Raskolnikov, he writes, "Unlike because no sorrow—cold."[29] Whereas Raskolnikov goes mad with guilt, Lancelot feels nothing, either in the moment or after. As Lancelot slits the throat of his wife's lover, he recalls "casting about for the feeling and not finding one" (242). He informs Percival, "The truth is that during all the terrible events that night at Belle Isle, I felt nothing at all. Nothing good, nothing bad, not even a sense of discovery. I feel nothing now except a certain coldness" (253).[30] This "cold" feeling, which Lancelot references several times, alludes to St. Augustine's definition of evil as *privatio boni* or the absence of good.[31] Because Lancelot cannot understand the meaning of this nothingness, he concludes, "There is no unholy grail" (ibid.). Percy had brainstormed such a story as early as 1951; he records in his notes the idea of "The Young Man in search of evil. . . . But the answer always faith as an answer. The search fails."[32] Since its inception, Lancelot's quest for evil is destined not to succeed because, for Percy, evil is nothingness.

---

28. Percy, SHC 70.1.
29. Percy handwrote this paragraph as an insert into the later manuscripts (Ibid. 79.239).
30. On the page before Lancelot's description of the cold, he mentions recently reading Augustine's *City of God*.
31. Percy, SHC 164.22.
32. Dowie, "Lancelot and the Search for Sin," 255.

Percy not only cast Lancelot colder than Raskolnikov; Percy also made the universe itself amoral. Just as Lancelot is apathetic about his crimes, his society casts no blame on him for committing them. Rather than calling his acts evil, people have labeled them "aberrant behavior" (*Lancelot* 3). Lancelot himself boasts, "Everyone's either wonderful or sick and nothing is evil" (138). The contrast between Dostoevsky's and Percy's novels emphasizes the drastic changes that had taken place in the hundred years that separated them. In his article "Lancelot and the Search for Sin," William J. Dowie writes, "Lancelot's story then is one of crime and no punishment. . . . Dostoevsky at least gave Raskolnikov, who also was judged temporarily insane, eight years in Siberia. . . . Not only is Lancelot unable to hold himself responsible for his actions but society is equally impotent to deal satisfactorily with human evil."[33] The different endings of the two novels indict the twentieth-century readers, for Lancelot's society neither recognizes his crime nor demands punishment, and even the movement toward redemption is rather vague.

The redemption in *Crime and Punishment* occurs through the conduit of Sonya. Although Schwarz connects Dostoevsky's Sonya and Percy's Anna, the link actually reveals greater contrast. Sonya is Dostoevsky's archetypal prostitute with a heart of gold who compels Raskolnikov to confess and repent; her love for him transforms him into a better man. In contrast, Anna, who resides in an adjoining cell to Lancelot, has been traumatized into silence by being gang-raped. Without consulting her, Lancelot absorbs her into his future plans: "I want to go with her, a mute, psychotic, totally ravaged and defiled woman, take her to a little cottage . . . and there take care of her" (*Lancelot* 62–63). He considers Anna purged, a "new Virgin" because she has been violated: "Her ordeal has made her like a ten-year-old" (159). In a parallel fashion to those who raped her, Lancelot objectifies this woman. For Lancelot a woman may either "be a lady or a whore" (179). With her dying breath, his wife Margot informs Lancelot that he prescribed an either-or classification to her life that did not fit: "With you I had to be either—or—but never a—uh—woman" (245). A woman like Sonya from *Crime and Punishment* defies Lancelot's either-or dichotomy, for she is both a saint and a prostitute. Because Lancelot cannot see women—or men—as holistic persons, he misses his opportunity to love Anna as she is. Lancelot fails to find redemption where Raskolnikov did.

In further contrast to Dostoevsky's novels, *Lancelot* is much more explicit in its use of sex. In his notes on Dostoevsky, Percy questions, "Would D have

---

33. Percy, SHC 449.8.

written more explicit sexual scene if he were truly modern?"[34] Then he asterisks and underlines the phrase "Sexuality of Notes," in reference to *Notes from Underground,* as though saving the topic for class conversation. In his manuscript notes, Percy writes in German "the only thing is sex,"[35] foreshadowing Lancelot's pronouncement, "The secret of life is violence and rape, and its gospel is pornography" (*Lancelot* 224). John Desmond documents a letter in which Percy announces the theme of *Lancelot* as "the incapacity of the postmodern consciousness to deal with sexuality."[36]

Percy demolishes a middle ground between the Catholic doctrine of sexual intercourse as a sacramental act committed within a marriage and that of debauchery. After Lancelot discovers that his wife has cheated on him, he determines to find proof that she is perpetually committing adultery in his home, only to uncover that his daughter Lucy is also being seduced into sexual immorality by their celebrity guests. At one point, in a side note, Lancelot remarks that his son is a homosexual, as though adding to the list of sexual deviations. The combination of the evidence, including Anna's story of gang-rape, has led him to conclude that man is nothing more than "a walking genital" (*Lancelot* 223) and that "man's happiness lies for men in practicing violence upon women and that woman's happiness lies in submitting to it" (224). To prove his theory, Lancelot takes advantage of Raine, one of the actors visiting his home, who is under the influence of drugs: in a fairly graphic scene, he takes her from behind to emphasize his power over her.

Not only is sex in *Lancelot* another form of violence but it also underscores the cold complacency of society. In a negative review of *Lancelot,* Brainard Cheney, whose review of *The Moviegoer* Percy applauded, accused Percy of writing pornography. In response to Cheney, Percy writes:

> If you think I write pornography—as astute as you are—and as vulnerable as I (or any serious writer) is—you may be right, and if you are right, that is a serious matter. You are imputing to me an offense for which I must take responsibility. The treatment of sex in a novel is always a difficult matter ... always caught between the requirements of honesty and giving scandal—Pornography is scandal in my book.[37]

---

34. Because of Percy's handwriting, the spelling of "more" and "modern" is questionable.
35. Percy, SHC 70.6.
36. Quoted in Desmond, "Demonic Self," 90.
37. Letter to Cheney, 1977. Vanderbilt University, Special Collections. Cheney Papers. Box 14. Folder 21.

Percy admits in this letter that he scandalizes readers with his pornographic images, as much as with his accounts of violence, because he believes horrifying readers is necessary to shake them out of complacency. When Percy queries, in his introduction to *Lanterns on the Levee*, whether his Uncle Will would have been shocked at the "sexual revolution" of the 1970s, he concludes that only the "complacency" would have unnerved him (*Signposts* 58). It is this complacency that Percy confronts with his graphic sex scenes.

Percy does not "outdostoevsky" Dostoevsky intentionally, but the comparison with *Crime and Punishment* should reveal how he supersedes him in the depictions of evil. He does so not to glory in the darkness but to decry it so loudly that his readers beg for the light again. Instead of creating an Underground Man who burrows in his cell or a philosophic nihilist who in the end repents his grievous acts, Percy combines the two in Lancelot and thus shows the evil at the heart of these antiheroes.

THE DARKNESS AND THE LIGHT FROM *THE BROTHERS KARAMAZOV*

If Dostoevsky ever accomplishes both darkness and light in one of his novels, it is in *The Brothers Karamazov* where the Grand Inquisitor rants about his ideology only to receive the kiss from Christ. In Dostoevsky's final novel, the "big one" as Percy saw it, he shows evil, suffering, and death, and counters it with goodness, forbearance, and resurrection. When Percy subconsciously echoes the Grand Inquisitor, he follows suit by invoking as well Dostoevsky's positive "Hurrah." Thus Lancelot outdoes the former in his evil machinations, only to hear the "Yes" of faith from Percival's lips.[38]

In a scene that many have been proposed as the apex of *The Brothers Karamazov*, Ivan Karamazov recites a poem that he has written entitled "The Legend of the Grand Inquisitor" to his brother Alyosha. Not only does the poem resemble *Lancelot* in its setting but also it establishes similar arguments. In "Fyodor Dostoevsky, Walker Percy, and the Demonic Self," John Desmond has suggested similarities between Ivan and Lancelot as well as Alyosha and Percival.[39] Ivan and Lancelot have both become doubters and cynics, though Ivan has yet to commit murder, and Alyosha and Percival are associated with religious orders, though at different stages of loyalty. When Alyosha sits down

---

38. John Desmond has argued that the "most pervasive influence and parallels" between Dostoevsky and Walker Percy occur "between *Lancelot* and *The Brothers Karamazov*" ("Demonic Self," 89).

39. Ibid.

to dine with his brother in the tavern, Ivan emphasizes their history together, "I remember everything, Alyosha" (*Brothers Karamazov* 210), and he proceeds to give evidence by ordering Alyosha's favorite, cherry jam. Similarly Lancelot proves his knowledge of Percival by listing the history of his nicknames, finishing in summary, "I remember a great deal about you" (*Lancelot* 10). However, Lancelot differs from his literary precursor by his age; whereas Ivan retains a hope and romantic idealism for life, Lancelot recalls this stage in his life with longing. In a way, Lancelot is Ivan twenty years later.

Moreover Ivan constructs his argument in "The Grand Inquisitor" as a dissent on behalf of the suffering in the world, primarily that of abused children. According to Ivan, God has constructed the world incorrectly, and he uses examples of tortured children to argue its unjust disharmony. For Ivan, though God may bring all into accord in some unverifiable afterlife, this future promise does not satisfy his present desire for justice. He exclaims, "I can't accept that harmony. And while I'm on earth, I make haste to take my own measures" (*Brothers Karamazov* 225). In this pronouncement, Ivan chooses his own way over God's way. Here Ivan foreshadows Lancelot. However, as Desmond indicates, "Unlike Ivan, Lance is not even theoretically concerned with suffering children."[40] While Lancelot presents a comparable solution to the problem of the world, namely his ability, like Ivan's, to correct the world himself, it is not suffering that he derides but immorality. He rejects the "whoredom" of women and the lack of chivalry among men (*Lancelot* 158). Echoing Ivan, Lancelot asserts, "I cannot tolerate this age" (157). Lancelot believes that he is not alone in this rebellion, and that millions will join him: "We shall not wait for [the world] to fester and rot any longer. We will kill it" (160). The "measures" that Ivan proposed to take are being fantasized by Lancelot. Yet whereas Ivan only longed to murder his depraved father, Lancelot picks up a Bowie knife.

In *The Brothers Karamazov*, Ivan's protest is religious: through the voice of his Inquisitor, Ivan derides Christ for not making the world better. While the dialogues in "The Grand Inquisitor" and *Lancelot* both occur in a prison cell, in Ivan's poem, Christ has been imprisoned. The Grand Inquisitor has arrested Christ with the intent to kill him and quietly dispose of him because he fears that the return of Christ will upset the world that he himself has redesigned. According to the Inquisitor, human beings are unhappy because they are too free. Their freedom makes them miserable. To save them from themselves, the Inquisitor has stepped in as their god and removed their freedom. He considers himself a martyr for the happiness of others. Although he once believed in the reality of Christianity, he "awakened and would not serve madness. [He]

---

40. Ibid., 101.

turned back and joined the ranks of those *who have corrected Thy* [Christ's] *work*" (*Brothers Karamazov* 240, emphasis original). Because Christ did not fulfill his promise—as the Inquisitor views it—to make the world good and human beings happy, the Inquisitor has deemed himself the better "Christ." The Inquisitor's logic will reappear in Lancelot's argument.

However, the freedom offered in the Inquisitor's world is a lie: it is slavery and death. Only the day before Christ's arrival, the Inquisitor has burned a hundred so-called heretics. The violence that accompanies the Inquisitor's reign is inevitable, as Ivan admits. Historically those groups that attempt to remake the world have begun with multiple murders: the Communists in Russia and the Fascists in Germany being only two examples. Percy invokes the Southern counterpart to these evil powers: in the South, the KKK tried to purify their societies by lynching and murdering Black Americans. Although Ivan is not proposing murder any more than those other idealist groups did, it is the logical outcome of his ideology.

In response to the recitation of "The Grand Inquisitor," Alyosha inquires how his brother will endure "such a hell" in his heart and head (*Brothers Karamazov* 243). Albert Camus rephrases the question in *The Rebel*—of which Percy owned two copies, "Can one live and stand one's ground in a state of rebellion?"[41] If Ivan's argument is taken to the extreme, he must conclude, as he has written elsewhere, "Everything is permitted" (*Brothers Karamazov* 244). Camus summarizes the argument thus: "As God and immortality do not exist, the new man is permitted to become God [which means] recognizing everything is permitted and refusing to recognize any other law but one's own."[42] In other words, the choice between God and the self is a false one because there is no self. Thus each person is his or her own god. And as god of his or her own universe, all is allowable—including the murder of Ivan's father or Lancelot's wife. According to Camus, "Everything is permitted and centuries of crime are prepared in that cataclysmic moment."[43] The crimes that Camus references include the Russian Revolution, the Nazi regime, the start of the Ku Klux Klan, and a number of other horrors in which the logic of the autonomous, all-powerful self prevails.

Across a majority of *Lancelot*'s manuscript, Percy has doodled swastikas, tying them in with its Southern foil: "Nazis+KKK."[44] In *The Fourth Ghost*, Robert Brinkmeyer claims, "For Percy, the specter of Nazi Germany provided, in the tumultuous 1970s, a means to interrogate the extremes to which south-

---

41. Camus, *Rebel*, 56.
42. Ibid.
43. Ibid., 59.
44. Percy, SHC 79.183.

ern antimodernism might extend."[45] Lancelot calls his new world or new age the "Third Revolution" but insists that the Nazis and Ku Klux Klan should not be associated with his plan: "Don't confuse it with the Nazis. . . . Don't confuse it with the Klan" (*Lancelot* 156). Rather, Lancelot's revolution will not be concerned with race or politics but with morality and dignity: he will replace all governments and religions and societies with "that stern rectitude valued by the new breed and marked by the violence which will attend its breach" (158). He is instituting an order of Stoic virtue, though it may be tainted with violence and death. Yet the mere protest that his new world should not be associated with these forerunners belies their connection.

Whereas Ivan disguised his plan for a new world under the dress of the church, Lancelot devises his new world as an answer to the failure of Christianity. He confesses to Percival, "I might have tolerated you and your Catholic Church, and even joined it, if you had remained true to yourself. Now you're part of the age" (*Lancelot* 157). Instead of using the Church as a front, Lancelot proposes a return to virtuous paganism. He asks Percival, "Which is a better world, this . . . fornicating Happyland U.S.A. or a Roman legion under Marcus Aurelius Antonius?" (158, obscenities omitted). In Percy's notes, he outlines his thesis: "*Our way didn't work, Good American class didn't work* . . . return to heroic paganism when disillusionment with old way."[46] Perhaps Percy had his Uncle Will in mind while writing. William Alexander Percy's memoir has been accused of Fascist and racist undertones.[47] In *Lanterns* Will Percy uplifts his ancestors for their Stoic virtues. In his chapter on *Lancelot*, Allen describes

---

45. Brinkmeyer, *Fourth Ghost*, 312.
46. Percy, SHC 70.9. Both in his notes and correspondence, Percy connects this idea with Ulysses. When Percy began writing *Lancelot*, he told Foote (Jul. 4, 1973) that his antihero would be "a noble murderer like Ulysses" (*Correspondence*, 176). However, Lancelot shares more in common with the Ulysses of Dante than that of Homer or Virgil. In Dante's retelling of Ulysses's story, the great hero has spent years at home but has grown bored of his life with his wife, son, and father. Instead he desires to "explore the world, and search the ways of life, / Man's evil and his virtue" (1.xxvi.97–98). Not only would Lancelot empathize with Ulysses's domestic malaise but also he would be inspired by his search for "evil" as well as for "virtue." In Alfred Lord Tennyson's poem "Ulysses," he depicts the man as an "idle king" (1) stuck with "an aged wife" (3), restless and longing to travel again. Through indirect discourse, Ulysses exclaims, "How dull it is to pause, to make an end / To rust unburnished, not to shine in use!" (22–23). In words that sound noble instead of sinful, he expresses his "desire / To follow knowledge . . . / Beyond the utmost bound of human thought" (30–32). Yet Ulysses's yearning here is for knowledge that is not his; he wants to surpass the limits of human understanding. Such a desire would be considered sinful by poets like Dante because he would equate it with the satanic impulse to be like God. In *Inferno*, Dante has cast Ulysses in the lower realms of hell among the fraudulent. Despite Ulysses's miserable ending, Lancelot would have prized him as Tennyson does, uplifting the noble man's courage to seek a better world.
47. Brinkmeyer, *Fourth Ghost*, 111–17.

how Percy "literally puts out the lanterns on the levee," lanterns that he deems to be Will Percy's "symbol of man's ability to confront the terrors of nature and to defeat them."[48] The problem with Will Percy's proposal is one Dostoevsky foretells of in "The Grand Inquisitor" and Walker Percy showcases in *Lancelot*: human beings cannot triumph over evil in the world because they themselves are the problem.

The choice between God and the self, in reality, is a choice between God and the devil. In Flannery O'Connor's novel *The Violent Bear It Away*, a devil whispers in the protagonist's ear, "It ain't the Jesus or the devil. It's Jesus or you" (*Collected Works* 354).[49] In the hopes of convincing the young boy that devils don't exist, the devil replaces the alternative to Jesus' authority with self-authority. However, in essence, the devil conflates the two alternatives. When a person assumes to be a law unto herself, she imitates the demonic. In *I See Satan Fall Like Lightning*, literary critic René Girard declares, "If we don't see that the choice is inevitable between two supreme models, God and the devil, then we have already chosen the devil and his mimetic violence."[50] Both "The Grand Inquisitor" and *Lancelot* reveal how the choice for the self over God will promote demonic violence.

In "The Grand Inquisitor" Ivan recasts Christ's victory over Satan's temptation in the desert as the great mistake that Christ made. For the Grand Inquisitor, Satan offered human beings happiness, which Christ hindered: "[If] there has ever been on earth a real stupendous miracle, it took place on that day, on the day of the three temptations" (*Brothers Karamazov* 232). The Inquisitor maintains that the answer to all of mankind's problems lies in Satan's questions. Thus the Inquisitor rejects Christ and chooses Satan instead. In imitation of his new god, the Inquisitor masquerades as a religious authority who controls his flock of sheep, only burning a hundred or so of them when necessary for keeping order.

Near the conclusion of his narrative, like the Grand Inquisitor before him, Lancelot refers to the demonic temptation of Jesus in the desert, as recorded in the gospels.[51] He confronts Percival, "You act as though I were Satan showing you the kingdoms of the world from the pinnacle of the temple" (*Lancelot* 254). Lancelot correctly views himself through Percival's eyes. In *The Brothers Karamazov*, Ivan is visited by a devil. Although he proposes, via the Inquisitor, to follow Satan, Ivan actually treats his demonic nightmare quite contemptuously. When the devil visits him, Ivan, in a fury, throws a glass at him, at

---

48. Allen, *Southern Wayfarer*, 109, 125.
49. *Collected Works* by Flannery O'Connor will be cited in text throughout the book.
50. Girard, *I See Satan Fall Like Lightning*, 42.
51. Matthew 4:1–11, Mark 1:12–13, Luke 4:1–13, New International Version.

which the demon then laughs and accuses Ivan of imitating Martin Luther. The connection between the Reformer and Ivan offers some hope that he has not become completely possessed. In contrast to Ivan's vehement encounter, Lancelot wishes for the reality of the devil: "Do you think I wouldn't be pleased to meet the devil? Ha, I'd shake his hand like a long-lost friend" (139). In this way, Lancelot seems as demon-possessed as the Grand Inquisitor.

Ultimately by trying to outdo the evil in Dostoevsky's fiction, Percy created a character who is little more than the devil himself. When Lancelot is expelled from his home during the explosion at Belle Isle, he describes himself "wheeling slowly up into the night like Lucifer blown out of hell, great wings spread against the starlight" (*Lancelot* 246). In his quest for evil, Lancelot has become more and more like the devil. Throughout the story, Lancelot has lamented not only the rejection of God but also the absence of Satan. In the context of his quest for evil, Lancelot pursues the question, "God may be absent, but what if one should find the devil?" (139). In *The Brothers Karamazov*, the devil inquires of Ivan, "Does proving there's a devil prove that there's a God?" (603). Though the devil mocks the logic of this question, the answer appears to be "yes." According to Lancelot, "If there is such a thing as sin, evil, a malignant force, there must be a God!" (*Lancelot* 52). In Percy's notes on Dostoevsky, he corroborates his antihero's logic:

> By appealing to the irrational in man, the spiteful, even the demonic D[ostoevsky] is almost saying this: man is not merely an organism not because he is made in image of God and has a soul—but because he is capable of acting like the devil himself.[52]

If a human being is capable of "acting like the devil," as Lancelot does in Percy's fourth novel, he inversely proves that goodness exists as an alternative. These thoughts are deeply rooted in an Augustinian definition of evil. As previously mentioned, according to Augustine, evil is a perversion of the good and therefore cannot exist without it. Thus the "existence" of evil proves the reality of good.

CONCLUSION

Both Ivan and Lancelot relate their stories to their priestly interlocutors because they want a different answer than the ones they have proposed. Before Ivan begins his confession to Alyosha, he admits, "Perhaps I want to be healed

---

52. Percy, SHC 450.9.

by you," and he smiles "like a gentle child" (*Brothers Karamazov* 217). There is no trace of cynicism or irony here, for Ivan is telling the truth. He desires for his brother to refute his argument and to offer him another way. The Underground Man had made this same solicitation of his reader: "Destroy my desires, wipe out my ideals, show me something better, and I will follow you" (*Notes* 30). Locked in his either-or dialectic, the Underground Man pleads for a *tertium quid*, a third option that is neither the cold calculating rationalism nor the fervent unrealistic romanticism. Similarly, Ivan implies a desire for more than the dialectical either-or that he himself constructs. Although Ivan concludes his poem, "*Dixi*," which means, "I have spoken," he adds an epilogue that reveals his desire for Christ to have the last "word" (*Brothers Karamazov* 241). He appends his argument with a scene in which the Inquisitor "longed for Him to say something," a longing that Ivan shares (243). Rather than speak, Christ kisses the old man's lips before he departs. Alyosha, too, then kisses Ivan, proving his love for his brother, despite the latter's fallacious ideology. When they part, Ivan promises that he will seek out Alyosha again "to have one more talk" (244). For Ivan the argument is not finished.

The conclusion of *Lancelot* correlates with "The Grand Inquisitor" because here, too, the "silent Christ" figure, Percival, receives the last word. Throughout the dialogue, Lancelot has interchanged "Christ" and "Jesus" with "Percival": "Christ, what were we talking about? Oh yes, Percival, you wanted to know what happened? Jesus, what difference does it make?" (*Lancelot* 163). Although Percy disguises these moments as profanity, he intends the names to suggest Percival's role in relation to Lancelot. The name interchange alludes to "The Grand Inquisitor": "You are silent. Christ. . . ." (106). In her article on the connection between "The Grand Inquisitor" and *Lancelot*, Linda Whitney Hobson remarks, "In this subtle way, even the mechanics of the text allude to Dostoevsky's parable."[53] Moreover she points out how the silence of Percival (except in his dozen words at the conclusion) imitates that of Christ in Ivan's poem. When Lancelot finishes his story, he repeats Ivan's words, "I've finished" (257). However he no longer controls the narrative. Rather, he asks questions and waits for the answer: "Is there anything you wish to tell me before I leave?" (ibid.). Like Alyosha, Percival offers a contrary answer to his friend's protest.

For Percival, Lancelot's narrative has demonstrated the reality of sin, evil, and the demonic, and thus, inversely, the reality of the God that he previously doubted. Lancelot observes that his friend has changed while listening to his

---

53. In a letter dated Sept. 25, 1976, Foote tells Percy that he hopes to accomplish this feat in his next novel (*Correspondence*, 219). Percy had already completed *Lancelot*; Hobson, "'The Grand Inquisitor' and *Lancelot*," 129.

story: he notices that Percival has again donned his priestly garments, and he even spied him praying in the cemetery. Through Lancelot, the reader hears of Percival's plans to "take a little church in Alabama [where he will] preach the gospel, turn bread into flesh, forgive the sins of Buick dealers, administer communion to suburban housewives" (*Lancelot* 256). In contrast to Lancelot's abstract blueprint to save the world, Percival will live in the concrete world and work among specific human beings. Like Father Zosima or Alyosha in *The Brothers Karamazov*, Percival does not offer an argument to counter Lancelot's conclusions. Instead Percy describes what his life will look like. The "yes" at the conclusion of *Lancelot* is like the kiss after Ivan's recitation of "The Grand Inquisitor"; it is an expression of love that cannot be debated. As in *The Brothers Karamazov*, so in *Lancelot*: there is another talk to come.

CHAPTER 6

Echoed Prophecies in *The Second Coming* and *The Thanatos Syndrome*

VERY LITTLE of *The Second Coming*, Walker Percy's fifth novel, alludes to Dostoevsky, so it would be disadvantageous to stretch my argument to analyze this text in the same way that I have done to Percy's previous works. However, Percy claimed that his final novel, *The Thanatos Syndrome*, was "Dostoyevsky's idea."[1] That Dostoevsky affected every one of Percy's novels before *The Second Coming* and that the great Russian's ideology lay at the core of Percy's final novel without bearing any significance for his fifth book seems unlikely. What becomes clear when a reader ties the two novels together is that the fifth novel makes ready the way for the sixth; the underlying argument of *The Second Coming* comes to fulfillment in *The Thanatos Syndrome*. Thus, "Dostoyevsky's idea" motivates both novels in different ways.

Percy faces at least two criticisms as a novelist: that his works are repetitive and that they are didactic, more philosophical than artistic. His last two novels bear the brunt of those critiques. His biographer Jay Tolson accuses Percy of showing "signs of slippage" in these sequels.[2] As an old man with strengthened religious devotion, some say, he wrote novels that read more like undercover ideological pamphlets. Dostoevsky encountered similar charges in

---

1. Percy, *More Conversations*, 203.
2. Tolson, *Pilgrim in the Ruins*, 452.

his lifetime, although critics, such as Mikhail Bakhtin, have attempted to show how his polyphonic style subverts his ideological positions. "It is clear," Kieran Quinlan claims, "that Percy also falls into the camp of those who, according to Bakhtin, show 'the tendency to monologize Dostoevsky's novel,' which 'remains to this day so strong.'"[3] For Quinlan, Percy not only reads Dostoevsky as an ideologue but also writes as one. From this perspective, Percy reduces Dostoevsky's work to single issue positions, and in his own fiction, writes under the authoritarian restrictions of his Catholic faith. Thus, to Quinlan and likeminded critics, *The Second Coming* and *The Thanatos Syndrome* merely repeat themes of the past—Bill Barrett and Tom More continue their searches—and without the polyphony or artistry of Dostoevsky.

To counter these assumptions about *The Second Coming* and *The Thanatos Syndrome,* I consider Percy's task in light of Dostoevsky's role as an artist. From Dostoevsky, Percy learned that an artist continually explores the same ground, asks the big questions, and never makes authoritative pronouncements. He saw that Dostoevsky considered writing as a form of discovery. In his notebooks for his fiction,[4] Dostoevsky outlines characters and themes that repeatedly manifest in different forms throughout his novels. Prince Myshkin, for instance, began as a Christ figure, the predecessor of Alyosha Karamazov, but also morphed into sketches for an anti-Christ figure, the starting place for Stavrogin's character.[5] Such allowance for his characters' freedom exhibits Dostoevsky's openness in his writing to discovery. According to René Girard, to see Dostoevsky this way is to understand what it means to be a novelist. One should not divide the thinker from the writer. "For Dostoevsky writing is a means of knowing, an instrument of exploration," Girard writes. "To say this is to say again that Dostoevsky is essentially a novelist."[6] Percy too fits this definition of novelist, one who repeats his ideas in writing because each novel is, as Percy puts it, "an adventure in discovering."[7]

Moreover, Percy's disposition toward discovery should clear Percy's name from any indictments that he is a rabid ideologue. After all, ideologues know all the answers, whereas Percy, like Dostoevsky, sought for answers. They considered novel writing to be a means for asking questions. In an essay on Her-

---

3. Quinlan, *Last Catholic,* 98. Quinlan quotes Bakhtin's *Problems of Dostoevsky's Poetics,* which refers in this instance to *The Brothers Karamazov.*

4. Percy did not have access to Dostoevsky's notebooks, but he read Frank's *Seeds of Revolt,* numerous introductions to Dostoevsky's works about Dostoevsky's process, as well Steiner's *Tolstoy or Dostoevsky* and other critiques of Dostoevsky.

5. George Steiner assesses the notebooks for the sources of Dostoevsky's major characters in *Tolstoy or Dostoevsky.* See for example pages 179 and 292.

6. Girard, *Resurrection,* 48.

7. Percy, *More Conversations,* 16.

man Melville that Percy penned in 1983 (in between *The Second Coming* and *The Thanatos Syndrome*), he praises Dostoevsky for not being "afraid to deal with ultimate questions" (*Signposts* 200). In this same essay, Percy implies that he himself is in conversation with Dostoevsky, writing to him, for him, against him.[8] Percy sees all writers in conversation with one another, what he calls "the ineffable sociability in writing. Intertextuality, if you please" (199). Although he speaks directly about Melville's fictional responses to Hawthorne's fiction, Percy concludes that all writers converse with another through their fiction. If Percy is, in fact, writing to other writers, whether Dostoevsky or Kierkegaard, Camus or Dante, his writing cannot be monologic.

For both Percy and Dostoevsky, novels are not only ways of exploring ultimate questions in conversation with readers and previous writers but they also are stories with ethical significance and possibilities for transformation. By retelling Dostoevsky's stories and responding to his ideas, Percy emphasizes his belief in the moral import of stories. Author of *Retelling/Rereading: The Fate of Storytelling in Modern Times*, Karl Kroebe, explains that such a viewpoint only appears countercultural in a modern or postmodern setting. Kroebe defends the continual retelling of story as a method to "preserve ideas, beliefs, and convictions without permitting them to harden into abstract dogma."[9] Although Dostoevsky and Percy write to investigate the questions of their faith, their methods defy dogmatism. In opposition to those, like Quinlan, who blame Percy of subsuming his stories under the weight of theology, the method of narrative itself engages "uncertainties and confusion of contingent circumstance," in Kroebe's words, and "allows us to test our ethical principles in our imaginations."[10] Such conceptions of novels and novel writing counter Dostoevsky's and Percy's less empathetic critics.

Finally, Percy's two last novels emphasize the difference between a genius and an apostle, a distinction that affected Percy's conversion to Catholicism and that he cites numerous times throughout his fiction as necessary to understanding his role as a writer. Percy claims that Kierkegaard's essay "The Difference between a Genius and an Apostle" is the "most important single piece that Kierkegaard wrote" and "was tremendously important" to him.[11] Kierkegaard argues that the genius and apostle occupy two separate spheres: the former speaks to the immanent world whereas the latter prophesies to the

---

8. I don't think it's a stretch to take Percy's claim and fill in the blank with Dostoevsky: "No matter what the writer may say, the work is always written to someone, for someone, against someone" (*Signposts*, 199).
9. Kroebe, *Retelling/Rereading*, 9.
10. Ibid.
11. Percy, *Conversations*, 113.

transcendent. While the genius might say something profound, it will ultimately be exceeded and displaced by subsequent generations. However, the apostle pronounces eternal dicta. The primary difference lies in the source of authority. Only the apostle speaks on behalf of the divine. Whatever s/he says bears the weight of permanent truth. Thus St. Paul is qualitatively different from Shakespeare. And if what St. Paul says is true, then woe to the reader who does not adhere to his claims. For Percy, this essay revealed the divine authority and truth behind the words of the Gospels. It also took the burden off his shoulders as an artist to ever say anything authoritatively and removed any anxiety of influence. Sykes notes, "[Kierkegaard's] essay loomed so large for Percy as a Christian writing fiction because it describes the limits of art for communicating faith."[12] In *The Second Coming* and *The Thanatos Syndrome*, the issue of authority, especially in regard to one's words, is central.

"DOSTOYEVSKY'S IDEA": FROM THE DEGRADATION OF LANGUAGE TO THE DEATH OF MILLIONS

The upsurge of apocalyptic films in 2010–16, such as *The Hunger Games* or *Divergent*, would have delighted Walker Percy, whose final novel is an apocalyptic sequel to *Love in the Ruins,* and who himself professed, near the end of his life, that had he to do it all over again, he would have written movies.[13] More than the shared interest in the end of the world, these films nod at a theme that Percy thought was intricately tied to the apocalypse—the loss of meaning in language. Even the title *The Hunger Games* alludes to the problem of language, for the "games" in that world are a misnomer for the slaughter of innocent children by the ruling elite. Percy had become obsessed with language following the birth of his second daughter Anne who was born deaf. His essay collection *The Message in the Bottle* explores in great detail the acquisition of language and his theory on semiotics, and all of his novels make mention of language and its degradation. When watching television or viewing new films, or reading other writers, Percy highlights how texts dealt with the subject of language. In reading Dostoevsky's *The Idiot,* Percy remarks on the "the loss of the meanings in words!"[14] For his last two novels, Percy focuses in on this Dostoevskian theme.

In *The Brothers Karamazov,* Dostoevsky depicts how language that is deprived of signification can be used to justify any atrocity. At the climax

---
12. Sykes, *Aesthetic*, 113.
13. Percy, *More Conversations*, 136.
14. Percy, SHC 257.23.

of the novel, two lawyers represent identical facts in a case against Dmitri Karamazov for the murder of his father, although one of the lawyers does so by fraudulent rhetoric. By juxtaposing the two lawyers' speeches, Dostoevsky cautions his readers about the consequences of dishonest language. The prosecuting attorney delivers a strong oration based on the facts of the case, the history of Russian society, and the virtues of the court. He makes use of powerful metaphors, calling the courtroom a "temple of justice" and Russia a "troika" who needs to overturn her destructive course (*Brothers Karamazov* 687). Despite the truth of his speech, though, most of his listeners are left discontented. After the speech of the defense attorney, however, the audience weeps. In this account, Dmitri never murdered his father because Fyodor does not deserve to be called "father," and thus, "Such a murder is not a murder" (709). Because Fyodor acts unjustly toward his son, the defense attorney revokes the word "father" from him. He argues, "One must use words honestly, gentlemen of the jury, and I venture to call things by their right names" (706). By disconnecting the words from what they signify, the attorney himself willfully misnames things, denying that a "robbery" or "murder" even occurred. The subtitle of this chapter is called "An Adulterer of Thought," which indicates that Dostoevsky disapproved of this lawyer even though the audience loved him. The audience's reception of the defense attorney's speech betrays the problem with Dostoevsky's society as he saw it: instead of seeking the truth that correlates with reality, people were swayed by misused language. Dostoevsky saw that such rhetoric could be used to justify murder, even the murder of one's own father.

Having lived through the destruction caused by World War II, Percy would have identified with writers who understood Dostoevsky's argument, those such as George Orwell who, in "The Politics of the English Language," declares the misuse of language the propagator of fascism, or C. S. Lewis who, in *That Hideous Strength* and *The Abolition of Man*, mocks the politicians and academics for their intentional abuse of it while simultaneously warning the rest of us to take care with our words. If political leaders can call mass genocide "euthanasia" or "good deaths," then we all should be wary of how words are used. With his eye on this theme, Percy reads Dostoevsky's fiction and then composes *The Second Coming* and *The Thanatos Syndrome*.

For Percy as for Dostoevsky, language is degraded when it is twisted by ideologues to distort reality. In *The Second Coming*, Percy depicts with some optimism the recovery of language and the reaffixing of signifiers to signs. In *The Thanatos Syndrome*, by contrast, Percy presents a much more pessimistic vision of language disintegrating, with such evil consequences that human life is utterly devalued and the most deplorable violence results. In these two depictions of language, Percy is extending to his own culture the argument of Dostoevsky's *The Brothers Karamazov*.[15] While Percy pursuing the path led by Dostoevsky shows that humans always have two drives, one toward life and the other toward death, in these last two works, he exhibits a concern that perhaps, by employing the wrong words, we cannot tell the difference between the two.

In between these two publications, Percy published his most popular book *Lost in the Cosmos,* a nonfiction satire exposing the danger, as he saw it, in our inability to understand the language phenomenon. Although limited to pre-1990s scientific knowledge of language acquisition, Percy's emphasis on communication remains relevant for understanding Percy's unique anthropology. As John Sykes notes, "While Percy's theory of meaning is skewed by his failure to grasp the full implications of the sociality of language, this failure does not refute the metaphysical claim that supplies the essential theological point."[16] In other words, even though new evidence is found after Percy's death that refutes Percy's claims that only human beings use language metaphorically and socially, the emphasis on social signification is still relevant to Percy's anthropology. For Percy only human beings are symbol-makers. Thus language provides the key to understanding our humanity. Paraphrasing Percy's goal in *Lost in the Cosmos,* Sykes writes, "In other words, we must return to the activity of language as the clue to our place in the cosmos."[17] Without it, humans become susceptible to being classified as animals or computers. Yet the uniqueness of language exalts us as distinct creatures.

Moreover, language, in Percy's theory, is a social endeavor, impossible within the confines of one's mind. It depends on a tetradic relationship between signer, receiver, signed, and signified. The social nature of language gives hints of the necessity of communal relationship for understanding one's nature. And knowing one's nature, that is, what it means to be human, is only one step in the process of understanding the mysterious self. In the tradition of Socrates—though in a parodic version of it—*Lost in the Cosmos* seeks to convince the reader through a series of questions how little of the self is known. What Percy wanted to accomplish was a mirror that reflected the problems of the self to the reader. Whereas the majority of twentieth-century Americans live as though they are their own floating islands, the speaking act, the existence of language, defies such a quest for autonomy. This defiance is an important step in Percy's project. If people continue to be deceived by the lie

---

15. Percy explicitly credits *The Brothers Karamazov* for inspiring *The Thanatos Syndrome*: "It was Dostoevsky's idea" (*More Conversations,* 203).
16. Sykes, *Aesthetic,* 108.
17. Ibid., 97.

that they are autonomous selves, then, they will "fall prey to ideology and kill millions of people—unwanted people, old people, sick people, useless people, unborn people, enemies of the state—and do so reasonably, without passion, even decently, certainly without the least obnoxiousness" (*Lost in the Cosmos* 157).[18] The connection between language and genocide is not self-evident, and Percy's logic in this nonfiction work may not be convincing. However, these are the underlying principles behind the writing of *The Second Coming* and *The Thanatos Syndrome*.

In their indirect, fictional mode, these final novels embody prophecies that Percy put forth directly in his nonfiction. Both novels subtly allude to the prophecies that—in Percy's reading—Dostoevsky had put forth in *The Brothers Karamazov*, prophecies of atrocities such as the Holocaust and the Russian Revolution that had stemmed from the degradation of human language. Yet in Percy's novels, he not only echoed Dostoevsky's prophecies but also applied them to his own age, which he considered to be equally under threat of destruction from the degradation of language and its resulting violence. John Desmond asserts, "Percy set out in his writing to imagine the fateful consequences of Dostoevsky's prophesy as manifested in the postmodern apocalyptic age."[19]

Both *The Second Coming* and *The Thanatos Syndrome* are sequels to earlier works; the former examines the later life of Will Barrett from *The Last Gentleman*, while the latter follows the adventures of Tom More from *Love in the Ruins* after the world has unexpectedly continued to exist.[20] Taken together,

---

18. *Lost in the Cosmos* by Walker Percy will be cited in text throughout the book.
19. Desmond, "Demonic Self," 89.
20. Many critics dispute whether the book may be called a sequel to *The Last Gentleman*. Scott Rasnic objects to such a link being drawn: "Will Barrett of *The Second Coming* is hardly recognizable as the same burgeoning seeker we met at the end of *The Last Gentleman*" (*Sacraments*, 143). Joseph Schwartz concurs and numerates the protagonists Will I and Will II as separate entities. He asserts, "What appears to be a sequel is actually another variation of [Percy's] only subject—discovery" ("Will Barrett Redux?," 47). When Percy began writing *The Second Coming*, he did not consider Dostoevsky or *The Last Gentleman*. He admits that he didn't know the character was Will Barrett until roughly a hundred pages into writing the novel (*Conversations*, 281). Rather, Percy supports Schwartz's contention that the novel is "an adventure in discovering" (*More Conversations*, 16). Although a sequel to *The Last Gentleman*, which was inspired by Dostoevsky's *The Idiot*, *The Second Coming* does not resemble *The Idiot*.

Of all his novels, the only one for which Dostoevsky expressed a desire to write a sequel was *The Brothers Karamazov*. In the foreword to the novel, Dostoevsky outlines his plan: "The main novel is the second—it is the action of my hero in our day, at the very present time" (*Brothers Karamazov*, xvii). However, Dostoevsky died before he was able to write the second half of the life story that he planned on telling. In a footnote to Dostoevsky's prefatory note, Ralph Matlaw cites Anna Grigoryevna's contention that the second novel "was to take place in the 1880s. Dmitri returns from prison, and Alyosha has lived through a complex drama with

the novels show how the proper naming of reality leads to life while its abuse leads to death. In *The Second Coming,* Percy presents a love story in which the protagonists learn how to live, first by understanding each other's words and then by loving one another. In *The Thanatos Syndrome,* Percy depicts the alternative, a sort of living death ("the thanatos syndrome") that spreads like a virus from one person to another through deceitful misuse of language.

UNITING OF SIGNS AND SIGNIFIERS IN *THE SECOND COMING*

In *The Second Coming* Percy allegorizes the two drives of the human spirit in the two protagonists and creates a romance between a Will Barrett, man intending to die, and Allie, a woman discovering how to live. Interwoven in this fable is the question about the meaning of language, especially language about love and God, which become conflated in this tale. At this point in his career, Percy is no longer consciously seeking to imitate Dostoevsky's fiction, however, elements of the great Russian's stories appear and, when drawn together, create a map to reading *The Second Coming* as a prophecy in line with *The Thanatos Syndrome,* providing an antidote to the apocalyptic destruction of the latter, a conquering, as Percy will term it, of "eros over thanatos, life over death."[21]

The Brothers Karamazov ties love to truth-telling, an act in which words and meaning are united as one. Surrounded by people who do not say what they mean, the noble Father Zosima, by contrast, is called a "custodian of God's truth" (*Brothers Karamazov* 24). When the Karamazov family gathers in his cell, he reprimands their dissimulation. The worst pretender in this episode is Fyodor Karamazov, who plays the buffoon. Unabashedly he proclaims, "I have been lying, lying positively my whole life long, every day and hour of it. Of a truth, I am a lie, and the father of lies" (37). The admission, although partially truthful, is not penitent but self-glorifying. Not allowing Fyodor to scandalize him, Zosima compels him not to lie:

Lisa" (ibid.). The sequel would occur more than a decade after the action of the first, in which Alyosha would no longer be a youth. For critics Travis Kroeker and Bruce Ward, readers provide the sequel to *The Brothers Karamazov* with "the drama of our own lives" (*Remembering the End,* 28).

21. "I'm convinced that in *The Second Coming* there's a definite advance, a resolution of the ambiguity with which some of my other novels end: the victory, in Freudian terms, of eros over thanatos, life over death" (Percy, *Conversations,* 184).

> The man who lies to himself and listens to his own lie comes to such a pass that he cannot distinguish the truth within him, or around him, and so loses all respect for himself and for others. And having no respect he ceases to love. (36)

Zosima cautions Fyodor against the consequences of lying—loss of vision, respect, and ultimately love.

Accepting the premise that lying may lead a person to lose the capacity to love, Percy describes this world as inhabited by liars, frauds, and loveless individuals. However, he writes the other side of the story, where two people who seek true language fall in love. Will Barrett has lived an apparently successful life, while Allie seems to have failed at living. Both characters ponder the existential question of how to live. Barrett is plagued by the question in his subconscious; Allie writes the question boldly down on paper: "How do you live?" (*Second Coming* 93).[22] Both Barrett and Allie consider whether the difficulty of living fully might have to do with other people. Barrett declares, "My equally belated discovery is the total failure, fecklessness, and assholedness of people in general and in particular just those people I had looked to" (187). His other discovery is that he had spent his life depending on the authority of certain people who did not have any more answers for how to live than he did. Allie too stumbles upon this truth. She cannot understand which invisible hand might be writing the manual for human happiness: "Must one have a plan for the pursuit of happiness? . . . Who says? Who is doing the supposing?" and she concludes, "Why not live alone if it is other people who bother me?" (241). Despite the similarity of their questions, Barrett and Allie undertake different routes of discovery.

The Second Coming will rely on this issue of authority, as we watch Bill Barrett become disenchanted with the fraudulent world around him and hunger for truth. In a letter to Sutter, the errant elder son of the Vaught family from *The Last Gentleman* (who never appears in this sequel except indirectly as the addressee of Barrett's thoughts), Barrett condemns people for not living according to what they say they believe. He faults the religious alongside the atheists. Of Christians he asks, "[If] the good news is true, why are its public proclaimers such assholes and the proclamation itself such a weary used-up thing?" and he concludes that the unbeliever "is crazy as well as being an asshole" because he continues living without knowing why or how to do so (*Second Coming* 189). To avoid falling into either class of hypocrites, Barrett determines to undertake an investigation himself for the truth. Barrett closes

---

22. *The Second Coming* by Walker Percy will be cited in text throughout the book.

the letter with an admission that he does not know the meaning of the word "love." As Barrett closes his letter to Sutter, he adds a postscript requesting Sutter to tell his daughter Leslie that he loves her, despite not knowing what the word means. He professes, "I've always been suspicious of the word 'love,' what with its gross abuse and overuse. There is no cheaper word" (196). He rejects Leslie's touchy-feely "love" of everyone as false, but he cannot answer for himself what it is. The search for the meaning of the word "love" leads to love itself.

While Barrett is searching for the meaning of "love," Allie too is commencing her own quest. She has recently escaped an insane asylum where her parents incarcerated her because of her strange speech patterns. She observes, "People don't mean what they say" (*Second Coming* 82). For instance, when she encounters a street evangelist, she attempts a true conversation. The woman responds with a clichéd script, "I have a feeling a person like yourself might get a lot out of it" to which Allie asks, "Does that mean you know what I am like?" (33). In contrast to the stock phrases and idioms of other people, when Allie speaks, she searches for the right words, often creating her own syntactical, nonidiomatic phrasing to communicate what she means. Refusing to say things that she does not mean or to speak without literal truth, Allie sounds like an odd, or even crazy, woman to most others around her.

Only Barrett understands her strange—*honest*—form of communicating. After his first meeting with her, Barrett considers, "There was something odd about her speech" (*Second Coming* 76). Yet he understands her and can communicate with her. Moreover, she feels free to speak with him, although she does not know "why she felt so free to talk or not talk with him" (109). Like expatriates who meet in a foreign country, the two of them recognize each other's way of speaking and thus reciprocate. When Allie wants to use a word, she desires to know its meaning, and thus as she falls in love with Barrett, she questions the meaning of "love." She visits the library and pores through the great poets' thoughts on "love." After she records a litany of answers, including, "Love begets love" and "Love is blind," she deduces, "These people are crazier than I am!" (241). All of the abstract uses of the word "love" fall flat and empty for Allie, as they do for Barrett.

As a response to the emptiness around him, Barrett determines to take his life, a motif that, as we have seen, is repeated as often in Percy's work as in Dostoevsky's. Barrett has absorbed his father's definition of the human being as "born into a world of endless wonders, having no notion how he got here, a world in which he eats, sleeps, shits, fucks, works, grows old, gets sick, and dies, and is content to have it so" (*Second Coming* 189). His father committed suicide, and Barrett understands why, for such a life appears meaningless. He summarizes the apathy of the man who lives this way: "Not once in his entire life does it cross his mind to say to himself that his situation is preposterous, that an explanation is due him and to demand such an explanation and to refuse to play out another act of the farce until an explanation is forthcoming" (ibid.). Instead of accepting such a farcical existence, Barrett determines that suicide is the only alternative.

Barrett shares similarities with two of Dostoevsky's famous suicidal protagonists, Nikolai Stavrogin from *The Possessed* and Ivan Karamazov from *The Brothers Karamazov*. When Barrett plots the end of his life, he crafts a letter to Sutter, and the correspondence recalls Stavrogin's confession to Bishop Tikhon. Barrett declares that he does not require Sutter's approval for his course of action: "So certain am I of my own course of action that I do not require your approval" (*Second Coming* 187). So too Stavrogin dismisses the Bishop's authority: "I don't need you at all, because I've decided everything" (*Demons* 690). Both are speaking falsely, of course, as they contradict their words with their actions. Stavrogin's refusal of Tikhon resembles Barrett's resistance to receiving aid from Sutter. Of Stavrogin's false confessions, Rowan Williams writes, "To speak as if the other's response were already known and could be dealt with or circumvented in advance, which is what Nikolai wants to do, is to be condemned to death."[23] Because Stavrogin subconsciously recognizes that this attempt at confession would fail, he seeks first for Bishop Tikhon to read the document and offer him absolution. In this relationship with another in which Stavrogin may speak without predicting the other's response, and in which the other actively listens in order to understand, here might he find forgiveness. Similarly, Barrett will only receive what he desires from a conversation with a listener who acknowledges the meaning of his words. Because of the way in which Barrett silences Sutter in this letter, the experiment that he describes is as doomed as is Stavrogin's confession.

Additionally, the reasons that Barrett gives for quitting life echo Ivan Karamazov. Ivan proposes that he cannot understand the world as it is created, and therefore he rejects it: "I don't accept this world of God's, and, although I know it exists, I don't accept it at all" (*Brothers Karamazov* 216). He assumes that the world was created by God, though he doubts it was a very good God. His primary evidence against the world as God created it is human suffering, namely that of children, which shall be explored further in the discussion of *The Thanatos Syndrome*. Ivan couches his argument against the suffering of children with his disapproval of human beings in general: "One can love one's neighbors in the abstract, or even at a distance, but in close quarters it's almost impossible" (218). Like Barrett, Ivan detests other people. He speaks of beg-

---

23. Williams, *Dostoevsky*, 109.

gars with rancid breath and ugly faces. Because other people are unlovable, especially in their suffering, Ivan decries a world in which we must all live and put up with one another. Suicide is the only form of rebellion adequate to face such a shameful reality. He admits to his brother his future plan to "fling down the cup" of life when he turns thirty (211). Ivan justifies his decision to commit suicide with this proposition: "If God does not exist, then everything is permitted."

Once again Percy writes the inverse of Dostoevsky's proclamations, for Barrett plans to commit suicide to prove God's *existence*. Like Elijah Barrett escapes to a cave underground where he will wait for God to speak to him.[24] If God does not exist, then Barrett will die there. His experiment seems to be a lunatic undertaking, yet he is surprisingly content: "Who else but a madman could sit in a pod of rock under a thousand feet of mountain and feel better than he had felt in years" (*Second Coming* 211). In this uncomfortable environment—the dark, wet, underground—he feels pleasure. "In the bowels of Sourwood Mountain directly below normal folk playing golf and antiquing and barbecuing and simply enjoying the fall colors," Barrett contentedly awaits the Last Days (213). Allegorically, Barrett is waiting to hear God speak. He is waiting for true and authoritative speech, for proof that makes life worth living, or else, if such speech is impossible and God is nonexistent, then the apocalypse.

Thankfully, Barrett's Pascalian wager is interrupted by the most prosaic of troubles and another allusion to Dostoevsky's fiction. Barrett suffers an inexplicable toothache, a mysterious answer to his question for God's existence, but one that makes more sense in light of *Notes from Underground*. The toothache causes such excruciating pain that he forgets his search for God: "There is one cure for cosmic explorations, grandiose ideas about God, man, death, suicide, and such—and that is nausea. . . . What does a nauseated person care about the Last Days?" (*Second Coming* 213). This unconventional anomaly seems without basis: why a toothache? Dostoevsky's Underground Man's toothache may have provided the inspiration for Barrett's pain. Dostoevsky's protagonist informs his readers, "I had a toothache for a whole month" (*Notes* 14). He ponders the ironic pleasure one feels in such pain: "These moans express the pleasure of the one who is suffering. . . . In these moans there is expressed, first, all the futility of our pain, so humiliating for our consciousness" (ibid.). The Underground Man revels in the pain because there is no reason for it. He considers the search for reasons to be fruitless: "The reasons evaporate, the culprit is not to be found, the offense becomes not an offence but a *fatum*, something like a toothache, for which no one is to blame. . . . And

---

24. In 1 Kings 19: 8–18, Elijah goes to Horeb, "the mountain of God," and spends the night in a cave. An angel asks him to stand on the mountain and wait to hear the voice of God.

so you just wave it aside, because you haven't found the primary cause" (18). This unexpected and pedestrian cause of misery interrupts Barrett's suicidal mission. Percy writes, "In the case of Will Barrett, what went wrong could hardly be traced to God or man, Jews or whomever, but rather to a cause at once humiliating and comical: a toothache" (*Second Coming* 213). The experiment does not end with a clear answer from God but with the ambiguity of the toothache, which has no cause nor explanation. The narrator elaborates, "How does one ask a question, either a profound question or a lunatic question with such a pain in an upper canine that every heartbeat feels like a hot ice pick shoved straight up into the brain? The toothache was so bad it made him sick" (ibid.). The concrete experience trumps any abstract searching. Whether true or feigned desire inspires him, Barrett goes underground to hear from God about whether life was worth living, and the toothache acts as a catalyst that compels him instinctually to want to live.

In his attempts to exit the cave, Barrett falls into the greenhouse where Allie resides, and this exit alludes to yet another Dostoevsky novel, *The Idiot*. When Allie discovers the unconscious Barrett, she bathes him, and observing his body, recalls "paintings of the body of Christ taken down from the crucifix, the white flesh gone blue with death" (*Second Coming* 236). Her description sounds similar to that of Myshkin's reflection on the Holbein painting in Rogozhin's hallway. In *The Idiot*, when Myshkin sees this painting, he suddenly feels "oppressed" and wants to flee the house (218). For him from such an image, "a man could lose his faith" (ibid.). However, Allie suffers no oppression; she brings Barrett's pale flesh into her home and begins to revive him. Before Barrett's arrival, she had felt herself slipping into her former boredom with life. She pondered, "Can I live happily in a world without people?" (*Second Coming* 239). When Barrett appears unexpectedly and needs her help, she returns to herself. In community with him, she feels as though she is living. The greenhouse is a verdant metaphor for the conversations between Allie and Barrett and their developing love.

By enacting the word "love," Barrett and Allie discover its meaning. As Barrett moves to kiss Allie for the first time, she wonders whether *this* action is love: "Will I for the first time in my life get away from my everlasting self sick of itself to be with another self and is that what *it* is" (*Second Coming* 257). There is no antecedent for "it," though the implication is "love," the word they both have been searching to understand. While she still cannot answer for sure, she contemplates whether "loving [Barrett is] the secret, the be-all not end-all but starting point of [her] very life, or is it just one of the things creatures do like eating and drinking" (258). Love can best be expressed in concrete action. For Percy, the moments of passionate love are signs of what love is, love that has a divine source. "There were signs of coming close, to *it,* for the first time, like the signs you recognize when you are getting near the ocean for the first time. Even though you've never seen the ocean before, you recognize it" (ibid.). Through her love for Barrett, Allie longs for the font of love, for the ocean that she's never seen, for the divine love that she glimpses when she kisses him.

Barrett too seeks a source for the love he experiences with Allie. As Barrett comes out of a medicated stupor, he observes, "Things took on significance" (*Second Coming* 326). The signs are aligning with what they signify, to use Percyean language. The word "love" now means finding and caring for Allie. He professes, "The single truth is I love you" (355). Barrett aligns love with the "truth," with reality as he now comprehends it. Allie asks him, "Is what you're saying part and parcel of what you're doing?" (ibid.). And he affirms that it is: that love is not only saying but doing. Both Barrett and Allie have discovered that words must signify, people must say what they mean, and especially love is an active and concrete thing, not merely a clichéd expression. Barrett's search for such a source leads him to church. Unsurprisingly Barrett's first thought upon waking in Allie's greenhouse is, "I'm in church" (227). Throughout *The Second Coming,* his developing love for Allie is paired with religious longings. Although such a move from romance to church may appear incongruous, Rowan Williams clarifies the natural connection: "Erotic satisfaction fully enjoyed is one of the most powerful glimpses we can have of what union with God is like—a point entirely consonant with a great deal in the tradition of Christian contemplation."[25] Throughout Christian history, writers have connected the physical experience of human love to the transcendent knowledge of divine love, and Percy joins this lineup.

LOVE, TRUTH, AND AUTHORITY AT THE END OF *THE SECOND COMING*

The Second Coming reads as a romance novel, but one with moral elements and spiritual questions resonant of Dostoevsky's fiction, and its conclusion exposes the meaning behind its plot. Barrett approaches a priest to sacramentalize his relationship with Allie, desiring for the priest's authority, a new concept in the question between truth, love, life, and God. Barrett demands to know whether Father Weatherbee has any authority. In response to Barrett's question, the priest responds, like Jesus telling a parable, with a story.

---

25. *The Lion's World,* 56.

He tells Barrett of his missionary trip to Mindanao where everyone believed the Gospel as he preached it. Astonished at their belief, Weatherbee reflects, "They said that if I told them, then it must be true or I would not have gone to so much trouble" (*Second Coming* 359). This connection between truth and authority excites Barrett, who has discovered that authority relies on truth.

In chapter 7 of Matthew's gospel, Jesus instructs the people according to the "Law of the Prophets,"[26] but with imperatives to "do" and "not do" certain actions. He concludes his sermon with the mandate, "Therefore everyone who hears these words of Mine and acts on them, may be compared to a wise man who built his house on the rock."[27] The parable suggests that the person who not only listens but acts according to Jesus' teachings will stand firm against troubles in life. Jesus emphasizes that his words have concrete meaning in this reality, and thus they demand action. It is this claim that amazes the crowds, those who have become inundated by scribes who preach abstract doctrine without any correlation to how to live life. By speaking words that connect to reality, Jesus speaks truth. Moreover, Jesus names himself "the truth."[28] In *Truth and Method*, Hans Gadamer asserts that authority rests on what "can, in principle, be discovered to be true."[29] Moreover the person who possesses authority should be the one who knows the truth, who "has a wider view of things or is better informed—i.e., once again, because he knows more."[30] There is a necessary link between authority and truth.

In *The Last Gentleman,* Barrett heard a similar assertion from Father Boomer, though he did not understand its meaning at the time. When Jamie is dying, Father Boomer is called to offer him extreme unction. He tells Jamie an outline of the truths of the Gospel, basically a brief version of the affirmations of the Nicene Creed, to which Jamie responds with wide-open eyes, "Is that true?" (*Last Gentleman* 403). As evidence to support the truth of his claim, Father Boomer says, "If it were not true, then I would not be here. That is why I am here, to tell you" (404). The truth has demanded action from both priests, and they rest their authority on the truth of the statements they make as well as their corresponding actions.

The desire for truth has led Barrett not only to Allie, who speaks only what she means, but also to Father Weatherbee, who acts in accordance with the truth he asserts. The novel ends with Barrett wondering what the two have to do with one another, how does his love for Allie relate to his question-

---

26. Matthew 7:12.
27. Matthew 7:24.
28. John 14:6.
29. Gadamer, *Truth and Method,* 281.
30. Ibid.

ing Weatherbee. He queries, "Is [Allie] a gift and therefore a sign of a giver? Could it be that the Lord is here, masquerading behind that simple holy face [of Weatherbee]?" (*Second Coming* 360). Barrett has unveiled the association between loving persons and knowing God. At the beginning of the novel, he detested all people. He concurred with Ivan Karamazov, who says, "For anyone to love a man, he must be hidden, for as soon as he shows his face, love is gone" (*Brothers Karamazov* 218). However, it is Allie's face with "gray eyes" and Father Weatherbee's with his one white spinning and other bloodshot eye that Barrett loves (*Second Coming* 360, 358).

The Second Coming ends with this happily-ever-after scenario in which Barrett finds love and God. Because of its celebratory ending, Percy felt that he had "made a breakthrough in this book."[31] He declares *The Second Coming* his "first unalienated novel" because it ends with a "definite advance, a resolution of the ambiguity with which some of [his] other novels end."[32] However, is such an ending appropriate for a work of fiction? In his assessment of Dostoevsky, Williams maintains that such an ending is merely a pretense of closure: "Every morally and religiously serious fiction has to project something beyond that ending or otherwise signal a level of incompletion, even in the most minimal and formal mode, indicating [an] as yet untold story."[33] Dostoevsky writes the type of ending that Williams here defends, in which his characters' stories feel unfinished. For example, at the conclusion of *Notes from Underground*, the narrator remarks, "The 'notes' of this paradoxalist do not end here. He could not stop himself and went on" (130). This conclusion allows for the reader to continue the story. In another example, *Crime and Punishment* sums up the hero's story with a sentence that suggests a sequel: "It might make the subject of a new story, but our present story is ended" (551). Although the narrator does not feign any mystery over Raskolnikov's fate—he will be renewed, in the narrator's terms, and initiated into Sonia's faith, the story of Raskolnikov and Sonia is only beginning. Percy's first four novels share similar endings with much of Dostoevsky's fiction in that whether or not the hero undergoes a conversion, there exists some element of hope, usually inspired by Christian truth. However, Schwartz contends that not only Percy's endings but also Dostoevsky's are unambiguous:

> Percy's endings are always special in the affirmation (and sometimes celebration) they give to the reader. I think he is indebted principally to Dostoevsky

---

31. Percy, *Conversations*, 197.
32. Ibid., 183–84.
33. Williams, *Dostoevsky*, 46.

and Tolstoy for this. The ending of *The Brothers Karamazov* is in particular a rich model for him.[34]

Although Percy's endings clearly resonate with hope, the characters do not sound finished any more than Dostoevsky's heroes do. Readers do not expect Binx and Kate to live happily after, but to talk of their new life together would be to begin a new story. Like Dostoevsky, Percy concludes his novels at appropriate stopping places, though the moments feel *in media res*.

Whereas Percy considered the ending to *The Second Coming* as resolute, Jay Tolson argues that the novel still leaves questions unanswered. Tolson calls Percy's novels "dialectical, or dialogic" because they are

> unresolved, disturbingly so, perhaps none more than *The Second Coming*, even though it appears to be the most firmly resolved of all his novels. The questions raised by *The Second Coming* impel the reader to think beyond the immediate text and to consider its relationship to other fictional works created by Percy.[35]

I concur with Tolson. *The Second Coming* only depicts one side of the dichotomy between love of people (eros) and love of death (thanatos); it shows readers what life looks like when love conquers death. However, the other side of the story waits to be told, and Percy tells it in *The Thanatos Syndrome*, where death is the pervasive drive.

THE LOSS OF MEANING TO THE LOSS OF LIFE

Percy wrote *The Thanatos Syndrome* to caution his contemporaries about the ways in which the degradation of language—what Father Smith describes as "words deprived of their meaning"—could lead to the devaluation of human life (117). Percy's justification for this project, if not his inspiration, came directly from Dostoevsky: In a 1988 interview, Percy defends his "right to issue a warning" about this moral danger by saying, "It's a noble tradition going back to Dostoevsky."[36] Percy saw *The Brothers Karamazov* as a prophecy of the twentieth century's ideologically driven atrocities. He perceived that the novel diagnosed and explained those atrocities with a startling foresight. Although Percy denied seeing himself as a prophet, in *Thanatos Syndrome*, his final pub-

---

34. Schwartz, "Will Barrett Redux?," 45.
35. Tolson, *Pilgrim in the Ruins*, 425.
36. Percy, *More Conversations*, 198.

lished novel, he set out to write a work that did the same for his own time as Dostoevsky had for his—but going even further than Dostoevsky had.

According to Percy, *The Brothers Karamazov* is a great novel because it not only spoke to nineteenth-century culture but also envisioned the future. Percy lauds the book for how it "prophesies and prefigures everything—all the bloody mess and issues of the 20th century."[37] Percy knew that if he was to accomplish an analogous task in his own novels, he must diagnose the twentieth century, explaining what Dostoevsky saw and how it came to be, as well as see further than his predecessor. Quoting Ivan Karamazov, Percy applies the character's philosophical conclusion to the twentieth century: "'If God does not exist, all things are permitted.' And that explains so much of what has happened in this century. Dostoevsky forecast communism and what would take place with the rise of all the ideologies."[38] In his final novel, he takes "Dostoevsky's idea" and extends it further, for "not even Dostoevsky imagined what man without God is capable of."[39] Percy chronicles how Dostoevsky's vision came to be and then surpasses it with his own predictions.

In *The Thanatos Syndrome*, the residents of Feliciana, Louisiana, become unsuspecting lab rats in a social engineering experiment called the Blue Boy Project, in which scientists Bob Comeaux and John Van Dorn are releasing enough heavy sodium into the water supply to make everyone into "ideal" human beings. Comeaux works at a so-called Qualitarian Center, in which he kills children younger than two years old as well as senile or unwanted elders. He calls his actions "pedeuthanasia" or "gereuthansia," rejecting the less human terms "infanticide" and "senicide" (*Thanatos Syndrome* 35, 36). In Percy's construction of this dialogue of Comeaux, he satirizes a passage from Frederic Wertham's *A Sign for Cain*, a study of the execution of slow-witted, sick, or unwanted children in Germany in the 1930s and 1940s. Wertham cites various euphemisms for the killing of children: "'help for the dying,' 'mercy deaths,' 'mercy killings,' 'destruction of life devoid of value.' . . . They all became fused in the sonorous and misleading term 'euthanasia.'"[40] Like the Weimar doctors or the Nazi SS officers, Percy's scientists use deceptive vocabulary to justify their misdeeds.

Percy echoes C. S. Lewis when he connects the Nazis' evil with the degradation of language. Lewis's novel *That Hideous Strength* shares with *The Thanatos Syndrome* the theme of how the dissolution of language leads to the devaluation of human life. In his defense of his novel, Lewis writes,

---

37. Ibid., 224.
38. Ibid.
39. Ibid., 203.
40. Wertham, *Sign for Cain*, 155.

> All men at times obey their vices: but it is when cruelty, envy, and lust of power appear as the commands of a great super-personal force that they can be exercised with self-approval. The first symptom is in language. When to "kill" becomes to "liquidate" the process has begun.[41]

Lewis wrote this novel at the end of World War II, after witnessing Hitler—"a great super-personal force"—fill the role of Dostoevsky's Grand Inquisitor and kill millions of people per his instruction. What aids these good-intentioned murderers is language without significance, what Father Smith describes as "words deprived of their meaning" (*Thanatos Syndrome* 117).[42]

Although the primary theme of *The Thanatos Syndrome* follows the legacy of *The Brothers Karamazov*, the early ideas for the plot were sparked by the conclusion of *Crime and Punishment*. During his illness in the prison hospital, Raskolnikov has a dream of "microscopic creatures that lodged themselves in men's bodies" (*Crime and Punishment* 547). However, this body snatcher dream does not make the humans crazy. They become more like Stepford Wives than aliens:

> Never had people considered themselves so intelligent and unshakeable in the truth as did these infected ones. Never had they thought their judgments, their scientific conclusions, their moral convictions and beliefs more unshakeable. . . . Each thought that the truth was contained in himself alone. . . . They did not know whom or how to judge, could not agree on what to regard as evil, what as good. (ibid.)

The most frightening part of the vision is that these possessed creatures sound similar to twentieth-century American citizens. Ironically, while the citizens of Feliciana do lose themselves in the Blue Boy experiment, it is the scientists who more closely resemble the possessed of Raskolnikov's vision.

Knowing that he was tackling a large theme, Percy considered, what would Dostoevsky do with such a topic? Percy feared that a writer could not adequately take on such a large subject as the Holocaust. After reading William Styron's *Sophie's Choice*, he writes on August 29, 1979:

> He had a lot of nerve taking on the Holocaust. . . . I suspect that it can't be handled. . . . It would take a Dostoevski [sic] to do it, and he would by the utmost guile, indirection and circumspection.[43]

---

41. Lewis, "Letter to Professor Haldane."
42. *The Thanatos Syndrome* by Walker Percy will be cited in text throughout the book.
43. Percy, *Correspondence*, 258.

After Percy writes *The Thanatos Syndrome,* he investigates further the questions of evil at the Holocaust by elaborating on the section with the clearest connections to Dostoevsky, the confession of Father Smith. Unlike Stavrogin's confession from *The Possessed,* which is haunting for its coldness and lack of repentance, Father Smith's excerpt reads like Father Zosima's last words from *The Brothers Karamazov.* The confession of Father Smith was added to the manuscript later. Patrick Samway divulges, "Percy told me that he thought the theme of the novel was not explicit enough and that he progressively drew his inspiration for Father Smith's confession from Dostoevsky's *The Brothers Karamazov.*"[44] The confession supplies the indirection that Percy thought necessary for tackling such a large subject, and is the heart of the novel.

Like book six of *The Brothers Karamazov* in which Father Zosima's life and teachings are recorded by Alyosha Karamazov, the confession in *The Thanatos Syndrome* includes all of Father Smith's recollections of his experience in Germany in the 1930s as received by More. Both stories are narrated in the first person and, as different genres, stand apart from the structure of the novel. The account of Zosima's life is composed as a *zhitie* by Alyosha, which Joseph Frank defines as "the hagiographical biography of the life of a saint."[45] According to Leonard Stanton, Dostoevsky copied much of the *Life of Elder Leonid of Optina* by Father Kliment Zedergol'm when he sojourned at the Optina Putsyn monastery in 1878.[46] Malcolm Jones notes, "Dostoevsky probably imported directly (if in disguised form) [*Life of Leonid*] into the text of his novel."[47] The factual elder's hagiography becomes the fictional life of Father Zosima. Similarly, Percy draws Father Smith's confession from the true accounts of the Weimar doctors as given by Wertham in *A Sign for Cain,* as he admits in the prefatory note of *The Thanatos Syndrome.* Wishing to engage their current society, Dostoevsky and Percy draw on these factual accounts for their fictional versions.

The life stories in both novels offer competing views of reality: in *The Brothers Karamazov,* Father Zosima's biography presents the possibility of a "life in God," as the translator's subheading of the chapter defines it, whereas Father Smith's confession presents the alternative, life when God does not exist. Only moments before he reaches the bedside of his dying elder, Alyosha has listened to his brother Ivan's poem that defies the necessity of Christ, and indeed the truth of God's existence. Because Dostoevsky intended the notes on Zosima's life to counterweigh Ivan's poem "The Legend of the Grand

---

44. Samway, "Two Conversations," 28.
45. Frank, *Writer,* 880.
46. Stanton, "Zedergol'm's *Life of Elder Leonid,*" 443–55.
47. Jones, *Dostoevsky and the Dynamics of Religious Experience,* 149.

Inquisitor,"[48] Alyosha imbibes the parting words of his elder directly after attending to his brother's polemic. In contrast to Ivan's stance that all is permissible if God does not exist, the Father Zosima section embodies Dostoevsky's most profound beliefs about how one should live if God does exist. The two stories—one of an actual life and the other his brother's fictive creation—ring in Alyosha's ears as competing views of reality. Before conversing with his brother or recording the dying words of his elder, Alyosha confessed to Lise, his intended, "And perhaps I don't even believe in God" (*Brothers Karamazov* 202). The choice for whether to believe in God is now contextualized as a choice of how to live. As Alyosha must choose which life is better—Zosima's or Ivan's—the reader must choose which is more true.

Zosima's story counters Ivan's protest regarding the suffering children and its literary accompaniment, "The Legend of the Grand Inquisitor." In Ivan's vision of the world, Christ is irrelevant to saving the suffering. He writes his poem on behalf of the suffering, namely the innocent children who are tortured. With unnecessary detail, Ivan describes the horrors occurring across the world as he had read in newspaper articles. He has collected these stories and relates them with embellishment—stories of Turks blowing out babies' brains, children being torn apart by dogs, locked in closets and forced to eat excrement. Because of these stories, Ivan protests:

> It's not worth the tears of that one tortured child who beat itself on the breast with its little fist and prayed in its stinking outhouse, with its unexpiated tears to 'dear, kind God'! It's not worth it, because those tears are unatoned for, or there can be no harmony. (*Brothers Karamazov* 225)

For Ivan, a good God is impossible if children are suffering. The future eternal harmony after resurrection does not atone for the sufferings in this world. Many of Ivan's stories may be traced to historical records because Dostoevsky attempted to use factual newspaper accounts. Like Ivan, he too felt that suffering children were the greatest argument against the existence of God. Percy has collected his own list of suffering children in his fiction.[49] Like Ivan, More

---

48. Frank cautions readers against assuming that this life encompasses all of Dostoevsky's argument against Ivan's poem because the whole novel was to be seen as an answer to Ivan's protest (*Writer*, 880).

49. In *The Moviegoer* Lonnie Smith, Binx's little brother, is dying. Kate describes him as "hideously thin and yellow, like one of those wrecks lying on a flatcar at Dachau" (238). She connects the suffering Lonnie with those children tortured in the concentration camps in Germany. In *The Last Gentleman*, Will Barrett witnesses the young Jaime's death, though the event embarrasses him by its foulness. And in the prequel to *The Thanatos Syndrome*, Tom More experiences the death of his daughter Samantha.

must decide whether this suffering child is enough evidence to justify rebellion against his faith. His wife Doris criticizes his belief:

> "That's a loving God you have there," she told me toward the end, when the neuroblastoma had pushed one eye out and around the nosebridge so that Samantha looked like a two-eyes Picasso profile. (*Love in the Ruins* 72)

The same description of Samantha is repeated when she questions her father about whether his faith remains. She asks,

> "Papa, have you lost your faith?" . . . Samantha asked me the question as I stood by her bed. The neuroblastoma had pushed one eye out and around the nosebridge so she looked like a Picasso profile. (373)

By repeating the description of Samantha, Percy ties the two scenes together and juxtaposes the doubt of Doris against More's potential to remain faithful.[50]

When Father Smith begins his story, he sounds like a young Ivan. He does not disguise his disapproval of his father, though more so because his father was a romantic and not a buffoon as Fyodor Karamazov was. Father Smith's family life sounds very similar to that of Binx Bolling: both share romantic fathers and harsh, religious mothers. Moreover, Father Smith admits, "I found my fellow man, with few exceptions, either victims or assholes. I did not exclude myself" (*Thanatos Syndrome* 243). Ivan makes a similar confession to Alyosha, "I could never understand how one can love one's neighbors. It's just one's neighbors, to my mind, that one can't love, though one might love those at a distance" (*Brothers Karamazov* 217). These admissions of theoretical love are indicators of the "tenderness" that Father Smith indicts as "the first disguise of the murderer" (*Thanatos Syndrome* 128). He warns More that when combined, "a lover of Mankind and a theorist of Mankind" will become a Stalin or a Hitler—or a Grand Inquisitor—who will kill millions "for the good of Mankind" (129). Without irony or awareness, Ivan includes the fact that his Inquisitor burns "a hundred heretics" the day before Christ's arrival (*Brothers Karamazov* 229). Yet Ivan uplifts him as the one who suffers for others' happiness.

---

50. The description recalls Flannery O'Connor's depiction of Mary Ann from her "Introduction to *A Memoir of Mary Ann*": "The other side [of her face] was protuberant, the eye was bandaged, the nose and mouth crowded slightly out of place" (*Mystery and Manners*, 215). It is in this essay that O'Connor alludes to Ivan Karamazov's protest against God's goodness. She accuses him of using the suffering of children, such as that of Mary Ann—or in Tom More's case, Samantha—as evidence. Percy borrows directly from this essay in *The Thanatos Syndrome* when Father Smith echoes O'Connor's claim that "tenderness leads to the gas chambers."

Father Smith confesses his previous rebellion because he wants Tom More to avoid a similar revolt, a loss of faith that would lead to his joining Comeaux and Van Dorn's Blue Boy project and thus to more suffering children. More accidentally elicits Father Smith's confession when he attempts to break the priest out of a trance that he has slipped into. Before the confession begins, More seeks the priest's advice because "the best way to get in touch with withdrawn patients is to ask their help" (*Thanatos Syndrome* 233). He explains the Blue Boy project, its accompanying threats as well as the job offer to participate, and the evidence that such a project produces "social betterment." The topic of social betterment recalls the priest's worst memories from his youth when he agreed with the rationale of the Weimar doctors and the subsequent Nazi agenda.

Although Father Smith now sees through these façades of social betterment, he confesses how, in his youth, he identified with the cause.[51] Grabbing More's arm, he pulls him in close and says, "This is my confession. If I had been German and not American, I would have joined [the Nazis]" (*Thanatos Syndrome* 248). The priest acknowledges his own complicity in the atrocities of the Holocaust. In line with the teaching of Father Zosima that all are "responsible for all men's sins [and] are to blame for everyone and for all things," Father Smith takes this guilt upon himself (*Brothers Karamazov* 299). The narrator of *The Brothers Karamazov* hints at this truth in the opening chapter when, after delineating all of Fyodor Karamazov's various faults, he concludes, "As a general rule, people, even the wicked, are much more naïve and simple-hearted than we suppose. And we ourselves are too" (4). Rather than persecute Fyodor as the lone villain of the tale, the narrator includes himself and enlists the reader in the category of "wicked." At the end of the novel, when Ivan must testify in court, he admits his part in his father's murder: "[Smerdyakov] murdered him and I incited him to do it. . . . Who doesn't desire his father's death?" (651). With his confession, Ivan indicts the audience there and the reader of the story as also guilty.

In *The Thanatos Syndrome*, Father Smith accuses More, too, of complicity in the death of millions:

> You are a member of the first generation of doctors in the history of medicine to turn their backs on the oath of Hippocrates and kill millions of old useless people, unborn children, born malformed children, for the good of

---

51. Percy himself admitted to drawing this experience from his visit to Germany. As an undergraduate at Chapel Hill, Percy went on an excursion to Germany with a professor and a few students. Although not blind to the problems with Fascism, Percy was enamored with the Nazi youth program (Tolson, *Writer*, 117–19).

mankind—and to do so without a single murmur from one of you. (*Thanatos Syndrome* 127)

More ignores the diatribe as the ravings of a lunatic. He does not connect the priest's stories of the Holocaust with his own predicament over whether to join the Blue Boy project. The priest offers his confession in answer to More's dilemma. Although More seeks the priest's help about the decision, he does not register the connection between the story and his own life.

After Blue Boy has been unveiled as an illegal project, Bob Comeaux confronts More, accusing him of sharing liability for the project. To More's astonishment, Comeaux claims, "We were after the same thing, the greatest good, the highest quality of life for the greatest number" (*Thanatos Syndrome* 346). More has no argument against Comeaux's allegation, although he never assents to sharing such a desire. When Father Smith concedes that Comeaux's qualitarians "make considerable sense," More acquiesces, "It could be argued" (116). Father Smith has used this same phrase in his confession when he recalls reading a 1920s book by German doctors called *The Release of the Destruction of Life Devoid of Value*: "Their arguments made considerable sense to me" (246). This book motivated the Weimar doctors who executed children before and during the Nazi regime in Germany. While Father Smith acknowledges how he was seduced by the arguments of the Weimar doctors, and even more so with the patriotism of the young Nazis, More is blind to his potential culpability in Comeaux's project, an endeavor that shares the aims of those Weimar doctors. Father Smith goes as far as to call them, "The Louisiana Weimar psychiatrists" (252).

To emphasize the connection between the Weimar doctors and the Louisiana scientists, Father Smith adds a "footnote" to his confession. This footnote is drawn from Wertham's chapter entitled "The Geranium in the Window." Like the Weimar doctors, Comeaux defends his practice as promoting quality life. However, Father Smith connects it with his memory of a special department at Eglfing-Haar, a hospital outside of Munich. The room was used for euthanizing children of all ages, those with psychological or physical disabilities. In both Wertham's and Smith's accounts, what stands out in the bare room is the geranium plant: "It was a beautiful plant, luxuriant, full of bloom, obviously very carefully tended" (*Thanatos Syndrome* 253). The geranium indicts those who purport to increase the "quality of human life," but in reality care more for a plant than for the human lives under their protection. Smith cannot get the geranium out of his mind and repeats several times that its smell or "lack of smell" haunts him. At one point, he wonders whether he remembers the "smell of the geranium or a trace of the Zyklon B" (275), conflating the geranium with the poison used in the holocaust.

The allusion to Wertham's book also recalls Dostoevsky. Perhaps it did not register in Percy's consciousness that such a detail is also included in Stavrogin's confession from *The Possessed*. In this passage, which was initially censored, Nikolai Stavrogin comes to Father Tikhon's hermitage to confess his greatest sin. He admits to raping a ten-year-old girl who then hangs herself in despair. In both the scene of the rape and the hanging, Stavrogin concentrates on a geranium plant. When he violates Matryosha, he notes, "They had a lot of geraniums in the window" (*Demons* 695). Later as he waits for her to commit suicide, he "began watching a tiny red spider on a geranium leaf, and became oblivious" (699). After listening to this confession, Tikhon makes two observations. First, he warns Stavrogin about artistically enhancing his confession, "Certain places in your account are stylistically accentuated; as if you admire your own psychology and seize upon every little detail just to astonish the reader with an unfeelingness that is not in you" (706). The extra details are reminiscent of Lancelot's description of his crimes on Belle Isle when he tries to convince Percival of his "coldness," or what Tikhon labels "unfeelingness." The geranium plant is a detail that denotes "unfeelingness." Moreover, Tikhon concludes, "There is not and cannot be any greater and more terrible crime than your act with the maiden" (707). Of all the deeds that Stavrogin confesses, the destruction of the young girl is by far the worst. When this confession is read alongside that of Father Smith, the geranium connotes the coldness of the Weimar doctors and emphasizes the horror of their acts against the children.

In addition to such subconscious allusions, Percy admits to choosing aspects of Dostoevsky's fiction that would benefit his audience. He knew that his novel, like Dostoevsky's *The Brothers Karamazov*, required a Zosima to counter the "Grand Inquisitor" vision that he was presenting. However, he did not want to create a saint because he knew that his readers would reject such an emblem of goodness as unreal. In a letter dated September 20, 1986, he confides in Foote: "Every time Fr. Smith opens his mouth he, I, is in trouble. . . . You can't get away with a Fr. Zossima [sic] these days and probably shouldn't."[52] Here is the method of indirection that Percy drew from Dostoevsky. Although Father Smith shares similar ideas to Zosima, Percy taints his priest's character. Smith seems insane, has a history of alcoholism, and calls himself a "failed priest" (*Thanatos Syndrome* 244). Like Percy's previous priests—Father Boomer, Father John, and Father Weatherbee—he is not a reverent man. Of Father Boomer, Percy admits, "I made him downright unpleasant, as unpleasant as I could. The doctrine of the church is that the sacraments are transmitted regardless of the character of the priest."[53] Percy creates objectionable priests to emphasize that

---

52. *Correspondence*, 292–93.
53. Percy, *More Conversations*, 6.

their "holiness"—or lack thereof—is not what merits love, any more so than it does in those to whom they deliver the sacraments. The point is the face of the other, the love Zosima and Father Smith require from others. The novel ends with Smith begging the doctors, "If you have a patient, young or old, suffering, dying, afflicted, useless, born or unborn, whom you for the best of reasons wish to put of his misery . . . send him to us" (*Thanatos Syndrome* 361). His congregants respond to this call to life over death with silence. Even More does not know what to make of this homily.

However, Percy hopes that his readers will respond better than More can, and he imitates Dostoevsky in writing an ending that calls for action. In the foreword to *The Brothers Karamazov*, Dostoevsky outlines his plan to write a sequel: "The main novel is the second—it is the action of my hero in our day, at the very present time" (*Brothers Karamazov* xvii), and his critics assert that readers act out that sequel in how they live after they close the book.[54] As readers, we not only continue the story of the characters—pondering whether Ivan finds faith or Dmitri reforms—but we choose whether to live the rest of the story, whether we echo the "hurrah" alongside the children at Ilyusha's grave, whether we will be transformed by Dostoevsky's story as we live our own lives. Percy models the ideal Dostoevskian reader by conversing with *The Brothers Karamazov* and then writing the next story. His novels take off from where Dostoevsky's story ends. When in *The Thanatos Syndrome* the church responds in silence, it is an invitation to the reader to finish Percy's story. Even the closing sentences of the novel echo this invitation. More is dialoguing with one of his patients who asks whether she may tell him something, to which he replies affirmatively, "Well?" (*Thanatos Syndrome* 372). The question is directed as much to her as to us. Thus, our reading of Percy, like his reading of Dostoevsky, concludes with open dialogue.

---

54. Dostoevsky died before he was able to write the second half of the life story that he planned on telling. In a footnote to Dostoevsky's prefatory note, Ralph Matlaw cites Anna Grigoryevna's contention that the second novel "was to take place in the 1880s. Dmitri returns from prison, and Alyosha has lived through a complex drama with Lisa" (*Brothers Karamazov*, xvii). The sequel would occur more than a decade after the action of the first in which Alyosha would no longer be a youth. For critics Travis Kroeker and Bruce Ward, readers provide the sequel to *The Brothers Karamazov* with "the drama of our own lives" (*Remembering the End*, 28). Williams makes a similar conclusion. He perceives that the reader replies to the novel "having digested the text in the continuing process of a reflective life" (*Dostoevsky*, 12).

CONCLUSION

Imitation Versus Anxiety

A Christian's Response to Harold Bloom's The Anxiety of Influence

AT THE CONCLUSION of Harold Bloom's *The Anxiety of Influence*, he unveils the theological assumptions behind his critical theory:

> The Protestant God, insofar as He was a Person, yielded His paternal role for poets to the blocking figure of the Precursor. . . . Poetry whose hidden subject is the anxiety of influence is naturally of a Protestant temper, for the Protestant God always seems to isolate His children in the terrible double bind of two great injunctions: "Be like Me" and "Do not presume to be too like Me." The fear of godhood is pragmatically a fear of poetic strength, for what the ephebe enters upon, when he begins his life cycle as a poet, is in every sense a process of divination.[1]

This Protestant God may as well be the Judeo-Christian God shared by the Roman Catholic and Orthodox traditions. Bloom dissects the Trinity into competing gods rather than distinct natures shared in a single deity. The Father rigs the game against the Son, and the Son must trump the Father. Although Bloom insists that he has no Oedipal suggestions in his theory, his use of the father-son tropes make it difficult not to see the allusion. Granted, Bloom was merely employing the language of his predecessor Roland Barthes, who, in "The Death of the Author," classifies the relationship as that between

---

1. Bloom, *Anxiety*, 152.

a father and his child.² A strong poet, like a strong critic, must commit patricide. It takes little imagination to jump from the death of the author to the death of the father, and thus, to the death of the theological father, God.

In Bloom's attack against the Protestant God, he finds Him deserving of death. God's death is a prerequisite for the freedom of the poet. While He remains, poets are bound on both sides by impossible chains, the commands, in Bloom's words, to imitate God while not to presume godlikeness. The two sanctions are at odds only when one misunderstands God's nature and thus the word "imitation." For Bloom, all imitation is slavish and weak. However, saints, in response to God-as-Christ's dictum to follow Him, uplift *imitatio Christi* as one's highest goal.³ To imitate God is to reach one's highest potential, to reclaim one's true self; it is an ascendant act that requires divine strength. Yet it is not a process of divination, in Bloom's way of defining it. Bloom praises Milton's Satan as the character who models this poetic divination, which counters the Gospel's account of this process.

The selflessness of God-as-Christ, the gratuity of divine self-abnegation, makes no sense to Bloom, who redefines it with his own "demonic parody."⁴ Instead of the humility and self-emptying described by St. Paul in Philippians 2:3–8, which he quotes nearly in full,⁵ Bloom redefines *kenosis* as making "the fathers pay for their own sins, and perhaps for those of the sons also."⁶ Rather than imitate the meaning found in his predecessor's work, the son should attempt to *empty* the parent-poet's poem of meaning in his new poem. Bloom finds a "double bind" because he cannot understand how impossible it would be for the one who is imitating Christ to presume godlikeness. In the Philippians letter that Bloom quotes, Paul asserts that Christ did not consider himself "to be equal with God." Therefore, any attempt to be like Christ will fulfill God's injunction not to presume to be like Him. It should be noted that Bloom does not completely quote Paul's letter, for he ellipses "on the cross" from the end of verse 8. In his version, the apostle's words end with "unto death . . . "⁷ and Bloom instructs readers that a "*kenosis* proper," or a Bloomian *kenosis,* is "not so much a humbling of self as of all precursors, and necessarily a defiance unto death." Such a conclusion lines up for a critic who admits a "distaste for the Crucifixion," a revulsion to humility, sacrifice, or its imitation.⁸

---

2. Barthes, "Death of the Author," 121.
3. Matthew 4:19, New International Version.
4. Bloom, *Anxiety,* 92.
5. Ibid., 91.
6. Ibid.
7. Ibid., 91–92.
8. Bloom, *Anatomy,* 5.

These theological assumptions stem from an aesthetic ideology and a Gnostic humanism that values autonomy, solipsism, and immortality, all of which are illusions. Bloom claims, "We need to stop thinking of any poet as an autonomous ego, however solipsistic the strongest poets may be."[9] Yet this very claim equates "solipsism" with strength and assumes "autonomy" as an unachievable ideal. Bloom asserts that a poet's intuitive desire is to prevent death, which only happens through strong poetry. However, this end directly opposes the Christian intention to die. In imitation of Christ's sacrificial death, Paul insists, "I have been crucified with Christ, and it is no longer I who live, but Christ lives in me."[10] This is the Christian definition of *kenosis*. The follower imitates the self-emptying of his God, so the God may dwell in him. Elsewhere Paul directs readers, "Be imitators of me, just as also I am of Christ."[11] The imitator desires that others imitate him in order to imitate Christ, like a domino effect. This is not Bloom's insistence that the prayer of the poet "is to be an influence, and not to be influenced," for the former only happens after the latter.[12] Imitating precedes influence.

Bloom admits that pre-romantic poets did not suffer this anxiety, but he does not draw the connection to the Christian worldview that dominated Western poetry before 1700. The anxiety of influence evolves in conjunction with the rising value of autonomy and the replacement of Christian religion with a romantic's devotion to art as faith, both of which Bloom shares.[13] For those writers like Dostoevsky and Percy, who adhere to the Christian ethos that precedes romantic poetry, not only is there no anxiety of influence but also there is an ideal of influence, an exaltation of imitation. Just as Christ says, "Follow me," and Paul says, "Follow me as I follow Christ," so every Christian writer desires to follow, to continue the trend, to imitate the *kenosis* of the predecessor and thus to offer an example of selflessness and charity to the next writer. By examining the ways in which Percy, in particular, modeled his Christian predecessor Dostoevsky, perhaps this book has shown a path back to Christian imitation. In contrast, the previous three hundred years of antagonistic striving for the illusion of originality, and in an attempt to undo the false claims of literary critics from the previous few decades who prize competition and anxiety, I have hoped to illustrate an old path as the better path and to invite critics and writers to follow me, as I have followed Him.

---

9. Idem, *Anxiety*, 91.
10. Galatians 2:20.
11. 1 Corinthians 11:1.
12. Bloom, *Anxiety*, 126.
13. In the culminating volume to his influence series, he writes, "Faith in the aesthetic ... is the little book's credo" (*Anatomy*, 4).

BIBLIOGRAPHY

Adelman, Gary. *Retelling Dostoyevsky: Literary Response and Other Observations*. Lewisberg, PA: Bucknell UP, 2001.

Allen, William Rodney. *Walker Percy: A Southern Wayfarer*. Jackson, MS: Mississippi UP, 1986.

Auden, W. H. *The Complete Works of W .H. Auden: Prose, 1939–1948*. Ed. Edward Mendelson. Princeton, NJ: Princeton UP, 2002.

Auerbach, Eric. *Mimesis: The Representation of Reality in Western Literature*. Trans. Willard R. Trask. Introduction by Edward Said. Princeton, NJ: Princeton UP, 2003.

Bakhtin, Mikhail. *Problems of Dostoevsky's Poetics*. Ed. and trans. by Caryl Emerson. With an introduction by Wayne C. Booth. Minneapolis, MN: Minnesota UP, 1984.

Barthes, Roland. *The Death of the Author*. Trans. Stephen Heath. New York: Hill and Wang, 1977.

Baxandall, Michael. *Patterns of Intention: On the Historical Explanation of Pictures*. New Haven, CT: Yale UP, 1985.

Berdyaev, Nicolas. *Dostoievsky: An Interpretation*. Trans. Donald Attwater. San Rafael, CA: Semantron Press, 2009.

Bloom, Harold. *The Anatomy of Influence: Literature as a Way of Life*. New Haven, CT: Yale UP, 2011.

——. *The Anxiety of Influence: A Theory of Poetry*. New York: Oxford UP, 1973.

——. *The Western Canon: The Books and School of the Ages*. New York: Riverhead Books, 1995.

Bloshteyn, Maria. "Dostoevsky and the Literature of the American South." *Southern Literary Journal* 37.1 (2004): 1–24.

——. *The Making of a Counter-Cultural Icon: Henry Miller's Dostoevsky*. Toronto, ON: University of Toronto, 2007.

Brinkmeyer Jr., Robert H. *The Fourth Ghost*. Baton Rouge: Louisiana State UP, 2009.

Camus, Albert. *The Myth of Sisyphus*. New York: Vintage, 1955. Percy 622. SHC.

——. *The Rebel: An Essay on Man in Revolt*. New York: Vintage, 1992.

Carel, Havi. *Life and Death in Freud and Heidegger*. Amsterdam: Rodophi, 2006.

Cervantes, Miguel de. *Don Quixote*. Trans. John Rutherford. Introduction by Roberto Gonzalez Echevarria. London: Penguin, 2003.

Chaucer, Geoffrey. *Troilus and Criseyde*. Trans. Nevill Coghill. New York: Penguin Books, 1971.

Cheney, Brainard. "To Restore a Fragmented Image." *Sewanee Review* 69.4 (Oct–Dec 1961): 691–700.

Ciuba, Gary. *Walker Percy: Books of Revelation*. Athens: Georgia UP, 2010.

Clayton, Jay, and Eric Rothstein. *Influence and Intertextuality in Literary History*. Madison: Wisconsin UP, 1991.

Coles, Robert. *Walker Percy: An American Search*. Boston: Little Brown and Company, 1978.

Contino, Paul. "'Descend that You May Ascend': Augustine, Dostoevsky, and the Confessions of Ivan Karmazov." In *Augustine and Literature,* edited by Robert Peter Kennedy, Kim Paffenroth, and John Doody. Lanham, MD: Lexington Books, 2006.

———. "Incarnational Realism and the Case for Casuistry: Dmitry Karamazov's Escape." In *Dostoevsky's* Brothers Karamazov: *Art, Creativity, and Spirituality,* edited by Pedrag Cicovacki and Maria Granik. Heidelberg: Universitatsverlag, 2010.

Correspondence of Shelby Foote and Walker Percy. Ed. Jay Tolson. New York: Center for Documentary Studies in Association with W. W. Norton & Co., 1997.

Cowdell, Scott. *René Girard and Secular Modernity*. South Bend, IN: University of Notre Dame Press, 2015.

Cox, Harvey. *The Secular City*. New York: Macmillan, 1966. Percy 515. SHC.

Cunningham, David. "*The Brothers Karamazov* as Trinitarian Theology." In *Dostoevsky and the Christian Tradition,* edited by George Pattison and Diane Oenning Thompson. 134–55. Cambridge, UK: Cambridge University Press, 2008.

Dale, Corinne. "*Lancelot* and the Medieval Quests of Sir Lancelot and Dante." In *Walker Percy: Art and Ethics,* edited by Jac Tharpe. Jackson: Mississippi UP, 1980.

Dante. *Inferno*. Trans. Anthony Esolen. New York: Modern Library, 2005.

Davison, Ray. *Camus: The Challenge of Dostoevsky*. Reed Hall: Exeter UP, 1997.

de France, Marie. *The Lais of Marie de France*. Trans. Glyn S. Burgess and Keith Busby. London: Penguin, 1991.

Desmond, John. "Fyodor Dostoevsky, Walker Percy, and the Demonic Self." *Southern Literary Journal* 44.2 (Spring 2012): 88–107.

———. "Revisioning *The Fall*: Walker Percy and *Lancelot*." *Mississippi Quarterly* 47.4 (Fall 1994).

———. "Walker Percy and Suicide." *Modern Age* (Winter 2005): 58–63.

———. *Walker Percy's Search for Community*. Athens, GA: University of Georgia Press, 2004; reprt. 2010.

Dostoevsky, Fyodor. *The Brothers Karamazov*. Ed. Ralph E. Matlaw. Trans. Constance Garnett. Chicago: Chicago UP, Norton Critical Edition, 1976.

———. *Crime and Punishment*. Trans. Richard Pevear and Larissa Volokhonsky. New York: Vintage, 1993.

———. *Demons*. Trans. Richard Pevear and Larissa Volokhonsky. New York: Vintage, 1995.

———. *The Idiot*. Trans. Constance Garnett. New York: Modern Library, 1935. Illustrated by Boardman Robinson. Percy 620. SHC.

———. *The Idiot*. Trans. David Magarshack. London: Penguin, 1958. Percy 621. SHC.

———. "Letter to A. N. Maikov." Excerpted in *Dostoevsky's* The Devils: *A Critical Companion*, edited by William J. Leatherbarrow. Evanston, IL: Northwestern UP, 1999.

———. *Notes from Underground*. Trans. Richard Pevear and Larissa Volokhonsky. New York: Random House, Inc., 1993.

———. *The Possessed*. Trans. Constance Garnett. Foreword by Avrham Yarmolinsky. Includes "At Tikhon's." New York: Modern Library, 1936. Percy 626. SHC.

———. *Selected Letters of Dostoevsky*. Ed. Joseph Frank and David L. Goldstein. New Brunswick, NJ: Rutgers UP, 1987.

———. *The Short Novels of Dostoevsky*. Intro by Thomas Mann. New York: Dial Press, 1945. Percy 628. SHC.

Douthat, Ross. *Bad Religion: How We Became a Nation of Heretics*. New York: Simon & Schuster, 2012.

Dowie, William J. "Lancelot and the Search for Sin." In *The Art of Walker Percy: Stratagems of Being*. Barton Rouge: Louisiana State UP, (1979): 245–59.

Duff, William. *An Essay on Original Genius*. London: Forgotten Books, 2016.

Elfenbein, Andrew. "Defining Influence." *Modern Language Quarterly* 69.4 (Dec 2008): 433–36.

———. "On the Discrimination of Influences." *Modern Language Quarterly* 69.4 (Dec 2008): 481–508.

Elie, Paul. *The Life You Save May Be Your Own: An American Pilgrimage*. New York: Farrar, Straus, and Giroux, 2004.

Eliot, T. S. "Tradition and the Individual Talent." In *Selected Prose of T. S. Eliot*, edited by Frank Kermode. 37–44. Boston, MA: Mariner, 1975.

Flowers, Ronald Bruce. *Religion in Strange Times: The 1960s and 1970s*. Macon, GA: Mercer UP, 1984.

Fox-Genovese, Elizabeth, and Eugene D. Genovese. *The Mind of the Master Class: History and Faith in Southern Slaveholders' Worldview*. Cambridge, UK: Cambridge UP, 2005.

Frank, Joseph. *Dostoevsky: A Writer in His Time*. Ed. Mary Petrusewicz. Princeton, NJ: Princeton UP, 2010.

———. *Dostoevsky: The Miraculous Years*. Princeton, NJ: Princeton UP, 1996.

———. *Dostoevsky: The Seeds of Revolt, 1821–1849*. Princeton, NJ: Princeton UP, 1979.

———. *Dostoevsky: The Stir of Liberation, 1860–1865*. Princeton, NJ: Princeton UP, 1986.

———. *The Mantle of The Prophet, 1871–1881*. Princeton, NJ: Princeton UP, 2003.

Franklin, Simon. "Nostalgia for Hell: Russian Literary Demonism and Orthodox Tradition." In *Russian Literature and Its Demons*, edited by Pamela Davidson. New York: Berghahn Books, 2000.

Frost, Robert. "New Hampshire." http://www.americanpoems.com/poets/robertfrost/768. Accessed June 20, 2017.

Gadamer, Hans Georg. *Truth and Method*. New York: Bloomsbury Academic, 1989.

Girard, René. *I See Satan Fall Like Lightning*. Trans. and with a foreword by James G. Williams. Maryknoll, NY: Orbis Books, 2008.

———. *Resurrection from the Underground: Feodor Dostoevsky*. East Lansing: Michigan State University Press, 2012.

Gordon, Caroline. Letter to Robert Giroux (Mar. 11, 1966). Vanderbilt University. Special Collections. Lytle papers. 2.17.

Guardini, Romano. "Dostoevsky's Idiot, A Symbol of Christ." Trans. Francis X. Quinn. *Cross Currents* 6.4 (Fall 1956): 359–82.

———. *The Essential Guardini: An Anthology of the Writings of Romano Guardini.* Selected and with an introduction by Heinz R. Kuehn. Archdiocese of Chicago. Chicago: Liturgy Training Publications, 1997.

———. "The Legend of the Grand Inquisitor." Trans. Sally S. Cunneen. *Cross Currents* 3.1 (Fall 1952): 58–86.

Hobson, Linda Whitney. "'The Grand Inquisitor' and *Lancelot.*" In *Walker Percy: Novelist and Philosopher,* edited by Jan Nordby Gretlund and Karl-Heinz Westarp. 119–30. Jackson: Mississippi UP, 1991.

Holy Bible, New International Version. Nashville, TN: Cornerstone Bible Publishers, 1999.

Huizinga, Johan. *The Waning of the Middle Ages.* Oxford, UK: Benediction Books, 2010.

Jackson, Robert Louis. *Dialogues with Dostoevsky: The Overwhelming Questions.* Redwood City, CA: Stanford University UP, 1993.

Jones, Malcom V. *Dostoevsky and the Dynamics of Religious Experience.* London: Anthem Press, 2005.

Juvan, Marko. *History and Poetics of Intertextuality.* West Lafayette, IN: Purdue University Press, 2009.

Kjetsaa, Geir. *Dostoevsky and the New Testament.* Oslo: Solum, 1984.

Kirsch, Arthur. *Auden and Christianity.* New Haven, CT: Yale UP, 2005.

Kobre, Michael. *Walker Percy's Voices.* Athens: Georgia UP, 2000.

Kroebe, Karl. *Retelling/Rereading: The Fate of Storytelling in Modern Times.* New Brunswick, NJ: Rutgers UP, 1992.

Kroeker, Travis P., and Bruce K. Ward. *Remembering the End: Dostoevsky as Prophet to Modernity.* Boulder, CO: Westview Press, 2001.

Landon, Philip. "Great Exhibitions: Representations of the Crystal Palace in Mayhew, Dickens, and Dostoevsky." *Nineteenth-Century Contexts: An Interdisciplinary Journal* 20.1. (July 2008): 27–59.

Lawson, Lewis A. "From Tolstoy to Dostoyevsky in *The Moviegoer.*" *Mississippi Quarterly* 56 (2003): 411–19.

Leatherbarrow, William, ed. *Dostoevsky's* The Devils. Evanston, IL: Northwestern UP, 1999.

LeClair, Thomas. "Walker Percy's Devil." In *The Art of Walker Percy: Stratagems of Being,* edited by Panthea Reid Broughton. 157–68. Baton Rouge: Louisiana State UP, 1979.

Lewis, C. S. "A Letter to Professor Haldane." In *Of Other Worlds: Essays and Stories,* edited by Walter Hooper. Boston, MA: Houghton Mifflin Harcourt, 2002.

Lubac, Henri de, S. J. *The Drama of Atheist Humanism.* Trans. Edith M. Riley, Anne Englund Nash, and Mark Sebanc. San Francisco, CA: Ignatius Press, 1983.

Luschei, Martin. *The Sovereign Wayfarer: Walker Percy's Diagnosis of the Malaise.* Baton Rouge: Louisiana State UP, 1972.

Mann, Thomas. Introduction to *The Short Novels of Dostoevsky.* New York: Dial Press, 1945. Percy 628. SHC.

BIBLIOGRAPHY

Maritain, Jacques. *Art and Scholasticism with Other Essays.* Las Vegas, NV: Filiquarian Publishing, 2007.

McCullers, Carson. "The Russian Realists and Southern Literature." *Decision* 2 (July 1941): 15–19.

Miller, Don. *Blue Like Jazz: Nonreligious Thoughts on Christian Spirituality.* Nashville, TN: Thomas Nelson, 2003.

Milton, John. *Paradise Lost.* Ed. Gordon Teskey. New York: Norton Critical Edition, 2004.

Murray, Sarah-Jane K. *From Plato to Lancelot.* Syracuse, NY: Syracuse UP, 2008.

Newkirk, Terrye. "Via Negativa and the Little Way: The Hidden God of *The Moviegoer.*" *Renascence* 44.3 (1992): 183–202.

Nietzsche, Friedrich. *The Gay Science.* Trans. Walter Kaufmann. New York: Vintage, 1974.

Nikoliukin, A.N. *Vzaimosviazi literature Rossii I SShA; Turgenev, Tolstoi, Dostoevskii I Americka.* [*Interrelations of Russian and American Literatures: Turgenev, Tolstoy, Dostoevsky and America.*] Moscow: Nauka, 1987.

O'Connor, Flannery. *Collected Works.* Ed. Sally Fitzgerald. Ann Arbor: Michigan UP, 1988.

———. *Mystery and Manners.* New York: Farrar, Straus & Giroux, 1962.

O'Gorman, Farrell. "Confessing the Horrors of Radical Individualism in *Lancelot*: Percy, Dostoevsky, Poe." In *A Political Companion to Walker Percy,* edited by Peter Augustine Lawler and Brian A. Smith. 119–44. Lexington: University of Kentucky Press, 2013.

Pattison, George. "Reading Kierkegaard and Dostoyevsky Together." In *Dostoevsky and the Christian Tradition,* edited by George Pattison and Diane Oenning Thompson. 239–255. Cambridge, UK: Cambridge UP, 2008.

Percy, Walker. *Conversations with Walker Percy.* Ed. Lewis A. Lawson and Victor A. Kramer. Jackson: Mississippi UP, 1985.

———. Introduction to *Walker Percy: A Comprehensive Descriptive Bibliography.* Linda Whitney Hobson, ed. New Orleans, LA: Faust Publishing Company, 1988.

———. Introduction to *Walker Percy: Novelist and Philosopher.* Ed. Jan Nordby Gretlund and Karl-Heinz Westarp. Jackson: Mississippi UP, 1991.

———. *The Last Gentleman.* New York: Farrar, Straus & Giroux, 1966.

———. *Lancelot.* New York: Farrar, Straus & Giroux, 1977.

———. *Lost in the Cosmos: The Last Self-Help Book.* New York: Picador, 2000.

———. *Love in the Ruins.* New York: Farrar, Straus & Giroux, 1971.

———. *The Message in the Bottle.* New York: Farrar, Straus & Giroux, 2000.

———. *More Conversations with Walker Percy.* Ed. Lewis A. Lawson and Victor A. Kramer. Jackson: Mississippi UP, 1993.

———. *The Moviegoer.* New York: Random House, Inc., 1961.

———. *The Second Coming.* New York: Picador, 1999.

———. *Signposts in a Strange Land.* Ed. with an introduction by Patrick Samway. New York: Farrar, Straus & Giroux, 1991.

———. *The Thanatos Syndrome.* New York: Picador, 1999.

Pevear, Richard. Foreword to *Notes from Underground.* By Fyodor Dostoevsky. Trans. Richard Pevear and Larissa Volokhonsky. vii–xxiii. New York: Random House, 1993.

Princeton University, Firestone Library (PFL). Caroline Gordon Papers. Summer 2010.

Quinlan, Kieran. *Walker Percy: The Last Catholic Novelist*. Baton Rouge: Louisiana State UP, 1998.

Radzinsky, Edvard. *Stalin: The First In-Depth Biography Based on Explosive New Documents from Russia's Secret Archives*. New York: First Anchor Books, 1997.

Rasnic, Rhea Scott. *Walker Percy and the Catholic Sacraments*. Dissertation. Baylor University, 2007. Proquest.

Ratzinger, Joseph Cardinal. *Introduction to Christianity*. San Francisco, CA: Ignatius Press, 1990.

Reynolds, L. D., and N. G. Wilson. *Scribes and Scholars: A Guide to the Transmission of Greek and Latin Literature*. Oxford, UK: Oxford University Press, 1991.

Samway, Patrick. "Two Conversations in Walker Percy's *The Thanatos Syndrome*: Text and Context." In *Walker Percy: Novelist and Philosopher,* edited by Jan Nordby Gretlund and Karl-Heinz Westarp. 24–32. Jackson: Mississippi UP, 1991.

———. *Walker Percy: A Life*. Chicago: Loyola Press, 1999.

Schwartz, Joseph. "Will Barrett Redux?" In *Walker Percy: Novelist and Philosopher,* edited by Jan Nordby Gretlund and Karl-Heinz Westarp. 42–53. Jackson: Mississippi UP, 1991.

Simmons, Ernest Joseph. *Introduction to Russian Realism*. Bloomington: Indiana UP, 1965.

Solzhenitsyn, Alexander I. "A World Split Apart—Commencement Address Delivered at Harvard University, June 8, 1978." http://www.orthodoxytoday.org/articles/SolzhenitsynHarvard.php. Accessed May 7, 2017.

Southern Historical Collection (SHC), Wilson Library, University of North Carolina-Chapel Hill. Walker Percy Papers. Summer 2010, 2011.

Stanton, Leonard. "Zedergol'm's *Life of Elder Leonid of Optina* as a Source of Dostoevsky's *The Brothers Karamazov*." *Russian Review* 49 (1990): 443–55.

Steiner, George. *Real Presences*. Chicago: Chicago UP, 1991.

———. *Tolstoy or Dostoevsky: An Essay in the Old Criticism*. 2nd ed. New Haven, CT: Yale UP, 1996.

Stern, Karl. *Pillar of Fire*. New York: Harcourt, Brace, & Co., 1951. Percy 2278. SHC.

Sykes Jr., John D. *Flannery O'Connor, Walker Percy, and the Aesthetic of Revelation*. Columbia: Missouri University Press, 2007.

Tate, Allen. "Narcissus as Narcissus." *Essays of Four Decades*. Wilmington, DE: Intercollegiate Studies Institute, 1999.

Taylor, Charles. *A Secular Age*. Cambridge, MA: Belknap of Harvard UP, 2007.

Tennyson, Alfred Lord. "Ulysses." Portable Poetry. N.p., n.d. http://www.portablepoetry.com/poems/alfredlord_tennyson/ulysses.html.

Thompson, Diane Oenning. "Problems of Biblical Word in Dostoevsky's Poetics." In *Dostoevsky and the Christian Tradition,* edited by Thompson and George Pattison. 69–102. Cambridge, UK: Cambridge UP, 2008.

Tolson, Jay. *Pilgrim in the Ruins: A Life of Walker Percy*. New York: Simon & Schuster, 1992.

Vanderbilt University, Special Collections. Brainard Cheney Papers. Summer 2010.

Wall, Alan. *Myth, Metaphor, and Science*. Chester, UK: Chester Academic Press, 2009.

Webb, Max. "Binx Bolling's New Orleans: Moviegoing, Southern Writing, and Father Abraham." In *The Art of Walker Percy: Stratagems of Being,* edited by Panthea Reid Broughton. 1–23. Baton Rouge: Louisiana State UP, 1979.

Wertham, Frederic. *A Sign for Cain: An Exploration of Human Violence*. New York: Macmillian, 1967. Percy 2505. SHC.

Williams, Rowan. *Dostoevsky: Language, Faith and Fiction.* Waco, TX: Baylor UP, 2008.

———. *The Lion's World.* New York: Oxford UP, 2013.

Wilson, Colin. *The Outsider.* Boston, MA: Houghton Mifflin, 1956. Percy 2562. SHC.

Wilson, Franklin Arthur. "Walker Percy's Bible Notes and His Fiction: Gracious Obscenity." *Renascence* 59.3 (Spring 2007): 197–213.

Yarmolinsky, Avrahm. Foreword to *The Possessed.* By Fyodor Dostoevsky. Trans. Garnett. New York: Modern Library, 1936. Percy 626.

Young, Edward. *Conjectures on Original Composition.* Scholar Press, 1966.

INDEX

Adelman, Gary, 110, 163
aesthetic, ix, 10, 18, 20, 24, 26, 32–39, 43, 51, 84, 109, 137, 139, 152
Allen, William Rodney, x, 6, 23, 34, 37, 77, 80, 83, 101, 118, 129, 130, 163
anxiety, 11–16, 58, 61, 137, 160–62
Auden, W. H., 79–80, 163
Auerbach, Eric, 38, 163

Bakhtin, Mikhail, 39, 48–49, 58, 119, 135, 163
Barthes, Roland, 12, 160–61, 163
Baxandall, Michael, 14, 163
Berdyaev, Nicolas, 77, 92, 163
Bloom, Harold, 11–15, 58, 60, 110, 157, 160–63
Bloshteyn, Maria, 3, 60–61, 163
Brinkmeyer, Robert H., Jr., 128–29, 163
Brothers Karamazov, The (Dostoevsky), 1–5, 8, 10, 19–20, 22, 27, 32, 35, 37, 39, 43, 49, 50, 53–54, 56, 73, 100–101, 104, 107, 114, 117–19, 122, 126–27, 133, 135, 137, 139–41, 150–53, 156, 158–59, 164

Camus, Albert, 104, 110, 118–19, 128, 136, 163
Carel, Havi, 76, 163
Catholic, ix, 1–2, 7, 9, 21–25, 27–28, 31, 33–34, 36, 53, 60, 83, 87, 103, 109, 125, 129, 135, 160
Cervantes, Miguel de, 67–68, 74, 79, 116, 163
Chaucer, Geoffry, 12–13, 164
Cheney, Brainard, 43, 47–48, 115, 125, 164
Ciuba, Gary, 97, 164
Clayton, Jay, 11–12, 164

Coles, Robert, 59, 98, 164
Comprehensive Descriptive Bibliography, A (Percy), 166
Contino, Paul, 32–33, 37, 164
Conversations with Walker Percy (Percy), 15, 22, 29, 42, 43, 53, 56, 57, 67, 86, 88, 117, 136, 140–41, 149, 167
Cowdell, Scott, 17, 164
Cox, Harvey, 91, 164
Crime and Punishment (Dostoevsky), 4–5, 26–27, 31–32, 64, 68, 114–15, 117–18, 121–22, 124, 126, 149, 152, 164
Cunningham, David, 56, 164

Dale, Corinne, 164
Dante, Alighieri, 12–15, 36, 38, 87, 129, 136, 164
Davison, Ray, 118, 164
de France, Marie, 13, 164
demon, 5, 9, 92, 100–102, 106, 114–16, 131
demonic, 3–4, 9, 88, 92, 95, 100–103, 111, 114–15, 125–26, 130–32, 140, 161, 164
Demons (Dostoevsky), 19, 144, 158, 164
Desmond, John, 3–4, 52, 104, 118, 125–27, 140, 164
Devil, 87, 91, 93, 95, 99–103, 106, 109, 115, 119, 130–31, 165–66
Dostoevsky, Fyodor, ix–x, 1–12, 14–23, 25–39, 41–44, 46–53, 56–61, 63–68, 70–72, 74–75, 77–80, 83–84, 86–94, 97–102, 104–5, 107–19, 121–41, 143–54, 158–59, 162–64
Douthat, Ross, 90, 165

• 170 •

Dowie, William J., 123–24, 165
Duff, William, 11, 165

Elfenbein, Andrew, 4–5, 11, 165
Elie, Paul, 65, 165
Eliot, T. S., 58, 113, 165
evil, 7, 9, 25, 57, 60, 71, 80, 87, 95, 101–3, 108, 117, 122–24, 126, 128–32, 138, 151–53
existential, 7, 22, 44, 51, 63, 88, 142
existentialism, 29
existentialist, 7, 9–10, 15, 22, 26, 104

Flowers, Ronald Bruce, 90, 165
Fox-Genovese, Elizabeth, 68, 165
Frank, Joseph, 2, 44, 48, 55, 64, 67, 77–78, 88, 97, 135, 153–54, 165
Franklin, Simon, 102, 165
Frost, Robert, 165

Gadamer, Hans Georg, 148, 165
Genovese, Eugene D., 165
Girard, René, 17, 130, 135, 165
gloss, 13, 34, 41, 53, 56, 61, 62
Gordon, Caroline, x, 23–24, 27, 28, 33–36, 59–61, 64, 68, 71–72, 83, 115, 166
Guardini, Romano, 33, 61, 70, 85, 95, 166

Hobson, Linda Whitney, 132, 166
Holy Bible, 166
Huizinga, Huizinga, 68, 166

Idiot, The (Dostoevsky), 3–4, 9, 18, 25, 32, 59–72, 75–83, 137, 140, 146, 164
imitate, 10, 12, 16–17, 21, 28, 30, 35, 43, 61, 83, 94, 110, 118, 130, 132, 141, 159, 161–62
imitation, 16, 20–21, 23, 25, 38, 62, 87, 109, 161–62
incarnate, 10, 25–26, 39, 103
incarnated, 3, 32–33, 72
incarnation, 26, 32–33, 35–39, 46, 77, 83–84, 95, 97
influence, ix, 2–5, 7, 9–21, 28, 31, 34–35, 41–43, 45, 50–51, 58, 60–61, 68, 88–89, 95, 97, 100, 109, 113–14, 116, 118, 125–26, 137, 160, 162
intertextuality, 11–12, 16, 62, 136

"Introduction to Walker Percy." See *Comprehensive Descriptive Bibliography, A*; *Novelist and Philosopher*

Jackson, Robert Lewis, 33, 166
Jones, Malcom V., 42, 153, 166
Juvan, Marko, 62–63, 166

Kirsch, Arthur, 79–80, 166
Kjetsaa, Geir, 95, 166
Kobre, Michael, 48–49, 118–19, 166
Kroebe, Karl, 136, 166
Kroeker, Travis P., 141, 159, 166

Lancelot (Percy), 3–4, 9, 13, 19, 37, 111–33, 158
Landon, Philip, 94, 166
language, 6, 19, 29, 34, 37, 44, 52, 89, 91, 112, 137–42, 147, 150–52
Last Gentleman, The (Percy), 4, 18, 26, 28, 49, 59, 61–66, 68, 69, 71, 76–77, 79–82, 85, 94, 116, 140, 142, 148, 154, 167
Lawson, Lewis A., 3, 22, 43–44, 49, 57, 166
Leatherbarrow, William, 50, 87, 109, 166
LeClair, Thomas, 101, 166
"Legend of the Grand Inquisitor, The" (Dostoevsky), 154
Letter to A. N. Maikov (Dostoevsky), 92
Lewis, C. S., 138, 151–52, 166
Lost in the Cosmos: The Last Self-Help Book (Percy), 34, 104–5, 107, 139–40, 167
Love in the Ruins (Percy), 6, 9, 19, 86–94, 96, 98–109, 114, 137, 155, 167
Lubac, Henri de, 94–95, 98–99, 108, 167
Luschei, Martin, 94, 167

Mann, Thomas, 18, 21, 28, 30, 43–44, 167
Maritain, Jacques, 34–36, 71, 167
McCullers, Carson, 5, 167
medieval, 50, 61–62, 68
Message in the Bottle, The (Percy), 137, 167
Miller, Don, 20, 61, 107, 167
Milton, John, 13–14, 161, 167
model, 2–4, 9, 12, 14, 16–22, 29, 40, 42–44, 51, 53, 60–61, 65, 67, 89, 105, 116, 130, 150, 159, 161
modern, 5, 10–12, 14, 17–18, 20, 41–42, 46–47, 59–63, 87, 90, 92, 101, 104, 110, 115, 125, 136

More Conversations with Walker Percy (Percy), 2–4, 8, 15–16, 27, 31, 33, 42–43, 134–35, 137, 139–40, 150, 158, 167
Moviegoer, The (Percy), ix–x, 3, 6, 9, 15, 18, 22, 24, 33, 37, 38, 40–45, 48–58, 60, 63, 83, 87, 91, 94, 116, 125, 154, 167
Murray, Sarah-Jane K., ix, 13, 167

Newkirk, Terrye, 55, 57, 167
Nietzsche, Friedrich, 16, 167
Nikoliukin, A. N., 5, 167
Notes from Underground (Dostoevsky), 3, 8–9, 18–19, 30, 37, 41–42, 45, 47, 49–51, 55, 94–95, 112–16, 118–20, 145, 149
Novelist and Philosopher (Percy), 1, 166

O'Connor, Flannery, ix, 6–7, 15, 130, 155, 167
O'Gorman, Farrell, 3, 112–13, 119–20, 167
Orthodox, 23, 28, 65, 96–97, 160

Pattison, George, 29, 167
Percy, Walker, ix–x, 1, 3–14, 16–39, 41–86, 88–114, 116–18, 120–23, 126, 130, 134, 137, 140, 142, 152, 167
Pevear, Richard, 48, 167
Possessed, The (Dostoevsky), 3, 5, 30, 32, 86–93, 95–96, 98–100, 104–5, 108–9, 111, 117, 144, 152–53, 158, 165
Princeton University, Firestone Library, x, 60, 167
prophecy, 108–9, 141, 150
Prophet, 66, 95, 148, 150
prophetic, 92, 110, 170

Quinlan, Kieran, 53, 63, 87, 109, 135, 168

Radzinsky, Edvard, 92, 168
Rasnic, Rhae Scott, 140, 168
Ratzinger, Joseph Cardinal, 53, 168
Reynolds, L. D., 62, 168
Rothstein, Eric, 11–12, 164

Samway, Patrick, 24, 33, 60, 153, 168
satire, 14, 18, 63–64, 81, 110, 139
Schwartz, Joseph, 4, 106–7, 122, 140, 149–50, 168
Second Coming, The (Percy), 10, 31, 68, 84, 134–38, 140–42, 147, 149–50, 167

Selected Letters of Dostoevsky (Dostoevsky), 102, 165
sex, 72, 75, 87, 90, 112, 124–26, 125
sexual, 52, 72–74, 76, 90, 94, 112–13, 117, 123, 125–26
Short Novels of Dostoevsky, The (Dostoevsky), 30, 165
Signposts in a Strange Land (Percy), 7–8, 10, 15–16, 23, 29, 36–37, 40, 42–43, 46, 77, 81, 88, 93, 110, 121, 126, 136, 167
signs, 88, 107, 134, 138, 141, 146–47
Simmons, Ernest Joseph, 33, 168
Solzhenitsyn, Alexander I., 97, 168
South, 1, 5–7, 15, 24, 36, 39, 68–69, 73, 75, 89, 128
Southern, 2–8, 38, 59, 68, 128, 130
Southern Historical Collection, x, 8, 168
Stanton, Leonard, 153, 168
Steiner, George, 6, 14, 33, 71, 116, 135, 168
Stern, Karl, 23, 25–26, 168
Sykes, John D., Jr., 137, 139, 168

Tate, Allen, x, 23, 34, 36, 83, 168
Taylor, Charles, 17, 91–93, 168
Tennyson, Alfred Lord, 129, 168
Thanatos Syndrome, The (Percy), 10, 15, 19–20, 134, 135–41, 144, 150–56, 159, 167
Thompson, Diane Oenning, 78, 168
Tolson, Jay, 2, 8–9, 15, 24, 34–35, 65, 115, 119, 134, 150, 156, 168

Vanderbilt University, x, 59, 115, 125, 168
violence, 19, 63, 71, 76, 80–81, 86, 92, 109, 111–12, 121–23, 125–26, 128–30, 138
violent, 4, 6, 72, 76, 80–81, 92, 123

Wall, Alan, 168
Webb, Max, 39, 168
Wertham, Frederic, 151, 153, 157–58, 168
Williams, Rowan, 64, 80, 144, 147, 149, 159, 169
Wilson, Colin, 18, 23, 26, 28–30, 169
Wilson, Franklin Arthur, 38, 83–84, 169
Wilson, N. G., 62, 168

Yarmolinsky, Avrahm, 92, 169
Young, Edward, 11, 169

LITERATURE, RELIGION, AND POSTSECULAR STUDIES
Lori Branch, Series Editor

Literature, Religion, and Postsecular Studies publishes scholarship on the influence of religion on literature and of literature on religion from the sixteenth century onward. Books in the series include studies of religious rhetoric or allegory; of the secularization of religion, ritual, and religious life; and of the emerging identity of postsecular studies and literary criticism.

Walker Percy, Fyodor Dostoevsky, and the Search for Influence
    JESSICA HOOTEN WILSON

The Religion of Empire: Political Theology in Blake's Prophetic Symbolism
    G. A. ROSSO

Clashing Convictions: Science and Religion in American Fiction
    ALBERT H. TRICOMI

Female Piety and the Invention of American Puritanism
    BRYCE TRAISTER

Secular Scriptures: Modern Theological Poetics in the Wake of Dante
    WILLIAM FRANKE

Imagined Spiritual Communities in Britain's Age of Print
    JOSHUA KING

Conspicuous Bodies: Provincial Belief and the Making of Joyce and Rushdie
    JEAN KANE

Victorian Sacrifice: Ethics and Economics in Mid-Century Novels
    ILANA M. BLUMBERG

Lake Methodism: Polite Literature and Popular Religion in England, 1780–1830
    JASPER CRAGWALL

Hard Sayings: The Rhetoric of Christian Orthodoxy in Late Modern Fiction
    THOMAS F. HADDOX

Preaching and the Rise of the American Novel
    DAWN COLEMAN

Victorian Women Writers, Radical Grandmothers, and the Gendering of God
    GAIL TURLEY HOUSTON

Apocalypse South: Judgment, Cataclysm, and Resistance in the Regional Imaginary
    ANTHONY DYER HOEFER

CPSIA information can be obtained
at www.ICGtesting.com
Printed in the USA
BVHW070715180120
569784BV00001B/60